ABIGAIL FIELD MOTT'S
*THE LIFE AND ADVENTURES OF
OLAUDAH EQUIANO*

ReGENERATIONS
AFRICAN AMERICAN LITERATURE AND CULTURE

ALSO IN THIS SERIES:

Imperium in Imperio
Edited by Tess Chakkalakal and Kenneth W. Warren

Memoirs of the Life, Religious Experience, Ministerial Travels, and Labours of Mrs. Elaw
Edited by Kimberly D. Blockett

Appointed: An American Novel
Edited by Eric Gardner and Bryan Sinche

The Hindered Hand
Edited by John Cullen Gruesser and Hanna Wallinger

Sketches of Slave Life and From Slave Cabin to Pulpit
Edited by Katherine Clay Bassard

Memoirs of Elleanor Eldridge
Edited by Joycelyn K. Moody

The Colonel's Dream
Edited by R. J. Ellis

Freedom's Witness: The Civil War Correspondence of Henry McNeal Turner
Edited by Jean Lee Cole

A Nickel and a Prayer: The Autobiography of Jane Edna Hunter
Edited by Rhondda Robinson Thomas

Hearts of Gold
Edited by John Ernest and Eric Gardner

SERIES EDITORS

John Ernest, Professor and Chair of English, University of Delaware

Joycelyn K. Moody, Sue E. Denman Distinguished Chair in American Literature, University of Texas at San Antonio

ABIGAIL FIELD MOTT'S
The Life and Adventures of Olaudah Equiano

A SCHOLARLY EDITION

EDITED BY
Eric D. Lamore

WEST VIRGINIA UNIVERSITY PRESS / MORGANTOWN

Copyright © 2023 by West Virginia University Press
All rights reserved
First edition published 2023 by West Virginia University Press
Printed in the United States of America

ISBN 978-1-952271-84-7 (paperback) / 978-1-952271-85-4 (ebook)

Library of Congress Cataloging-in-Publication Data
Names: Mott, Abigail, 1766–1851, author. | Lamore, Eric D., editor.
Title: Abigail Field Mott's The life and adventures of Olaudah Equiano / edited by Eric D. Lamore.
Other titles: Life and adventures of Olaudah Equiano
Description: A scholarly edition. | Morgantown : West Virginia University Press, 2023. | Series: Regenerations | Includes bibliographical references.
Identifiers: LCCN 2022050110 | ISBN 9781952271847 (paperback) | ISBN 9781952271854 (ebook)
Subjects: LCSH: Equiano, Olaudah, 1745–1797. | Slaves—Great Britain—Biography. | Slaves—United States—Biography. | Africans—Biography.
Classification: LCC HT869.E6 M67 2023 | DDC 306.3/62092 [B]—dc23/eng/20230113
LC record available at https://lccn.loc.gov/2022050110

Book and cover design by Than Saffel / WVU Press

For my parents: Russ Lamore and Helen E. Spriggs

Contents

Acknowledgments ix
Introduction xi
A Note on the Text xxiii

*The Life and Adventures of Olaudah Equiano;
or, Gustavus Vassa, the African* 1

Explanatory Notes 39

Appendix A: Rethinking Textual Paradigms in
Early Black Atlantic Studies 59

Appendix B: Pedagogy, Politics, and Regulations at the
New York African Free Schools 103
   *An Address to the Parents and Guardians of the Children
Belonging to the New-York African Free-School* (1818) 103
   Charles C. Andrews, Letter to John B. Russwurm,
Freedom's Journal (1827) 113
   "A[frican] F[ree] S[chool]," *Freedom's Journal* (1828) 114
   A "[R]esolution," *Commercial Advertiser* (1828) 115
   Selections from Charles C. Andrews, *The History
of the New-York African Free-Schools* (1830) 116

Appendix C: Additional Works by and about Abigail Field Mott 129
   *A Short Account of the Last Sickness and Death of
Maria Mott* (1817) 129
   "G[eneral] R[emarks]" from Abigail Field Mott, *Observations on the
Importance of Female Education, and Maternal
Instruction* (1825) 138

Selections from Abigail Field Mott, *Biographical Sketches
   and Interesting Anecdotes of Persons of Colour* (1826) 147
Selections from Abigail Field Mott, *The Mother and
   Her Children* (1828) 154
"Report of [the] Ladies' Anti-Slavery Society of Albany,"
   The Albany Patriot (1845) 160
Abigail Field Mott, "[*Narrative*] of Douglass,"
   The Liberator (1845) 161
*Memoir of Purchase Monthly Meeting, Concerning
   Abigail Mott* (1852) 163

Appendix D: Selected Commentary on the Institution of Slavery
   in Books Published by Samuel Wood and Sons 191
"To the Reader," *The Penitential Tyrant* (1807) 191
"A Family [C]onversation on the Slavery of the Negroes,"
   The New-York Reader, No. 2 (1813) 194
"Master and Slave," *The New-York Reader, No. 3* (1819) 198

Acknowledgments

In the course of completing this scholarly edition, I have been extremely fortunate to have received a variety of support. Though Hurricane María derailed this project in the early hours of September 20, 2017, various parties at the University of Chicago spearheaded an important initiative to assist students, professors, and artists from Puerto Rico whose work was interrupted by the powerful storm. I classify my participation in this program as a transformative professional experience. I extend my gratitude to individuals at the University of Chicago, especially those working in the Office of the Provost and ones affiliated with the Center for the Study of Race, Politics, and Culture, for developing this program during one of the most precarious times in the archipelago's history. At the University of Chicago, Shadi Bartsch-Zimmer, Macol Cerda, and Jessica Velazquez welcomed me into the ideal intellectual environment at the Institute on the Formation of Knowledge; Tiana Pyer-Pereira effortlessly handled the logistics and always pointed me in the right direction; and Kenneth W. Warren, my faculty mentor, provided helpful advice as I worked my way through ideas on Olaudah Equiano, Abigail Field Mott, book history, and textual editing. The Bibliographical Society of America, Faculty Resource Network at New York University, Schomburg Center for Research in Black Culture, American Antiquarian Society, Library Company of Philadelphia, Haverford College, and Eccles Centre for American Studies at the British Library have generously supported this project as well.

I also wish to extend my deepest thanks to Vincent Carretta and John Saillant, both of whom wrote numerous letters of support for fellowships. Thank you for believing in me. Furthermore, I am grateful to Joycelyn K. Moody for her friendship as well as invitation to contribute a volume to the Regenerations Series. Derek Krissoff, director of West Virginia University Press, recruited an anonymous reviewer of the manuscript, whose commentary was productive in refining argumentation. I am appreciative of these efforts, including those of Sara Georgi and Sarah C. Smith. Lauren Stark (Schomburg Center for Research in Black Culture), Pat O'Donnell (Swarthmore College), Meredith A. Self (Columbia University), J. Eytan Shemtov (Free Library of Philadelphia), Amanda Zimmerman (Library of Congress), Christopher Ehrman (Library of Congress), Ted O'Reilly (New-York Historical Society), Laura E. Wasowicz (American Antiquarian Society), Marie Lamoureux (American Antiquarian Society), James Green (Library Company of Philadelphia), Connie King (Library Company of Philadelphia), Sarah Horowitz (Haverford College), Mary A. Crauderueff (Haverford College), Eva C. Karpinski (York University), Tomasz Mrozewski (York University), Andrew Diamond (Temple University), Rebecca Lloyd (Temple University), Emily Hipchen (Brown University), Roberta Trites (Illinois State University), Krista Roberts (Illinois State University), Jeremy Popkin (University of Kentucky), Johnhenry Gonzalez (Cambridge University), Andrew Walker (Wesleyan University), Sarah Jones (Temple University), Brian Boling (Temple University), Jordan Landes (Swarthmore College), A. Wynn Eakins (Library Company of Philadelphia), Sam Kirk (University of Pennsylvania), and Deborah Cordonnier (Princeton University) tracked down materials or responded to inquiries at just the right time. Emiko Hastings (University of Michigan) and Terese M. Murphy (University of Michigan) deserve special recognition. The scan of Mott's *Life and Adventures of Olaudah Equiano* appears courtesy of Hastings, Murphy, and their colleagues at the William L. Clements Library. Additionally, I am indebted to Fernando Gilbes Santaella and Matías J. Cafaro, colleagues at the University of Puerto Rico at Mayagüez, for continuing to invest in my scholarly work. My stellar students, Ángela Ramos Morales and Gabrielle Armstrong Velázquez, assisted with transcription. As always, from day one, Ricia A. Chansky, the ideal partner, supported me on this project and the ensuing adventures to Chicago, New York, Princeton, Worcester, Philadelphia, Haverford, and elsewhere.

Finally, I wish to recognize Sheila McMahon, senior project editor, and Anne McKenna, subsidiary rights and permissions manager, at the University of Wisconsin Press for allowing me to reprint parts of "Olaudah Equiano in the United States: Abigail Mott's 1829 Abridged Edition of the *Interesting Narrative*," my chapter in *Reading African American Autobiography: Twenty-First-Century Contexts and Criticism*, edited by Eric D. Lamore (© 2017 by the Board of Regents of the University of Wisconsin System, all rights reserved). Staff members at Cambridge University Press also permitted me to reprint some language from "The Circulation of Early Black Atlantic Literature," my chapter in *African American Literature in Transition*, vol. 1, edited by Rhondda Robinson Thomas (© 2022 by Cambridge University Press).

Introduction

This scholarly edition of Abigail Field Mott's *The Life and Adventures of Olaudah Equiano; or, Gustavus Vassa, the African. From an Account Written by Himself. Abridged by A. Mott. To Which Is Added Some Remarks on the Slave Trade*, an unauthorized, posthumous abridgment of Equiano's *The Interesting Narrative of the Life of Olaudah Equiano, or Gustavus Vassa, the African. Written by Himself*, published by Samuel Wood and Sons in 1829, alters the critical terrain upon which the best-selling autobiography has been traditionally studied. *Life and Adventures* may also be classified as an adaptation, a term that signifies "[a]n altered or amended version of a text," along with "[t]he action or process of altering, amending, or modifying something, [especially] something that has been created for a particular purpose, so that it is suitable for a new use."[1] Mott, a white Quaker, designed the adaptation not for European readers but for African American children studying at New York African Free Schools, one of the first educational systems to instruct individuals of African descent in the United States. Despite the global trajectory of Equiano's life story as well as the life writer's classification of himself as a "[citizen] of the world,"[2] most biographers, literary critics, and historians have closely aligned him and his autobiography with late eighteenth-century Britain. In this regard, they have argued that the mobilization of Equiano's life story fueled British anti-slave-trade and antislavery political agitation. Even though Equiano did not live to see the eradication of the transatlantic slave trade or the end of the institution of slavery in Great Britain and its colonies, his life story contributed to these important historic events.

The status of Equiano as an Afro-British subject may also be observed in scholarly editions of the *Interesting Narrative* in which editors have selected as copy-text[3] one of the nine authorized editions published in Great Britain.[4] Editors have privileged these editions because they underscore a variety of agential acts exercised by Equiano. To bring stability to his life and later to provide security for his family, Equiano copyrighted, marketed, and profited from these editions. In particular, the authorized ninth edition, published in London in 1794, has been the most rigorously studied because it was the last version published during Equiano's lifetime. This edition contains the autobiographer's final authorial revisions. Vincent Carretta selected this edition as copy-text for his revised Penguin Classics edition and anthology *Unchained Voices*. There is no doubt that Carretta's meticulous archival and editorial work has extended scholars' understanding of Equiano, along with several other early Black Atlantic lives and texts. Indeed, Carretta has set a new benchmark for scholarly editing in the field of early Black Atlantic studies. Nonetheless, Carretta's use of the authorized ninth edition as well as his editorial justification for selecting it as copy-text reinforce a textual paradigm that privileges authorial control to the near exclusion of other factors. In "A Note on the Text" in the Penguin edition, Carretta writes, "[n]one of the posthumous editions [of Equiano's *Interesting Narrative*] has any testamentary authority, and all are untrustworthy."[5] These editions should be dismissed because they contain, this logic holds, nonauthorial language and editorial intervention in the body of the text.

Other conceptualizations of Equiano and the *Interesting Narrative* are valuable, however. Reading only one authorized edition truncates the publishing history of the *Interesting Narrative* by discounting editions published in Britain after Equiano's death in 1797, including one printed with Phillis Wheatley's *Poems on Various Subjects, Religious and Moral*, and eliminating several geographical and cultural spaces outside of Britain where the best-selling book circulated in various formats. Ironically, the most compelling evidence for reading unauthorized editions reflecting the transatlantic, transnational publishing history of the *Interesting Narrative* may be found in numerous authorized editions. In chapter 12, Equiano observes that he was aware of the transatlantic, transnational publishing history of his autobiography. He writes, "Soon after I returned to London, where I found persons of note from Holland and Germany, who requested me to go there; and I was glad to hear that an edition of my [*Narrative*] had been printed in both places, also in New York."[6] Equiano articulates his view on unauthorized editions published in Holland (1790), New York (1791), and Germany (1792). Granted, Equiano does not expand on why he was "glad to hear" that publishers in the Atlantic world printed unauthorized editions of his life story. Nevertheless, to a certain degree, Equiano's remark signifies his desire to note the international appeal of the narrative. He likely envisions readers purchasing his book because they learned that the text was a best-selling life story in a variety of markets in the Atlantic world.

Understanding this passage as an instance in which Equiano boasts of his entrepreneurial savviness does not go far enough, though. It is also important to note that although Equiano knew that he would not make money from sales of these unauthorized editions, he still states that he was "glad to hear" that publishers in certain pockets of the Atlantic world were circulating unauthorized editions and that individuals from different countries, including the United States, were reading them. In this case, the indication is that the circulation of anti-slave-trade and antislavery arguments throughout the Atlantic world was more important than the acquisition of money from book sales. This sentence constitutes, as well, one of the hundreds of revisions Equiano made to authorized editions throughout a five-year period, beginning with the publication of the first edition, printed in London in 1789, and ending with the ninth edition, printed in London in 1794.[7] The first and ninth editions have traditionally been used as copy-texts for editions of the *Interesting Narrative* published in the twentieth century and twenty-first century, but the contents of a single authorized edition do not allow an individual to grasp the full extent to which Equiano continued to reshape his life story. These authorial revisions may be understood as important agential acts, yet scholars have not paid adequate attention to them, even though the current textual paradigm values authorial control.

Importantly, Equiano, beginning with the authorized fifth edition, offered this observation on the circulation of his life story, indicating that he remained fixed in remarking on the publishing and reading of unauthorized editions. This sentence signifies that Equiano continued to develop new insights on his autobiography as his life and contexts around him unfolded. Yet Equiano also comments on matters of textuality. That is, Equiano's opinion on unauthorized editions indicates that his view of textuality—his take on what constitutes a legitimate autobiographical text—runs counter to late twentieth-century and twenty-first-century scholars' consistent usage of authorial control as the main benchmark from which to judge the legitimacy of a text. This mismatch between scholars subscribing to a textual paradigm primarily valuing one authorized edition and Equiano's embrace of a wider conception of textuality reinforces Joseph Rezek's observation that "[s]cholarship on the early black Atlantic can benefit from more attention to the functions black writers assigned to print."[8] Therefore, the textual paradigm both embraces a limited range of authorial control and fails to capture adequately the dynamics of late eighteenth-century transatlantic and transnational print networks, ones that Equiano clearly understood. Given Equiano's provocative comment on unauthorized editions, it is time that twenty-first-century scholars reassess what texts have been read and what texts have been consistently overlooked in the canon of early Black Atlantic literature.

In fact, Equiano's autobiography is perhaps the most useful case study for illustrating the benefits of examining the transatlantic, transnational publishing history of a book related or written in English by an individual of African descent and first published before 1800. Thus, the nine authorized editions reveal an incomplete process concerning the production, distribution, and reception of the best-selling autobiography. Unauthorized editions, translated into Dutch, German, and Russian, printed in 1790, 1792, and 1794, have been largely overlooked.[9] Plus, during Equiano's lifetime and after his death, a variety of individuals on the other side of the Atlantic, including William Durell, Samuel Wood and Sons, and Isaac Knapp, published versions of the life story in the United States. Durell's 1791 unauthorized edition, Mott's 1829 unauthorized, posthumous adaptation, and Knapp's 1837 unauthorized, posthumous edition form the late eighteenth-century and nineteenth-century publishing history of the *Interesting Narrative* in the United States. Even though these editions of Equiano's life story printed in the United States provide compelling evidence of the transatlantic, transnational publishing history of this autobiography, many scholars have been hesitant to follow this book across the Atlantic. Most Equiano scholars have chosen not to study these editions because they were altered in ways that the life writer did not endorse, control, profit from, or, in some cases, see in his lifetime. In other words, nonauthorial intervention practices documented in these editions undermine Equiano's agential acts found in authorized editions.

This neglect of the transatlantic, transnational circulation of the autobiography largely stems from what Leon Jackson has identified as the disciplinary divide between scholars who study early Black Atlantic and African American literature and those who work in the fields of book history, print culture, and textual scholarship. As Jackson observes, "[s]cholars of slave culture and print culture have rarely shared agendas, nor have, more broadly, African American social, cultural, and literary historians and those within the community of book historians." Jackson also holds that "the more traditional theories of textual editing, bibliography, or authorial attribution" have not "generated cross-pollination."[10] Following Jackson, other scholars have remarked on the necessity of merging these disciplinary worlds. For instance, George Hutchinson and John K. Young have posited that "black literary history might be reread and re-edited from theoretical orientations focused on broader imaginings of textuality, without authorial intention as a guiding principle."[11] These models include what John Bryant calls a fluid text, or "any literary work that exists in more than one version."[12] Additionally, Lara Langer Cohen and Jordan Alexander Stein have maintained that "[t]o the extent that scholars of African American literature have addressed the matter of print, they have generally done so with a dependence on critical models that assume that print is a stabilizing technology that subtends the establishment of African American identity." Cohen and Stein have also argued that "such models hit their limits in many of the earliest African American texts, whose meandering plots, numerous plagiarisms, and multiple rewritings defy nearly any notion of textual stability."[13] Furthermore, Joycelyn K. Moody and Howard Rambsy II have called for more nuanced understandings of African American print culture, which they define as "a broad, diverse range of transactions and products concerning the contributions of black people across the range of proficiencies and expertise needed for the composition, illustration, publishing, printing, binding, typesetting, pricing, distribution, circulation, promotion, consumption, and reception of texts."[14]

To cite a final example, Eric Gardner and others have assessed Jerome McGann's corrected edition of Martin Delany's *Blake*, an incomplete novel, parts of which were first published serially in 1859 in the *Anglo-African Magazine*. The unique nature of this productive roundtable published in *American Periodicals: A Journal of History and Criticism* should prompt scholars to question why dialogue on the editing of an early Black Atlantic or African American text has not been more regularly pursued. It is time that "A Note on the Text" transforms from a brief, obligatory, and often overlooked statement to an expanded meditation on the editorial theory (or theories) to which the editor subscribes and the challenges associated with editing the text, especially if it is a challenging one like Delany's *Blake*. Two contributors' use of the word "definitive" to classify McGann's editorial work illustrates the still-present divide between textual scholars and those who study African American literature.[15] In this case, the divide is between textual scholars like McGann who have repeatedly argued against the idea of a definitive edition and specialists in African American studies repeatedly claiming that his editing of *Blake* is definitive. As McGann clarifies, "my edition of *Blake* is not a 'definitive edition.' For almost forty years, I have been arguing that there is no such beast as a definitive edition, a fact made especially clear in the case of *Blake*, which stops at its highly uncertain, unresolved ending."[16] Peter L. Shillingsburg has insisted that "[t]he word *definitive* should be banished from editorial discussion."[17]

The transatlantic, transnational publishing history of Equiano's *Interesting Narrative*, including Mott's adaptation, provides a fertile space for textual editors, book historians, bibliographers, and print culture specialists, along with early Black Atlantic and African American literary scholars, to have meaningful conversations. Both the preference for authorized editions and commitment to Equiano as an Afro-British subject have prohibited this important dialogue from taking place. In fact, many scholars insist that the unauthorized, posthumous, and abridged editions of Equiano's life story published in the United States do not belong to a canon. Though numerous scholars regularly teach Equiano in a variety of courses, they almost always assign their students an authorized edition of the *Interesting Narrative* (or parts of one) published in Great Britain, especially if they adopt scholarly editions or anthologies.[18] Therefore, they rarely question when, why, and how this seminal autobiography and autobiographer became part of the African American and United States literary canons. Mott's *Life and Adventures* marks one of the entry points of Equiano's autobiography into these canons.

Some scholars even contend that editions published in the United States possess little—if any—significance because they trouble their conceptions of Equiano as a politically astute Afro-British subject and the autobiography as a late eighteenth-century British text. For instance, James Walvin writes about the presence of Equiano in books published in the United States, including Mott's *Biographical Sketches and Interesting Anecdotes of Persons of Colour. To Which Is Added, A Selection of Pieces in Poetry*, one of the first anthologies dedicated to the lives of Diasporic Africans, African Americans, and Indigenous persons, published by Mahlon Day in 1826. Walvin claims that United States abolitionists "stripped" Equiano "of many of his defining experiences and qualities." Walvin also points to Mott's *Life and Adventures* as evidence that the *Interesting Narrative* "remained a severely edited piece, with many of the key sections deleted, and was clearly aimed at promoting American abolition."[19] This point has contributed to stagnation in understanding the publishing history of the *Interesting Narrative* in the United States. Scholars still know relatively little about how the autobiography circulated in the United States, who read the life story (or portions of it), how readers responded to the book, and what purposes this text served on the US side of the Atlantic. Indeed, as S. E. Ogude observes, "[t]here are many questions about Equiano which have not been satisfactorily answered."[20]

Nonauthorial subjects like Durell, Mott, and Knapp may be more productively understood as individuals who ensured that the *Interesting Narrative* did not experience textual death after Equiano's passing, though posthumous editions were also printed in Great Britain.[21] Rather than envisioning them as men and women who corrupted Equiano's book, nonauthorial agents involved in the production and dissemination of unauthorized, posthumous, and abridged editions published in the United States enhanced the life span of this life story. As Joanna Brooks observes, "books need movement and movements. Books must move to live. They need constituencies, or dynamic social contexts. If books get stranded between places, between communities, they will have brief life spans."[22] The publishing history of Equiano's autobiography in the United States underscores, as well, Cathy N. Davidson's arguments that "one book is actually many books," and the field of book history reveals "the many varied ways in which one book can enter into [cultures] by addressing different kinds of readers with different tastes, needs, and literary expectations."[23]

Another more productive approach in studying the publishing history of the *Interesting Narrative* in the United States may be found in Julie Sanders's work on adaptation studies. Sanders compares some adaptations with the editorial practice of "trimming and pruning." This description accurately captures *Life and Adventures* insofar as Mott likely used Durell's two-volume "First American Edition" as the base text from which to craft the adaptation. Sanders also identifies one purpose of adaptation as "mak[ing] texts 'relevant' or easily comprehensible to new audiences and readerships via the processes of proximation and updating." When Mott abridged—and rewrote some of—Equiano's autobiography for African American children, multiple African Free Schools existed in New York. Moreover, this editorial work occurred after the illegalization of the transatlantic slave trade in the United States. Thus, Mott packaged Equiano's life story to align the book with multiple subjects taught at New York African Free Schools, including reading, writing, mathematics, and geography, and imparted guidance on the ways these Black children could experience life as free persons. In abridging Equiano's life story, Mott also eliminated or altered scenes from Durell's edition. However, Sanders adds that the purpose of adaptation studies is "not about making polarized value judgements, but about analyzing process, ideology, and methodology." "[I]t is usually," Sanders maintains, "at the very point of infidelity that the most creative acts of adaptation" occur.[24] When examining Mott's *Life and Adventures*, readers are charged not with the task of bemoaning the length of the edition or the ways the text departs from authorized editions but with investigating how and why Mott reworked Durell's unauthorized edition for African American children studying at New York African Free Schools.

When scholars have pursued the relationship between Equiano, the North American colonies, and United States, they have typically weighed in on the hotly contested authenticity debate. This controversy is over whether the life writer was born in Africa, as he claims in his autobiography, or in the Carolinas, as two archival documents suggest.[25] The debate on the authenticity of Equiano's African origins has resulted in privileging certain archival documents, namely the parish register of Saint Margaret's Church in London and muster list from the *Racehorse*.[26] According to these documents, Equiano may have fabricated his birth in Africa. In other words, instead of drawing upon his recollections of a free life in Africa, capture and enslavement by other Africans in his Eboe nation, forced travel west through the continent of Africa, and survival of the Middle Passage, among others, Equiano may have used the experiences of Diasporic

Africans who certainly experienced these events to shape the early chapters of his life story.[27] Equiano heard many orally related autobiographical narratives from enslaved persons with whom he interacted in the Atlantic world, especially while working in the West Indies for his final master, Robert King, a Quaker. In authorized editions, Equiano even quotes some of this testimony. In this manner, critics may categorize the *Interesting Narrative* as a collaborative life story containing orally related accounts of Diasporic Africans along with the life story of Equiano or Gustavus Vassa. Clearly, the debate over Equiano's African origins is a complex case involving the politics of witnessing and the ethics of life writing. Given the ramifications of this controversy, especially on the interpretation of the opening chapters from the *Interesting Narrative*, this conversation will likely continue for some time, especially if additional archival documents surface.

Until now, however, the presence of "Gustavus Vassa" (or variations thereof) on a parish register and muster list has overshadowed other archival texts that yield new ways to understand Equiano's relationship to the North American colonies and United States. Mott's *Life and Adventures* offers readers an adaptation published thirty-two years after Equiano's death, yet brevity does not always equate simplicity. Nor does Mott's editing of Equiano's life story for African American children undermine the text's place in the canon of eighteenth-century British literature. Rather than diminishing the spirit of the authorized editions or Equiano's status as an Afro-British subject, Mott's adaptation allows scholars to uncover a more complicated—and, yes, interesting—narrative on how different readers at different historical periods and in different countries consumed different editions of the autobiography for specific purposes. Simply put, Mott's trimming of the late eighteenth-century life story for early nineteenth-century Black children in New York adds new depth to—instead of deflating—Equiano's autobiography.[28] Like Equiano's life and authorized editions, Mott's adaptation emerges from the components of Black Atlantic culture that Paul Gilroy has identified as "movement, transformation, and relocation."[29]

Ushering in a new era of textuality in early Black Atlantic studies, this book supports scholars and students as they attend to the pertinent contexts that shaped Mott's *Life and Adventures*. Numerous notes on the adaptation contain relevant passages from Durell's edition that allow readers to track Mott's nonauthorial revision practices and comprehend this manifestation of the *Interesting Narrative* as fluid text. Additionally, the documents comprising the appendixes yield even more insights into Mott's adaptation. Readers can engage with the most thorough analysis of Mott's *Life and Adventures* to date with the essay "Rethinking Textual Paradigms in Early Black Atlantic Studies." Appendix B, "Pedagogy, Politics, and Regulations at the New York African Free Schools," aids scholars and students in developing a more sound grasp of the nineteenth-century educational institution attended by Black children. Mott visited the New York African Free Schools on several occasions. For example, the authors of *An Address to the Parents and Guardians of the Children Belonging to the New-York African Free-School, By the Trustees of the Institution*, published by the Woods in 1818, outline what they viewed as important policies for African Americans; selections from Charles C. Andrews's *The History of the New-York African Free-Schools, from Their Establishment in 1787, to the Present Time; Embracing a Period of More Than Forty Years: Also a Brief Account of the Successful Labors, of the New-York Manumission Society: With an Appendix*, published by Mahlon Day in 1830, include a valedictory speech, dialogue, and poetry performed or written by Black students; Andrews's letter to John Russwurm, published in a November 1827 issue of *Freedom's Journal*, provides evidence of the white educator at a New York African Free School receiving issues of the first African American newspaper; and an article published in February 1828 in the *Commercial Advertiser* indicates that trustees of the New York African Free Schools sent students' work to members of the American Colonization Society, who advocated for individuals of African descent to abandon the United States and move to Liberia.

Appendix C, "Additional Works by and about Abigail Field Mott," offers readers a diverse series of texts punctuating the white Quaker's interest in death, children, editing, education, and political activism. *A Short Account of the Last Sickness and Death of Maria Mott, Daughter of Richard and Abigail Mott, of Mamaroneck, in the [S]tate of New-York*, published by the Woods in 1817, features the Quaker elder's first attempt at writing for children; parts from *Biographical Sketches*, published by Mahlon Day in 1826, demonstrate the white editor's knowledge of the instruction of African Americans in New York along with an African Free School alumna's letters from Haiti; a report published in 1845 in *The Albany Patriot* of an organization to which Mott belonged, the Ladies' Anti-Slavery Society of Albany, along with a review of Frederick Douglass's first autobiography published in 1845 in *The Liberator* showcase Mott's participation in antislavery politics; and a selection from *The Mother and Her Children, or Twilight Conversation*, published by Day in 1828, illustrates a pseudo-fictional familial unit discussing Equiano's autobiography, among other topics. Finally, texts in appendix D, "Selected Commentary on the Institution of Slavery in Books Published by Samuel Wood and Sons," reveal how the New York printers and booksellers disseminated information on the dynamics of slavery, instructed children on this important topic, and attempted to mold young readers into antislavery agents. As a whole, then, this book equips scholars and students with the necessary texts and annotations to have more productive classroom conversations on the editing and reading of Equiano's *Interesting Narrative* in the United States and the life story's links to education, abolition, and resettlement.

NOTES

1. *Oxford English Dictionary*, s.v. "adaptation, *n.*"
2. Olaudah Equiano, *The Interesting Narrative and Other Writings*, ed. Vincent Carretta, rev. ed. (New York: Penguin, 2003), 337.
3. W. R. Owens, in *The Handbook to Literary Research*, ed. Delia da Sousa Correa and W. R. Owens, 2nd ed. (London: Routledge, 2010), defines this term as "the copy of a manuscript or printed version of a text that is chosen by an editor as the basis for a critical edition" (210).
4. Consult, for instance, Olaudah Equiano, *The Life of Olaudah Equiano, or, Gustavus Vassa[,] the African*, ed. Paul Edwards, 2 vols. (London: Dawsons, 1969); Olaudah Equiano, *The Interesting Narrative of the Life of Olaudah Equiano*, ed. Angelo Costanzo (Peterborough, Ontario: Broadview, 2001); Olaudah Equiano, *The Interesting Narrative of the Life of Olaudah Equiano, or Gustavus Vassa, the African[.] Written by Himself*, ed. Werner Sollors (New York: W. W. Norton, 2001); Equiano, *The Interesting Narrative and Other Writings*; Olaudah Equiano, *The Interesting Narrative of the Life of Olaudah Equiano[,] Written by Himself with Related Documents*, ed. Robert J. Allison, 2nd ed. (Boston: Bedford/St. Martin's, 2007); and Olaudah Equiano, *The Interesting Narrative of the Life of Olaudah Equiano, or Gustavus Vassa, the African[.] Written by Himself*, ed. Shelly Eversley (New York: Modern Library, 2004). Edwards, Costanzo, Sollors, and Allison use the authorized first edition as copy-text; Carretta and Eversley use the authorized ninth edition as copy-text. Editors of early Black Atlantic anthologies also include an authorized edition of the *Interesting Narrative*. See Henry Louis Gates Jr. and William L. Andrews, eds., *Pioneers of the Black Atlantic: Five Slave Narratives from the Enlightenment, 1772–1815* (Washington, D.C.: Civitas, 1998), 185–365; and Vincent Carretta, ed., *Unchained Voices: An Anthology of Black Authors in the English-Speaking World of the Eighteenth Century*, expanded ed. (Lexington: University Press of Kentucky, 2004), 185–318. Gates and Andrews use the authorized eighth edition, printed in Norwich in 1794, as copy-text; Carretta uses the authorized ninth edition as copy-text.
5. Equiano, *The Interesting Narrative and Other Writings*, xxxi.
6. Equiano, 235.
7. On Equiano's authorial revisions, consult Carretta's superb notes in the revised Penguin edition: *The Interesting Narrative and Other Writings*. Carretta is the only editor of Equiano's autobiography to document the full range of ways in which the life writer revised the nine authorized editions. In *The Limits of Autobiography: Trauma and Testimony* (Ithaca: Cornell University Press, 2001), Leigh Gilmore comments that "[s]everal [life] writers have taken the project of self-representation to be open-ended, susceptible to repetition, extendible, even, perhaps, incapable of completion" (96). Gilmore's comments provide an important lens through which to understand Equiano's "returning to the autobiographical scene" (96).
8. Joseph Rezek, "The Orations on the Abolition of the Slave Trade and the Uses of Print in the Early Black Atlantic," *Early American Literature* 45, no. 3 (2010): 655.
9. Members of the Equiano Society in London have examined the Dutch and German editions. For these investigations, consult "Equiano Articles" on the society's webpage (https://equiano.uk/).

10. Leon Jackson, "The Talking Book and the Talking Book Historian: African American Cultures of Print—The State of the Discipline," *Book History* 13 (2010): 252, 253.
11. George Hutchinson and John K. Young, introduction to George Hutchinson and John K. Young, eds., *Publishing Blackness: Textual Constructions of Race Since 1850* (Ann Arbor: University of Michigan Press, 2013), 2.
12. John Bryant, *The Fluid Text: A Theory of Revision and Editing for Book and Screen* (Ann Arbor: University of Michigan Press, 2002), 1.
13. Lara Langer Cohen and Jordan Alexander Stein, introduction to Lara Langer Cohen and Jordan Alexander Stein, eds., *Early African American Print Culture* (Philadelphia: University of Pennsylvania Press, 2012), 2.
14. Joycelyn K. Moody and Howard Rambsy II, "Guest Editors' Introduction: African American Print Cultures," *MELUS* 40, no. 3 (2015): 2.
15. For the use of "definitive," see Katy L. Chiles, "Defining *Blake*," *American Periodicals: A Journal of History and Criticism* 28, no. 1 (2018): 75, 76, 77; and Sharada Balachandran Orihuela, "Black Revolution and Martin Delany's *Blake*," *American Periodicals: A Journal of History and Criticism* 28, no. 1 (2018): 80.
16. Jerome McGann, "A Response to My Colleagues," *American Periodicals: A Journal of History and Criticism* 28, no. 1 (2018): 87.
17. Peter L. Shillingsburg, *Scholarly Editing in the Computer Age: Theory and Practice*, 3rd ed. (Ann Arbor: University of Michigan Press, 1996), 90; emphasis in original.
18. For instance, editors of *The Norton Anthology of American Literature* (New York and London: Norton, 2013) and *The Norton Anthology of African American Literature* (New York and London: Norton, 2014) use the authorized first edition, published in London in 1789, as copy-text.
19. James Walvin, *An African's Life: The Life and Times of Olaudah Equiano, 1745–1797* (London: Continuum, 2000), 190.
20. S. E. Ogude, introduction to Paul Edwards, ed., *Equiano's Travels*, 2nd ed. (Oxford: Heinemann, 1996), xiii.
21. For a concise overview of the publishing history of the *Interesting Narrative*, see "Bibliographical Note," in *Black Atlantic Writers of the Eighteenth Century: Living the New Exodus in England and the Americas*, ed. Adam Potkay and Sandra Burr (New York: St. Martin's, 1995), 162–65.
22. Joanna Brooks, "The Unfortunates: What the Life Spans of Early Black Books Tell Us about Book History," in Cohen and Stein, *Early African American Print Culture*, 48.
23. Cathy N. Davidson, introduction to Cathy N. Davidson, ed., *Charlotte Temple* (New York: Oxford University Press, 1986), xxxii, xxviii.
24. Julie Sanders, *Adaptation and Appropriation* (London: Routledge, 2016), 18, 19, 20.
25. On the identity debate, consult, for instance, Vincent Carretta, "Olaudah Equiano or Gustavus Vassa? New Light on an Eighteenth-Century Question of Identity," *Slavery and Abolition: A Journal of Slave and Post-Slave Studies* 20, no. 3 (1999): 96–105; Paul Lovejoy, "Autobiography and Memory: Gustavus Vassa, Alias Olaudah Equiano, the African," *Slavery and Abolition: A Journal of Slave and Post-Slave Studies* 27, no. 3 (2006): 317–47; Cathy N. Davidson, "Olaudah Equiano, Written by Himself," *Novel: A Forum on Fiction* 40, nos. 1–2 (2006–2007): 18–51; Vincent Carretta, "Response to Paul Lovejoy's 'Autobiography and Memory: Gustavus Vassa, Alias Olaudah Equiano, the African,'" *Slavery and Abolition: A Journal of Slave and Post-Slave Studies* 28, no. 1 (2007): 115–19; Paul Lovejoy, "Issues of Motivation—Vassa/Equiano and Carretta's Critique of the Evidence," *Slavery and Abolition: A Journal of Slave and Post-Slave Studies* 28, no. 1 (2007): 121–25; and Brycchan Carey, "Olaudah Equiano: African or American?," *1650–1850: Ideas, Æsthetics, and Inquiries in the Early Modern Era* 17 (2008): 229–46. For a classroom-friendly model on the spectrums of the identity debate, see

Brycchan Carey's website, "Where Was Equiano Born? (And Why Does It Matter?)" (http://www.brycchancarey.com/equiano/nativity.htm).
26. Vincent Carretta includes, in *Equiano, the African: Biography of a Self-Made Man* (New York: Penguin, 2006), the parish register (89) and the *Racehorse* muster list (149).
27. If this scenario is the case, then Equiano violated what Philippe Lejeune has called the autobiographical pact, a seminal concept in auto/biography studies. Defining the genre of autobiography, Lejeune, in *On Autobiography*, trans. Katherine Leary (Minneapolis: University of Minnesota Press, 1989), writes, "In order for there to be autobiography (and personal literature in general), the *author*, the *narrator*, and the *protagonist* must be identical" (5; emphases in original).
28. For commentary on the word "depth" in Equiano studies, see Jessica L. Hollis, "Flat Equiano: A Transatlantic Approach to Teaching *The Interesting Narrative*," in *Teaching Olaudah Equiano's Narrative: Pedagogical Strategies and New Perspectives*, ed. Eric D. Lamore (Knoxville: University of Tennessee Press, 2012), 69–93.
29. Paul Gilroy, *The Black Atlantic: Modernity and Double Consciousness* (Cambridge: Harvard University Press, 1993), xi.

A Note on the Text

In 1829 Samuel Wood and Sons, a prominent New York publisher, printed and sold *The Life and Adventures of Olaudah Equiano; or, Gustavus Vassa, the African. From an Account Written by Himself. Abridged by A. Mott. To Which Is Added Some Remarks on the Slave Trade*, an adaptation of Olaudah Equiano's *Interesting Narrative*, a best-selling autobiography first published in London in 1789. Abigail Field Mott, a white Quaker woman, adapted Equiano's life story for Black children studying at New York African Free Schools, an educational system created by members of the New York Manumission Society. The Woods sold the text as one of their "Juvenile Books" designed for child readers. Extant evidence does not indicate that the Woods printed a second edition. However, different-colored covers of extant copies likely indicate that the Woods issued the book in multiple runs. Notwithstanding some of the limitations of a facsimile edition, I have chosen to present Mott's book in this manner since it preserves the visual-verbal dynamics found in *Life and Adventures*, ones designed to enhance the interpretive skills of child readers. On selected pages of the adaptation, the Woods printed a visual image and a page number below it that invited young readers to return to pages they had already read or move forward to pages they had not yet read to establish meaningful visual-verbal connections. For the reproduction, I have selected the copy of the adaptation housed at the William L. Clements Library at the University of Michigan because of the condition of this book compared to other extant copies. For more information on Equiano, Mott, New York African Free Schools, the Woods, and *Life and Adventures*, consult the explanatory notes on the adaptation and essay in appendix A.

THE
LIFE AND ADVENTURES
OF
OLAUDAH EQUIANO;
OR,
GUSTAVUS VASSA,
THE AFRICAN.
FROM AN ACCOUNT WRITTEN BY HIMSELF.

ABRIDGED BY A. MOTT.

TO WHICH IS ADDED
SOME REMARKS ON THE SLAVE TRADE.

NEW YORK:
Published by Samuel Wood & Sons,
No. 261 Pearl-street.

R. & G. S. WOOD, PRINTERS.

GUSTAVUS VASSA.

THE
LIFE AND ADVENTURES
OF
OLAUDAH EQUIANO;
OR
GUSTAVUS VASSA,
THE AFRICAN.

FROM AN ACCOUNT WRITTEN BY HIMSELF.

ABRIDGED
BY A. MOTT.

TO WHICH ARE ADDED
SOME REMARKS ON THE SLAVE TRADE, &c.

"AM I NOT A MAN AND A BROTHER."

"Ah pity human mis'ry, human wo!
"'Tis what the happy to the unhappy owe."

NEW YORK:
PUBLISHED BY SAMUEL WOOD & SONS,
No. 261 Pearl-street.

R. & G. S. WOOD, PRINTERS.
1829.

PREFACE.

HAVING, for several years, been one of the Committee to visit the Female Department of the African Free School in New York; and having also been occasionally at that for boys, I have observed that the tickets given to the pupils, as rewards for attention to their studies, have a very favourable tendency. A specific value being given to those tickets, they become a sort of currency in the schools, and are received by the teachers in payment for toys and other articles which are provided as premiums for the scholars. Similar observation induces me to believe that there is scarcely any thing which can be given to a child as a premium for good behaviour which has a better tendency than a book. This belief prompted me to attempt an abridgement of the Memoirs of Gustavus Vassa, the African; which, as they contain many interesting circumstances, may not be thought unsuitable for distribution in those schools.

Whether or not the design of these extracts meet the approbation of the Trustees of the African Schools, I think it will be an interesting little work for children of any class, and I have therefore placed it in the hands of the publisher.

A. M.

Hickory Grove, 6th mo. 1825.

GUSTAVUS VASSA.

I OFFER here neither the history of a saint a hero, nor a tyrant. I believe there are few events in my life that have not happened to many. Did I consider myself a European, I might say my sufferings were great; but when I compare my lot with that of many of my own countrymen, I acknowledge the mercies of Providence in the occurrences of my life.

That part of Africa known by the name of Guinea, to which the trade for slaves is carried on, extends along the coast above 3400 miles, from Senegal to Angola, and includes a number of kingdoms; the most considerable of which is Benin, as it respects its extent, wealth, and richness of soil. It is bounded on the sea coast 170 miles—and its interior seems only to be terminated by the empire of Abyssinia, near 1500 miles from its beginning. In one of the most remote and fertile provinces of this kingdom I was born, in the year 1745. My father was one of those chiefs styled Embrenche, signifying a mark of grandeur.

As our country is one where nature is prodigal of her favours, our wants are few and easily supplied. In our buildings we study convenience rather than ornament. The houses never exceed one story in height, and are built of wood and thatched with reeds. The walls and floors of the lodging rooms are generally covered with mats. The dress of both sexes is nearly the same; it being generally a long piece of calico or muslin wrapped loosely round the body. Women, when not employed with the men in tilling the ground, spin, weave, and dye the cloth, then make it into garments:—with this cloth our beds are also covered. Our manner of living is very simple; the land being uncommonly rich and fruitful, produces many kinds of vegetables in abundance. We have plenty of Indian corn, cotton, and tobacco. Pine apples grow very large without culture, and we have a variety of delicious fruits. All our industry is exerted in improving these blessings of nature. We are all habituated to labour from our earliest years: every one contributing to the common stock, and being unacquainted with idleness, we have no beggars.

Our tillage is exercised in a large common, and all the people resort thither in a body. As they do not use beasts, their instruments of husbandry are hoes, axes, shovels, and pointed irons. They generally take their weapons of defence also, for fear of surprise by their enemies. Our meat consists of bullocks, goats, and poultry; our vegetables, plantains, eddas, yams, beans, and Indian corn. The ceremony of washing before eating is strictly enjoined; and cleanliness is considered a necessary part of our religion. We believe there is one Creator of all things, and that he governs all events.

My parents had one daughter and a number of sons, of which I was the youngest. As I generally attended my mother, she took great pains in forming my mind and training me to exercise. In this way I grew up till about eleven years of age, when an end was put to my happiness in the following manner:

When the grown people were gone to labour, the children generally collected together to play, and one of them climbing up a tree, looked out and gave the alarm, if he saw the kidnappers approaching, as it was not uncommon for them to make use of such opportunities, and carry off all they could catch. But one day when all our people were gone to their work, and only myself and dear sister were left to watch the house; two men and a woman came and seized us both, and stopping our mouths that we should not cry, ran off with us into the woods, where they tied our hands, then carried us as far as they could before dark, and coming to a small house, they halted for the night. They offered us some food, but we could not eat, being quite overcome by fatigue and grief: our only relief was sleep, which allayed our trouble for a short time. The next morning we left the house and continued travelling all day. For some time we kept in the woods, but coming into a road, and seeing some people

Page 5.

Page 6.

at a distance, we had hopes of being released; and I began to cry for assistance. This made them tie me faster, and stop my mouth, and they soon put me into a sack. They also tied my sister's hands again, and stopped her mouth until we got out of sight of the people. When night came they offered us victuals again, but we refused them: the only comfort we had was in being in each other's arms, and bathing each other with our tears. But alas! we were soon deprived of even the comfort of weeping together. The next day proved to be one of great sorrow indeed, for my sister and myself were separated, while we lay clasped in each other's arms. It was in vain that we besought them not to part us—She was torn from me and carried away, while I was left in a state not to be described. I grieved continually, and for several days did not eat any thing but what they forced into my mouth.

After many days' travelling, and often changing my keepers, I fell into the hands of a chieftain in a pleasant country. This man had two wives, and several children, and they all used me well, and tried to comfort me; particularly the first wife, who was some like my mother. Although we had travelled many days, these people spoke the same language we did. My master being a smith, I worked his bellows. I was also indulged in going with the maidens to the spring for water, and sometimes a small distance alone. The latter circumstance induced me to think of making my escape, and, as I had observed that our journeying was towards where the sun went down, I knew that my father's abode must be towards the place of its rising. Being oppressed with grief for my connexions, and my love of liberty great, I determined to take the first opportunity to make my escape: but in this I was disappointed. The houses and villages being skirted with woods and bushes, which were so thick that a person could easily conceal himself among them, I got into one of these thickets; but the whole neighbourhood was soon in search of me, and they came several times so near that I could understand what they said; and finding by that, that my home was farther off than I had supposed it to be, and the way so difficult that I should probably perish in the woods, I gave it up, and abandoned myself to despair. However, when night came on, the idea of being devoured by wild beasts induced me, hungry and faint as I was, to creep to my master's kitchen, and lie down in the fire-place, where I was found in the morning; and being reprimanded by my master, he ordered me to be taken care of.

Not long after, I was sold again, and carried to a great distance. As I had acquired a little of several languages, from the time I left my own nation, I found some one that could understand me until I came to the seacoast. To my great surprise, one evening, on our journey, my dear sister was brought to the same house. We were both so overcome we could not speak, but clung to each other and wept, which affected all who saw us; and when they knew that we were brother and sister they indulged us with being together. One of the men at night lay between us, and allowed us to hold each other's hand across him. This comfort, small as it may appear to some, was not so to us—but it was of short duration. Alas! when morning came we were again separated, and I never saw her more. My anxiety for *her* was greater than for myself. I remembered the happiness we had enjoyed together in our childish sports, and the indulgencies of maternal care, and fear that her sufferings would be great, made a deep and lasting impression on my mind, and her image was so indelibly fixed, that neither time, adversity, nor prosperity, has ever been able to remove it.

I was sold again, and travelling as before, we passed through a very fertile country, where, for the first time, I met with cocoa-nuts and sugar-cane. In one place I stayed nearly two months, and received much kindness; but in an unexpected moment I was obliged to relinquish these joys also. This change proved as painful as it was unexpected—for it soon discovered to me an element I had not before seen, and until then had no idea of. It also made me acquainted with such cruelties and hardships as I can never think or reflect upon but with horror.

All the nations and people I had hitherto seen, resembled my own; but now, after a lapse of six or seven months from the time I was kidnapped, I arrived at the sea-shore, and the first object that I saw was a SLAVE SHIP riding at anchor, waiting for her cargo. When I was taken on board, being roughly handled, and closely examined by those men whose complexion and language differed so much from any I had ever seen, I was apprehensive I had got into a world of bad spirits; and being quite overpowered with fear and anguish, I fell on the deck and fainted. After I came to a little, they offered me a small portion of spirits; but their horrid looks, red faces, and long hair, made me so fearful, that I refused to take it: however, they made me take a little. Having never tasted any before, the strange feeling it produced, threw me into great consternation—but I was not long in this reverie; being soon, with many of my country people, put under the deck into a loathsome and horrible place. We wished for death rather than life, and often refused to eat, for which we were beaten. At length understanding we were not always to remain in this dreadful situation, but were going to the country of these white people, to work for them. I became more reconciled; thinking that if nothing worse than working was to be my lot, it was not so desperate.

After enduring more hardships than I can now relate, and which are inseparable from this iniquitous traffic, we arrived at Barbadoes and anchored off Bridge-Town. When we were taken on shore we were put into a pen, like so many sheep. On a signal being given, the buyers rushed into the yard and made their choice; and, like *ministers of destruction*, separated friends and relatives without remorse. But the cries of those so separated were very moving to those *capable* of feeling. Must every feeling of tenderness be sacrificed to *avarice*—must parents lose their children, brothers their sisters, husbands their wives, and be prevented from cheering their gloom with the small comfort of being together, and mingling their sufferings! This separation, while it has no advantage, aggravates the distress, and adds fresh horrors even to the wretchedness of slavery.

I stayed but a short time here, when I, with some others, were shipped for North America. We were better treated than when on our voyage from Africa, and soon landed up a river in Virginia, where we were separa-

Page 8.

Page 15.

ted, and I was quite alone, as it respected my suffering shipmates. I was placed on a plantation to weed grass and gather stones; but my master being unwell, I was sent for to fan him while he slept. In his room I saw many strange things; such as a watch, whose noise alarmed me, and the pictures seemed to gaze me in the face. I thought it was a way they had to keep their great men after they were dead. These things, with a black woman that I saw as I entered the house, who was cooking, and had a large iron on her head, which locked her mouth so that she could scarcely speak, and could not eat or drink, frightened me extremely, but when my master awoke I was relieved by being sent out of the room.

Some time after this, Michael H. Pascal, who commanded a trading ship, called the Industrious Bee, came to my master's, and taking a fancy to me, purchased and sent me on board of his ship. It was a fine one, laden with tobacco and destined for England. My knowledge of the English language was still imperfect; but being very desirous of knowing the place of our destination, I made such inquiries as I could, when some of the people made me believe I was going to my native country; which, with the thought that I should have so many wonderful things to tell of when I got home, made me very happy.

These white men, and their treatment of me, was so different from that which I had before received on ship board, rendered me very comfortable; and on board this ship I received my name of Gustavus Vassa: before, I had been called Jacob. But as it respected going home I was soon undeceived, when we came in sight of the English coast.

On our passage a lad named Richard Baker, whom we mostly called Dick, showed me many kindnesses, instructing me in the English language, &c. Our friendship terminated about two years after, with the termination of his life. It was early in the spring of 1757 when I arrived in England. One morning when I went on deck, I found it covered with snow. As I had never seen any before, I thought it was salt—ran to the mate and told him somebody had thrown salt all over the deck. He told me to bring some of it to him, which I did, and he desired me to taste of it: I did so, and was surprised with its coldness;

and more so, when I saw a heavy shower of it fall from the clouds the same day.

I had often seen my master and Dick employed in reading; and I had a desire to talk to the books, as I thought they did, and learn how all things had a beginning. For that purpose I often took up a book and talked to it, then placed it close to my ear in hopes it would answer me. And when I found it remained silent, I was much concerned.

The summer following I was taken by a press gang on board of the ship-of-war called the Roebuck. When I came on board I was surprised at the number of men and guns, but as my knowledge increased, my surprise diminished. We were several times on the coasts of France and Holland; we also went to Scotland and the Orkneys. When we returned to England I was so afflicted with chilblains that I was sent to the hospital, where I came near losing one of my legs from an apprehension of mortification.

My master being appointed lieutenant of the Namur, we sailed with the fleet for America; and after having many engagements with the French, by sea and land, we returned to England about the close of the year 1758. During my stay here I received much kindness; was sent to a school where I made much progress in reading, &c.

The Namur being again ready for sea, we were ordered on board and sailed for the Mediterranean. In this voyage we had some close engagements with the French, in which many of my companions fell victims, and I narrowly escaped with my life; which at times made a serious impression on my mind, and I returned thanks to Providence for my preservation. My desire for learning continuing, some of my shipmates taught me, so that I could read in the Bible; and one of them, a sober man, explained many passages to me.

I had now served my master faithfully a long time, and his kindness to me gave hopes that when we arrived again in England I should be free, which I ventured to tell him; but he was offended, for he had determined to send me to the West-Indies. Accordingly, soon after our arrival in England, at the close of the year 1762, he found a vessel bound to one of these islands, and taking me on board gave me in charge to the captain. I remonstrated with him; telling him he had taken all my wages and my prize money, and I thought I ought now to have my freedom; but to no purpose. Taking my only coat from my back, he got into his boat and went off. I followed them as long as I could, with aching eyes, and a heart ready to burst with anguish. I wept for some time, and with earnest supplication besought the Lord not to abandom me in my distress, nor cast me off forever. In time, my grief began to subside a little, and I became more calm

The Captain, whose name was Doran, calling me to him, told me if I would work like the other boys in the ship, I would fare the better for it; but the remembrance of what I had seen in the West-Indies, and the tempestuous voyage we had, rendered me miserable indeed. Nor were my terrors abated, when, on the 13th of February 1763, we discovered the Island of Montserrat. These regions of sorrow, chilled me to the heart, and brought to my view nothing but misery, stripes, and chains. In this state of mind we came to an anchor; and, to complete my distress, two of the sailors robbed me of my money, about eight guineas, which I had collected by doing small jobs on board the ships of war, and which I hid when my master took my coat.

Helping to unload and load the ship, in a heavy surf, and under a hot sun, was painful and dangerous work; but when the ship was ready to sail for England, the captain sent for me, and with a trembling heart and faultering step I went to him, and found with him a Mr. Robert King, a quaker and a merchant. He told me the charge he had to get me a good master, and he had got me one of the best on the island. Mr. King also said he had bought me on account of my good character, and that he did not reside there altogether, but part of the time in Philadelphia, where he expected soon to go, and he would then put me to school, and fit me for a clerk. This conversation relieved my mind, and I thanked the captain for giving me so good a character. My new master soon asked me what I could do, saying he did not mean to treat me hard. I told him I could shave and dress hair pretty well. I could also refine wines, which I had learned on shipboard. I could write, and understood arithmetic as far as the Rule of Three.

I was, during our stay on the island, employed in managing the boats to load and unload vessels. My master often hired slaves of their masters to work for him, and found them victuals himself, because he thought what they were allowed was not sufficient for the work they did. This pleased them so well that they would work for him in preference to any other gentleman. Indeed the character which captain Doran had given me of him I found to be correct—he possessed an amiable disposition, was very charitable and humane. In my passing about the Island I had great opportunity of seeing the wretched situation, and dreadful usage of the poor slaves. This reconciled me to my own condition, and made me thankful for falling into the hands of such a kind master. He was several times offered a great price for me, which induced me to double my diligence, for I was very much afraid of falling into the hands of those men who did not allow their slaves a sufficient support, and treated them so cruelly.

Having obtained three pence I began a little trade, and as I passed about from one island to another, I soon gained a dollar, then more, and bought me a *Bible*. This, with my "Guide to the Indians," that I had given me in England, I loved above all other books. My success induced me to venture again, and being about to sail in a vessel of my master's for Georgia and Charleston, I took a small venture with me, and on my return sold what I had obtained very well. Thus I continued trading until the year 1765, when my master prepared for going to Philadelphia. This, with the offer he made of crediting me with a tierce of rum, and another of sugar, and encouraging me to industry, that I might get enough to purchase my freedom, which he promised I should have for what he gave for me, elated me very much, and I told him it was what I had hoped for.

In a short time we sailed, and arriving safe in port, I sold my venture pretty well. Finding things plenty and cheap, I again laid in my little store, and returned with the vessel to Montserrat, from thence to Georgia—back to Montserrat, and to Georgia the second time. This time, being in a yard one evening with some negroes, whose master coming home drunk, he, and a very rough white

Page 18.

Page 20.

man with him, beat me almost to death; though I gave a good account of myself, and he knew my captain. In the morning they took me to the jail. As I did not return to the ship in the evening, nor make my appearance in the morning, the captain became very uneasy, and making inquiry, learned where I was; and when he saw how I was mangled he could not help weeping. He soon took me to his lodgings, where with his kindness in watching me all hours of the night, and the skilful attention of an eminent physician, I recovered so as to get out of bed in about sixteen or eighteen days, and in four weeks, being able to go on duty, we sailed for Montserrat, where I continued until the beginning of the year 1766.

Every day now brought me nearer to my freedom and I longed to be at sea that I might be gaining something to obtain it. My master having purchased a larger vessel, in lading her he gave me an opportunity of taking more goods than I had done before; and we sailed again for Philadelphia, where we arrived in good time—and selling my goods to honest people I did very well.

Thus passing from one port to another, with my kind master's and captain's indulgence, and my own indefatigable industry, I at length obtained the sum required for my liberty; but how to make my master the offer of it I was at a stand. Nevertheless, one morning while he and the captain were at breakfast, I ventured, by telling him what he had promised, and that I had got the money—at which he was much surprised. The captain told him I had come honestly by it, and he must be as good as his word. Upon which he directed me to get a manumission drawn and he would sign it. At this my heart leaped for joy; and going to the office, I hardly knew whether my feet touched the ground or not. And when the whole was completed, and I was in reality *free*, I felt like another being—My joy was indescribable: but my master and captain entreated me not to leave them. Here my duty and inclination were at variance, and caused me a hard struggle. Gratitude for favours induced me to stay, though I longed to go to London and see my old captain Pascal, and let him know I was free.

Our first voyage was to Savannah in Georgia, by way of Eustatia. Here I met as usual with poor treatment, re-
2*

ceiving uncurrent money for my goods, and some other abuses hard for human nature to bear; but in due time we were ready for sailing. As we were taking some bullocks on board, one of them butted the captain in the breast so that he soon became unable to do duty, and died before we reached our port. This was a heavy stroke to me, for he had been my true friend, and I loved him as a father. The mate was also unwell, so that the principal management of the vessel devolved upon me. Having, by the kindness of the captain, learned a little of navigation, I found it useful, and we got in in safety. Many were astonished when they heard that I had brought the vessel into port, and they gave me the appellation of captain. By the captain's persuasion, I had now brought some turkeys, which I disposed of at three hundred per cent.

My old friend, the captain, being now gone, I set my heart again on going to England—but, by the entreaties of Mr. King, I consented to go one more voyage to Georgia, and about the last of January 1767, we took our departure in the Nancy with a new captain. Steering a more westerly course than usual, we in a few days got among the breakers, and our vessel was wrecked on the Bahama Banks. The night being dark we were in great consternation, but remained as quiet as we could until morning, when some of us prepared the boat, but others drank as if there was no danger. However, with the great exertions of a few, we all got on one of the Bahama Islands. When we came near the shore we saw several flamingoes on the beach, and supposing them to be cannibals we were very much alarmed, but they soon took to their wings and relieved us of our anxiety. On this and the adjacent islands we remained many days; and having some oranges, limes, and lemons, I planted some of the seeds in the good soil, as a token to any that might be cast away hereafter. In the day time we went out in search of fresh water, for want of which we suffered extremely; at night we returned to the same island. When we were almost famished with hunger, thirst, and fatigue, we to our great joy saw a sail; it proved to be a friendly one, and we were taken (but not without experiencing a severe gale) to New Providence It is impossible for any one who has not suffered such hardships, to conceive the joy we felt at these deliverances. The inhabitants were kind, and showed us a great deal of hospitality for more than two weeks; when we again got on board a vessel and sailed for Savannah where we arrived in a few days. From thence we went to Martinico, and so to Montserrat, where we arrived 23d of July, after an absence of six months; in which time I had experienced the delivering hand of Providence more than once, when all human means seemed hopeless.

After relating the loss of the vessel; our various difficulties, &c. to Mr. King, I informed him of my resolution to go to London; and although he would gladly have kept in his service, he gave me the following certificate:

Montserrat, —— 1767.

The bearer hereof, Gustavus Vassa, was my slave for upwards of three years, during which he always behaved himself well, and dischared his duty with honesty and assiduity.   R. KING.

When I had obtained this certificate, I parted with my kind master, with sincere gratitude, and soon embarked for England. We had a prosperous voyage, and when the captain paid me my wages I had thirty seven guineas. I soon found many of my old acquaintance, and particularly captain Pascal. He was surprised to see me, and asked me "How I came back." I said in a ship. To which he replied, "I suppose you did not *walk* on the water." We had some conversation about our old matters, but not to any satisfaction.

I now set my mind on getting some more learning, and attended school diligently for some time, but my money being mostly spent, I undertook to perfect myself in hairdressing. I also engaged with Dr. Charles Irving, who was celebrated for his success in making salt-water fresh. My wages, which were only twelve pounds a year, not being sufficient, I determined again to try the sea and having long a desire to see Turkey I engaged on board the Delaware, and we sailed in July, and went to Italy, and had a delightful sail among the Archipelago islands; from thence to Smyrna in Turkey. The mate also taught me more of navigation, which I was fond of. In a few months our ship was laden with a rich cargo of silks and other articles, and I returned to England well pleased with my voyage.

The May following we made a delightful trip to Portugal, where I saw many curiosities, and returned to London in July. Our next voyage was to Genoa, for which place we sailed in September. I also saw Naples, a beautiful city and very clean. When we had finished our business we went to Smyrna. Here I saw many caravans from India. Among other articles, they brought with them great quantities of locusts, a kind of pulse resembling French beans but longer, which are sweet and palatable. With another rich cargo we sailed in March, and arrived in England in July 1770.

The April following I went once more for the West-Indies with captain William Robertson, in the Granada Planter. We were at Madeira, Barbadoes, and the Grenadas. Here I met with my usual West-India treatment of hard dealing, and was not very well pleased with my voyage; but we soon returned to England. My next trip was to Jamaica, as steward, with captain David Watts. While on that Island I saw many cruelties inflicted on the poor slaves, and heard of many more. They retain many of the customs here, which are practised in Africa, particularly putting victuals, pipes and tobacco in the graves with their dead.

On my return to England, in August, I entered again into the service of Dr. Irving, where I remained until May 1773. An expedition was now fitting out to explore a North-east passage to India, conducted by the Hon. Constantine John Phipps, in his Majesty's sloop of war, the Race Horse. My master being anxious to accompany them, I attended him on board, 24th of May. We were soon joined by the sloop Carcass, captain Lutwidge, and on the 13th of June we were near Shetland. On the 20th we began to use Dr. Irving's apparatus for making salt water fresh. I attended the distillery, and frequently purified from 26 to 40 gallons a day. On the 28th we reached Greenland, where I was surprised to see that the sun did not go down. On the 29th and 30th we saw large plains of ice, and we fastened to one that was 80 yards wide. While here we killed manys different kind of animals, among which were nine bears. About the 1st of

August we got fast in the ice, but by sawing it away we relieved the vessels some. After we had been eleven days in this deplorable situation, hourly expecting to be crushed to pieces, the wind changed and the weather became mild, so that the ice gave way, and in about thirty hours with hard labour we got into open water, to our great joy and gladness of heart. On the 19th we left this dreary clime, which affords very little food and no shelter, and arrived at Deptford on the 30th of September, ending our Arctic voyage with about four months absence, imminent dangers, and rejoicing to be once more in England. I returned with Dr. Irving to London and staid some time. During this period I began to reflect seriously on the many dangers I had escaped, and particularly in my last voyage; and they made a lasting impression on my mind. My reflections were often turned to the awfulness of eternity, and I seemed a burden to myself. While in this state I thought of going again to Turky, but was disappointed. I asked many the way to Heaven, for I was convinced that no unclean thing could enter there. Some told me one way and some another; which only tended to confusion. I then took to my Bible, where I found it said, " No new thing happeneth under the sun," and I received some encouragement.

While under those serious impressions I made several voyages to Spain as steward. On board the first ship I heard much swearing, and I was very fearful I should fall into the habit again, and then there could be no hope of my salvation: confusion seized me and I was almost induced to cast myself overboard, but recollecting that " no murderer hath eternal life abiding in him," I paused, and was convinced that the Lord was better to me than I deserved. Some time after this many things which had occurred in my past life were presented before me, and I saw the hand of Providence in them to guide and protect me, though I knew it not. When I considered my state, and what a great debtor I was, I wept.

The Bible was now my companion and comfort. I prized it much, with many thanks to God that I could read it for myself. The worth of a soul cannot be told, and I viewed the unconverted people of the world in an awful state, being without God and without hope.

Page 23.

Page 29.

On our return from our last voyage we picked up eleven pitiable men. They were in a small boat without victuals, compass, water, or any thing else, and must soon have perished. As soon as they got on deck they fell on their knees and thanked God for their deliverance. Thus I saw verified what was written in the 107th Psalm. They told us they were Portuguese, and that their vessel had sunk with two of the crew in it.

Dr. Irving having a mind for a new adventure, to cultivate a plantation at Jamaica and the Musquito shore, wished me to accompany him; to which, with the persuasion of my friends, I consented; and in the month of November 1775 we sailed in the sloop Morning Star, David Miller, captain, and arrived at Jamaica the 14th of January. We went soon to the Musqueto shore and began to cultivate the land. After enduring many hardships, and the rainy season coming on and washing away what we had put in the ground, I obtained permission of the Doctor, and taking leave of him and my other friends, I set sail again for England; but meeting with disappointments and bad usage, it was a long time before we got even to Jamaica, where Dr. Irving had arrived before me. However, I soon after arrived at Plymouth and from thence went to London with a heart filled with thanks to God for his mercies. Such were the various scenes which I was a witness to, and the fortune I experienced until the year 1777. Since that period my life has been more uniform. Being weary of a seafaring life and the impositions I had met with in my commercial business, I shortly engaged once more at service, where I continued for the most part until 1784.

I once had a proposition made me to go as a missionary to Africa, and endeavour to convert my countrymen: but I had suffered so much by the intrigues of men, I feared they would serve me worse than Alexander the coppersmith did St. Paul, if I had attempted to go to Africa. I visited different parts of England, and had intercourse with many men of rank and respectability, and they treated me kindly.

In 1784 I embarked as steward on board the London, captain Hopkins, and made a trip to New York. I admired the place much. Provisions of every kind were plenty and cheap, but our stay was short. In March 1785 I sailed again for Philadelphia, where we arrived in May. I was very glad to see this favourite place, and my pleasure was much increased in seeing the worthy Quakers freeing and easing the labours of many of my countrymen. And it rejoiced my heart when one of those people took me to the Free School where I saw the children of my colour instructed, and their minds cultivated to fit them for usefulness. After my return to England, accompanied by some of my African brethren, we presented an address of thanks to some of the members of this society who had been also engaged in our behalf, and we were kindly received.

The next year I went again to Philadelphia in the Harmony, captain John Willet, and on my return I was informed that Government was preparing to send some of my countrymen to form a settlement on the coast of Africa, and that vessels were engaged to carry them to Sierra Leona. This filled me with prayers and rejoicing. I was sent for to meet a committee who were sitting on this subject. They proposed my going as superintendant. I pointed out many difficulties, particularly on account of the slave dealers; but they pressed me so hard, I consented to go as commissary, and proceeded immediately to my duty. After much difficulty and delay we set sail with 426 persons on board, and reached our destined port in June, just as the rainy season commenced. Having been closely confined for several months we were unprepared for such a season, and many of them died. Thus was the benevolent intention frustrated for that time, and I returned to England.

Since that period my life has passed in a more even tenor, and a great part of my study has been to assist in the cause of my much injured countrymen. In 1788 I had the honour of presenting the Queen with a petition in behalf of my African brethren, which was received most graciously by her majesty.

I now request the reader's indulgence, as I have aimed at simple truth in relating the chequered scenes of my life. I early learned to look for the hand of God in minute circumstances, and this has made them of importance to me. And to those who are desirous of doing justly, loving mercy, and walking humbly before God, there is scarce any book so trifling, but they may gather some instruction from it.

END OF GUSTAVUS VASSA.

NOTE. In a work that has lately come into my hands I find this additional information respecting Gustavus Vassa:

"About the time of writing his Narative he married and settled in London; and a son of his named Sancho, who received a good education, was assistant librarian to Sir Joseph Banks, and also secretary to the Committee for Vaccination." A. M.

The publishers have thought proper to enlarge this small work by adding the following Remarks upon the Slave Trade: not with a view to excite the indignation of any, but to give the young and the uninformed a correct idea of what the poor inhabitants of Africa suffer; for which their oppressors can give no better excuse, than that they are "guilty of a skin not coloured like their own."

REMARKS ON THE SLAVE TRADE.

IT must afford great pleasure to every true friend to liberty, to find that the cause of the unhappy Africans engrosses the general attention of the humane, in many parts of Europe; but we do not recollect to have met with a more striking illustration of the barbarity of the slave-trade, than in a small pamphlet lately published by a society at Plymouth, in Great Britain; from which the Philadelphia Society for Promoting the Abolition of Slavery, have taken the following extracts, and have added a copy of the plate, which accompanied it. Perhaps a more powerful mode of conviction could not have been adopted, than is displayed in this small piece. Here is presented to our view one of the most horrible spectacles—a number of human creatures, packed, side by side, almost like herrings in a barrel, and reduced nearly to the state of being buried alive, with just air enough to preserve a degree of life sufficient to make them sensible of all the horrors of their situation. To every person who has been at sea, it must present a scene of wretchedness in the extreme; for, with every comfort, which room, air, variety of nourishment, and careful cleanliness can yield, it is still a wearisome and irksome state. What then must

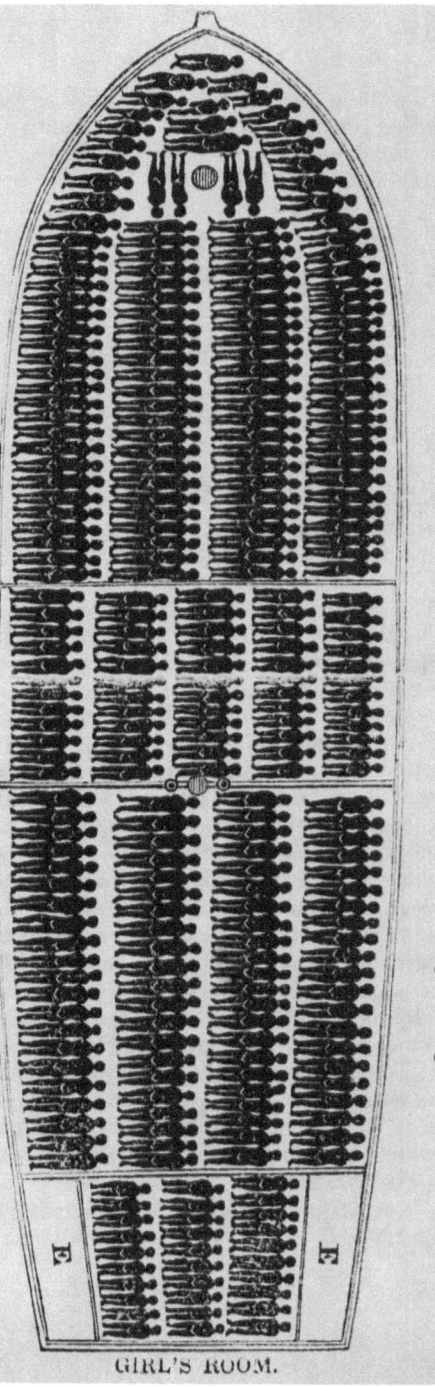

it be to those who are not only deprived of the necessaries of life, but confined down the greater part of the voyage to the same posture, with scarcely the privilege of turning from one painful side to the other, and subjected to all the nauseous consequences arising from sea-sickness, and other disorders, unavoidable amongst such a number of forlorn wretches! Where is the human being that can picture to himself this scene of wo, without, at the same time, execrating a trade which spreads misery and desolation wherever it appears? Where is the man of real benevolence, who will not join heart and hand in opposing this barbarous, this iniquitious traffic?

"The annexed plate represents the lower deck of an African ship, of two hundred and ninety-seven tons burden, with the slaves stowed in it, in the proportion of not quite one to a ton.

"In the men's apartment the space allowed to each is six feet in length, by sixteen inches in breadth. The boys are each allowed five feet by fourteen inches; the women, five feet ten inches by sixteen inches, and the girls four feet by twelve inches. The perpendicular height between the decks is five feet eight inches.

"The men are fastened together, two and two, by handcuffs on their wrists, and by irons riveted on their legs. They are brought up on the main deck every day, about eight o'clock; and, as each pair ascends, a strong chain, fastened by ring-bolts to the deck, is passed through their shackles; a precaution absolutely necessary to prevent insurrection. In this state, if the weather is favourable, they are permitted to remain about one third part of the twenty-four hours; and during this interval they are fed, and their apartment below is cleaned; but when the weather is bad, even these indulgences cannot be granted them, and they are only permitted to come up in small companies of about ten at a time, to be fed, when, after remaining a quarter of an hour, each mess is obliged to give place to the next in rotation.

When a ship arrives at a port in the West-Indies, the slaves are exposed to sale, except those who are very ill, they being left in the yard to perish by disease or hunger. The healthy are disposed of by auction; the sickly by scramble. The sale by scramble is thus described: the ship being darkened by sails, the purchasers are admitted, who, rushing forward with the ferocity of brutes, seize as many slaves as they have occasion for. In none of the sales is any care taken to prevent the separation of relatives or friends; but, husbands and wives, parents and children, are parted with as little concern as sheep and lambs by the butcher. *Abstract of the evidence laid before a committe of the British Parliament, pages* 46, *and* 47.

The field slaves are called out by day-light to their work: if they are not out in time, they are flogged. When put to their work they perform it in rows, and, without exception, under the whip of drivers, a certain number of whom are allotted to each gang. Such is the *mode* of their labour: as to the time of it, they begin at day-light, and continue, with two intermissions, (one for half an hour in the morning, the other for two hours at noon,) till sunset. Besides this, they are expected to range about and pick grass for the cattle, either during the two hours *rest* at noon, or after the fatigues of the day.

In the crop season, the labour is of much longer duration. Mr. Dalrymple says, they are obliged to work as long as they can: that is, as long as they can keep awake or stand. Sometimes through excess of fatigue, they fall asleep; when it has happened to those who feed the mills, that their arms have been caught therein and torn off. Mr. Cook, on the same subject, states, that they work in general, eighteen hours out of the twenty-four: he knew a girl lose her hand by the mill while feeding it: being overcome with sleep, she dropped against the rollers.

Abstract of the evidence, pages 55, 56.

All the facts that have been now adduced, are of unquestionable authority, having been extracted from the evidence laid before the house of Commons by eye-witnesses to the facts. Let now every honest man lay his hand on his breast, and seriously reflect, whether he is justifiable in countenancing such barbarities; or whether he ought not to reject with horror, the smallest participation in such infernal transactions. To the weaker sex, whose amiable characteristic it is, to be "tremblingly alive" to every tale of wo, the friends of the abolition return their warmest acknowledgments, for the zeal with which many of them have espoused the cause of humanity, and for the noble example they have shown, in rejecting the produce of slavery and misery.

When the cargo of a slave ship is brought to market, it frequently happens that the husband and wife, being sold to different purchasers, are violently separated, probably never to see each other more. When purchased, they are generally marked on the breast with a red hot iron. The poor victims are also sometimes fastened to a ladder to be flogged, which is occasionally laid flat upon the ground for severer punishment.

A SUBJECT

FOR CONVERSATION AND REFLECTION AT THE TEA-TABLE.

[*Originally published in England.*]

THE following beautiful pieces are the production of the pen of our deservedly admired, and charming poet, Mr. Cowper. The genuine poetic pathos they display, and the ardent love of freedom with which they glow, cannot fail of awakening the sympathy, and engaging the attention, of the benevolent admirers of the muses.

When we take a survey of the benefits we derive from the universal commerce carried on between distant nations, and notice its natural tendency to unite together in one grand whole, under one common parent, all the kindreds of the earth, we cannot but admire the wisdom of that Being who so governs and over-rules the passions and interested views of men, as to render these the means of his bestowing most extensive blessings on the human race. But when, in the progress of the survey, and after having contemplated with pleasure and exultation the manifold diffusive advantages, which, by such means, are enriching and felicitating the nations of the earth, from pole to pole, and from one end of heaven to the other; when, after having observed, successively, barbarism giving place to civilization, confusion to order, despotism to liberty, and wretchedness and misery succeeded by prosperity and happiness; when, after dwelling with rapture on this enchanting scene, our attention is directed to one particular, but extensive part of the globe, to the vas-

regions of Africa, what an accursed species of commerce do we see there encouraged! a TRAFFIC IN MEN! what different emotions do we feel! Our whole frame receives a sudden shock, and, instead of being elevated with admiration, or soothed with tranquil joy, we are lost in pensive melancholy, and are agitated with horror! The mind recovering a little the power of recollection, which it had thus well nigh lost, will naturally fall into the following train of

REFLECTIONS.

——   ——   ——   My ear is pain'd,
My soul is sick with every day's report
Of wrong and outrage with which earth is fill'd.
There is no flesh in man's obdurate heart:
It does not feel for man; the natural bond
Of brotherhood is sever'd as the flax
That falls asunder at the touch of fire.
He finds his fellow GUILTY of a skin
Not COLOUR'D like his own; and, having pow'r
T' enforce the wrong, for such a WORTHY cause,
Dooms and devotes him as his lawful prey:
And worse than all, and most to be deplor'd
As human nature's broadest, foulest blot,
Chains him, and tasks him, and exacts his sweat
With stripes, that mercy, with a bleeding heart
Weeps when she sees inflicted on a BEAST.
Then what is man? and what man seeing this,
And having human feelings, does not blush
And hang his head, to think himself a man.
  I would not have a slave to till my ground,
To carry me, to fan me while I sleep,
And tremble when I wake, for all the wealth
That sinews bought and sold have ever earn'd.
No! dear as freedom is, and in my heart's
Just estimation priz'd above all price,
I had much rather be myself the slave,
And wear the bonds, than fasten them on him.
  We have no slaves at home—then why abroad?
And they themselves, once ferried o'er the waves
That part us, are emancipate and loos'd.
Slaves cannot breathe in England: if their lungs
Receive our air, that moment they are free;
They touch our country and their shackles fall.
That's noble, and bespeaks a nation proud
And jealous of the blessing. Spread it then,
And let it circulate through every vein
Of all your empire: that where Britain's power
Is felt, mankind may feel her MERCY too.

After these noble sentiments, and such glowing poetic fire, in favour of liberty, and in detestation of oppression, it may not be unpleasing to present the reader, without entering into any minute detail of all the miseries which, by European avarice, cruelty, and wickedness, are entailed on the ill-fated and wretched Africans, with a simple and pathetic delineation of what may naturally be supposed to pass, at times, through the mind of the enslaved Negro. However incapable, he may be just in such a manner to speak the sentiments of his mind, yet, from his condition and circumstances, we may easily imagine that he, as a mere percipient being, must frequently feel like the following.

To enter more fully into the spirit of this, let the reader realize the situation of the poor and helpless African. Jaded with excessive fatigue, and sinking under the weight of inhuman punishments, he comes to his miserable hut, throws himself on his mat, and seeks relief from his woes in the forgetfulness of sleep. Scarce does he slumber, but he starts, awakened with the dreadful apprehension, that already the iron hand of oppression is about to repeat the accustomed wanton cruelties. Thus overpowered with fatigue and fear, nature refuses her wanted balm. A crowd of thoughts rush into his indignant mind; and, after long pondering his condition, he breaks forth into the following

COMPLAINT.

Forc'd from home and all its pleasures,
  Afric's coast I left forlorn;
To increase a stranger's treasures
  O'er the raging billows borne.
Men from England bought and sold me,
  Paid my price in paltry gold;
But, though theirs they have enroll'd me,
  MINDS are never to be sold.

Still in thought as free as ever,
  What are England's rights, I ask?
Me from my delights to sever,
  Me to torture, me to task?
Fleecy locks and black complexion
  Cannot forfeit nature's claim:
Skins may differ, but affection
  Dwells in white and black the same.

Why did all creating nature
  Make the plant for which we toil?
Sighs must fan it, tears must water,
  Sweat of ours must dress the soil.
Think ye, masters, iron hearted,
  Lolling at your jovial boards,
Think how many backs have smarted,
  For the sweets your cane affords!

Is there, as you sometimes tell us,
  Is there one who reigns on high?
Has he bid you buy and sell us,
  Speaking from his throne, the sky?
Ask him if your knotted scourges,
  Fetters, blood-extorting screws,
Are the means which duty urges
  Agents of his will to use.

Hark! he answers—wild tornadoes,
  Strewing yonder shores with wrecks,
Wasting towns, plantations, meadows,
  Are the voice with which he speaks.
He, foreseeing what vexation
  Afric's sons would undergo,
Fix'd their Tyrant's habitation
  Where his whirlwinds answer—No!

By our blood in Afric wasted,
  Ere our necks received the chain—
By the mis'ries which we tasted
  Crossing in your barks the main—
By our sufferings since ye brought us
  To the man-degrading mart,
All sustain'd with patience, taught us
  Only, by a broken heart—

Deem our nation brutes no longer,
  Till some reason you shall find
Worthier of regard, and stronger
  Than the colour of our kind.
Slaves to gold, whose sordid dealings
  Tarnish all your boasted pow'rs,
Prove that you have human feelings
  Ere you proudly question ours.

The distresses which the inhabitants of Guinea experience at the loss of their children, which are stolen from them by the persons employed in that barbarous traffic, is perhaps more thoroughly felt than described. But as

Page 29.

Page 29.

it is a subject to which every person has not attended, the following is an attempt to represent the anguish of a mother, whose son and daughter were taken from her by a ship's crew belonging to a country where the GOD OF JUSTICE AND MERCY is owned and worshipped.

"HELP! Oh, help! thou God of Christians!
   Save a mother from despair!
Cruel white men steal my children,
   God of Christians! hear my prayer.

From my arms by force they're rended,
   Sailors drag them to the sea—
Yonder ship at anchor riding,
   Swift will carry them away.

There my son lies pale and bleeding;
   Fast with thongs his hands are bound.
See the tyrants, how they scourge him;
   See his sides a reeking wound.

See his little sister by him,
   Quaking, trembling, how she lies!
Drops of blood her face besprinkle—
   Tears of anguish fill her eyes.

Now they tear her brother from her—
   Down below the deck he's thrown;
Stiff with beating---through fear silent,
   Save a single death-like groan.

Hear the little daughter begging,
   "Take me, white men, for your own!
Spare! Oh, spare my darling brother!
   He's my mother's only son."

See upon the shore she's raving:
   Down she falls upon the sands---
Now she tears her flesh with madness,
   Now she prays with lifted hands.

"I am young, and strong, and hardy,
   He's a sick and feeble boy---
Take me, whip me, chain me, starve me,
   All my life I'll toil with joy.

Christians, who's the God you worship?
   Is he cruel, fierce, or good?
Does he take delight in mercy?
   Or in spilling human blood?

Ah! my poor distracted mother!
   Hear her scream upon the shore"—
Down the savage captain struck her,
   Lifeless on the vessel's floor.

Up his sails he quickly hoisted,
　　　To the ocean bent his way;
　　Headlong plunged the raving mother,
　　　From a rock into the sea.

THE NEGRO BOY.

An African Prince on arriving in England, being asked what he had given for his watch, answered, "What I never will again. I gave a fine Boy for it."

　　When avarice enslaves the mind,
　　　And selfish views alone bear sway,
　　Man turns a savage to his kind,
　　　And blood and rapine mark his way:
　　　　Alas! for this poor simple toy
　　　　I sold a blooming Negro Boy.

　　His father's hope, his mother's pride,
　　　Though black yet comely to the view;
　　I tore him helpless from their side,
　　　And gave him to a ruffian crew;
　　　　To fiends that Afric's coast annoy
　　　　I sold the blooming Negro Boy.

　　From country, friends, and parents torn,
　　　His tender limbs in chains confin'd,
　　I saw him o'er the billows borne,
　　　And mark'd his agony of mind:
　　　　But still to gain this simple toy,
　　　　I gave away the Negro Boy.

　　His wretched parents long shall mourn,
　　　Shall long explore the distant main,
　　In hope to see the youth return,
　　　But all their hopes and sighs are vain;
　　　　They never shall the sight enjoy
　　　　Of their lamented Negro Boy.

　　Beneath a tyrant's harsh command,
　　　He wears away his youthful prime;
　　Far distant from his native land,
　　　A stranger in a foreign clime:
　　　　No pleasing thoughts his mind employ,
　　　　A poor dejected Negro Boy.

　　But he who walks upon the wind,
　　　Whose voice in thunder's heard on high;
　　Who doth the raging tempest bind,
　　　Or wing the lightning through the sky,
　　　　In his own time will sure destroy
　　　　The oppressors of the Negro Boy.

THE NEGRO'S PRAYER.

The following Prayer was penned by a Black Man, a slave, in the lower part of Virginia, and was presented by him to his master, which struck him with admiration and surprise, as he acknowledged to a Friend. Written in 1790.

Lord, if thou dost with equal eye
See all the sons of Adam die;
Why dost thou hide thy face from slaves?
Consign'd by fate to serve the knaves.

Stolen or sold in Africa,
Imported to America,
Like hogs and sheep in market sold,
To stem the heat and brook the cold,

To work all day, and half the night,
And rise before the morning light;
Sustain the lash, endure the pain,
Expos'd to storms of snow and rain.

Pinch'd both with hunger and with cold,
And if we beg, to meet a scold:
And after all the tedious round
At night to stretch upon the ground.

Has Heaven decreed that negroes must
By cruel men be ever curs'd;
Forever drag the galling chain,
And ne'er enjoy themselves again?

When will Jehovah hear our cries?
When will the sun of freedom rise?
When will a Moses for us stand,
And free us all from Pharaoh's hand?

What though our skin be black as jet,
Our hair be curl'd, our noses flat,
Must we for this no freedom have,
Until we find it in the grave?

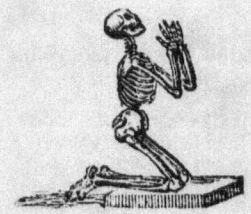

THE END.

C2
1829
Equiano, Olaudah.

Juvenile Books,

Published by Samuel Wood & Sons,

New York.

Rural Scenes,
Infant's Cabinet,
Choice Emblems,
Hedge of Thorns,
Alexander Selkirk,
Rational Dame,
Daisy,
Alice, the Negro Girl,
New York Cries,
Divine Songs,
Garden Amusements,
English History in Miniature,
Olaudah Equiano, or Gustavus Vassa,
Rose Bush,
Giddy Gertrude,
Esop's Fables,
School of Good Manners,
Way to Wealth,
Original Hymns,
Olio,
Decoy,
&c. &c. &c.

Explanatory Notes

Front Cover: "O[laudah] E[quiano]; [or], G[ustavus] V[assa], [the] A[frican]": This name refers to the well-known anti-slave-trade and antislavery activist in late eighteenth-century Britain. Equiano (c. 1745–1797) remains a household name because of his best-selling autobiography, *The Interesting Narrative of the Life of Olaudah Equiano, or Gustavus Vassa, the African. Written by Himself*, first published in London in 1789, considered by many scholars to be one of the most significant texts written in English by an individual of African descent. The term "[the] A[frican]" solidifies that Equiano's eyewitness testimony in the early chapters devoted to his youth in Africa derives from firsthand experiences. Plus, this language underscores that Equiano continued to identify himself with the continent on which he claims he was born. Scholars have debated whether Equiano was born in Africa or North America.

Front Cover: "F[rom] A[n] A[ccount] W[ritten] B[y] H[imself]": Abigail Field Mott (1766–1851), or "A. M[ott]," as the title indicates, likely used William Durell's unauthorized edition of Equiano's *Interesting Narrative*, published in New York in 1791, as the base text from which to construct *Life and Adventures*. On the title pages, volumes 1 and 2, Durell markets the book as the "First American Edition." In the list of subscribers, Durell includes the names of Mott's brother-in-law, Robert Mott, and two individuals associated with the first New York African Free School, John Murray Jr., a trustee, and Cornelius Davis, a teacher. The first New York African Free School opened in 1787. This educational system was one of the first to teach individuals of African descent in the United States. Abigail Field Mott visited New York African Free Schools on numerous occasions. To provide readers access to Mott's nonauthorial revision practices in *Life and Adventures*, I quote in these notes relevant passages from Durell's edition. I do not claim to highlight all of Mott's nonauthorial revisions. Nonetheless, the passages from Durell's edition provide an appropriate starting point for comprehending how Mott adapted Equiano's life story for African American children studying at New York African Free Schools. The phrase "W[ritten] B[y] H[imself]" indicates that Equiano had no help from a white editor or amanuensis in producing his life story.

Front Cover: "A[bridged]": According to the *Oxford English Dictionary*, this term may be understood as "[s]hortened, cut short; contracted, condensed."

Front Cover: "A. M[ott]": This name refers to Abigail Field Mott, a white Quaker elder, abolitionist, editor, author of children's books, advocate for educating women and girls, and visitor of New York African Free Schools. In addition to *Life and Adventures*, books co-written, edited, and written by Mott include *A Short Account of the Last Sickness and Death of Maria Mott, Daughter of Richard and Abigail Mott, of Mamaroneck, in the [S]tate of New-York* (New York: Samuel Wood and Sons, 1817), co-written with her husband, Richard Mott

(1767–1856); *Observations on the Importance of Female Education, and Maternal Instruction, with Their Beneficial Influence on Society. By A Mother* (New York: Mahlon Day, 1825); *Biographical Sketches and Interesting Anecdotes of Persons of Colour. To Which Is Added, A Selection of Pieces in Poetry* (New York: Mahlon Day, 1826), which includes a section on Equiano; and *The Mother and Her Children, or Twilight Conversation* (New York: Mahlon Day, 1828), which includes a familial discussion on Equiano. For these books or selections from them, see appendix C. Mott compiled at least some of the material for the posthumous *Narratives of Colored Americans* (New York: William Wood, 1875), which includes a section on Equiano. Nineteenth-century abolitionists in the United States were likely the most familiar with Mott's *Biographical Sketches*, an anthology documenting the diverse life experiences of Diasporic Africans, African Americans, and Indigenous subjects. According to Thomas Clapp Cornell, in *Adam and Anne Mott: Their Ancestors and Descendants* (Poughkeepsie, NY: A. V. Haight, 1890), Abigail married Richard Mott, an Orthodox Quaker minister, on January 17, 1787. The Motts had four children: Maria, born in 1799 and died in 1817; two sons named William, born in 1790 and 1796, both of whom died in infancy; and Robert F. Mott, born in 1794 and died in 1826 (212–13).

Front Cover: "T[o] W[hich] I[s] A[dded]": On the title page, this phrase reads, "T[o] W[hich] A[re] A[dded]."

Front Cover: Illustration: This image may have been created by the New York wood engraver and illustrator Alexander Anderson (1775–1870). Anderson's work appears in many children's books published by Samuel Wood along with Wood and Sons, and he created several illustrations depicting dogs, as demonstrated in Alexander Anderson's Scrapbooks, part of the New York Public Library Digital Collections. However, Anderson's signature does not appear in the image. The scene depicting an adult man, seated on a large stool while holding a ball, and child, standing with her right hand resting on the leg of the adult, training a dog, stands as a curious choice for the cover of Mott's book. The image captures one way to condition a dog to wait patiently, yet it also introduces the possibility of physical abuse to extract obedience from the animal, as the child holds in her left hand a whip. This illustration may indicate that the Woods marketed the book beyond the New York African Free Schools; white Quaker adults purchasing books for their children may have been another target audience. For this point, I am indebted to James Green. Unfortunately, I have been unable to locate other nineteenth-century books, published by the Woods or others, in which this image appears.

Front Cover: "Samuel Wood & Sons": This name refers to the New York publishing team consisting of Samuel Wood (1760–1844), Samuel S. Wood (1789–1861), and William Wood (1797–1877) from 1817 to 1836, according to the American Antiquarian Society's Nineteenth-Century American Children's Book Trade Directory. Samuel Wood, a Quaker and member of the New York Manumission Society, opened "one of the first children's book specialty shops in the United States." In "Writers of Juvenile Fiction," included in *The Bookman: An Illustrated Magazine of Literature and Life* (New York: Dodd, Mead, 1902), Carolyn Wells refers to Samuel Wood as "the pioneer printer of children's books in America" (350). Extant evidence does not indicate that the Woods printed a second edition of *Life and Adventures*. Nevertheless, different-colored covers from extant copies may indicate that the Woods printed Mott's book in multiple runs in 1829.

Front Cover: "No. 261 *Pearl-[S]treet*": This address pinpoints where Wood and Sons was located, in New York, from 1817 to 1836, according to the American Antiquarian Society's Nineteenth-Century American Children's Book Trade Directory. From 1814 to 1816, Wood and Sons was located at 357 Pearl Street.

Front Cover: "R. & G. S. Wood, P[rinters]": These names refer to Richard Wood (1801–1861) and George S. Wood (1802–1865), who assisted their father, Samuel Wood, with the production of *Life and Adventures*. According to the American Antiquarian Society's Nineteenth-Century American Children's Book Trade Directory, Richard Wood and George S. Wood printed a book as early as 1828, and their publishing firm owned Woodvale Water-Power Press in Morristown, New Jersey. By the mid-1840s, these two members of the Wood family regularly printed and sold books.

Frontispiece: This frontispiece, signed "AA," indicating that Alexander Anderson completed this work, parallels the visual images of Equiano in several authorized editions published in Great Britain and Durell's edition. In these frontispieces, Equiano looks directly at the reader, wears gentleman's clothes, and holds a Bible turned to Acts. However, in *Life and Adventures*, the language under the visual image of Equiano does not contain the name "Olaudah Equiano" nor the designation "the African," both of which may be found below frontispieces in authorized editions and Durell's edition.

Title Page: "'Am I N[ot] A M[an] and A B[rother]'" Illustration: Members of the London Committee Society for Effecting the Abolition of the Slave Trade utilized the image of the supplicant slave as its seal. In 1787, two years before the publication of the first authorized edition of Equiano's *Interesting Narrative*, Josiah Wedgwood (1730–1795), a British master potter and member of the society, created an antislavery medallion showcasing the image of the supplicant slave. Maurie D. McInnis, in *Slaves Waiting for Sale: Abolitionist Art and the American Slave Trade* (Chicago and London: University of Chicago Press, 2011), refers to the image as one of the "visual icon[s] of the first phase of the abolitionist movement" (29) in Great Britain, noting that the "supplicant slave was repeated endlessly. It was adopted by other artists and used on numerous objects, including collection boxes, plates, pitchers, snuff boxes, tea caddies, and tokens" (31). In *Alexander Anderson (1775–1870), Wood Engraver and Illustrator: An Annotated Bibliography*, vol. 2 (New Castle, DE: Oak Knoll, 2005), Jane Pomeroy indicates that this image may not be found in Anderson's proof books (1408). Samuel Wood used the image on the title page for the "enlarged" second edition of *The Penitential Tyrant; or, Slave Trader Reformed: A Pathetic Poem, in Four Cantos* (New York: Samuel Wood, 1807) and *The Mirror of Misery; or, Tyranny Exposed. Extracted from Authentic Documents, and [E]xemplified by Engravings* (New York: Samuel Wood, 1807). Wood also incorporates the image on the title pages of the 1811 and 1814 editions of *Mirror of Misery*. According to the title page of the 1814 edition, Wood printed and sold the book at his Juvenile Book-Store at 357 Pearl Street.

Title Page: "'Ah pity human mis'ry, human wo! / 'Tis what the happy to the unhappy owe'": Most of this language may be found in *The Odyssey of Homer. Translated from the Greek* by Alexander Pope (1688–1744), volume 2 (London: Printed for Bernard Lintot, 1725), 133. In Pope's book, the lines read: " . . . oh pity human woe! / 'Tis what the happy to th' unhappy owe." Pope's commentary on Book VII, line 200, "A wretched exile to his country send," which follows the two lines from the title page, may illuminate why the Woods used one part from this edition of the *Odyssey* below the supplicant slave. As Pope writes,

> *Ulysses* here speaks very concisely; and he may seem to break abruptly into the subject of his petition, without letting the audience either into the knowledge of his condition or person. Was this a proper method to prevail over an assembly of strangers? But his gesture spoke for him, he threw himself into the posture of a suppliant, and the persons of all suppliants were esteem'd to be sacred. (163; emphasis in original)

Samuel Johnson, in his 1755 *Dictionary*, volume 2, defines the word "suppliant" as "[a]n humble petitioner; one who begs submissively." He also uses the second definition to define the similar word "supplicant," which is likely more recognized by twenty-first-century readers. Wood used these slightly adjusted lines from Pope's *Odyssey* on the title pages of the 1807, 1811, and 1814 editions of *Mirror of Misery*, all of which appear under the same image of the supplicant slave.

Preface: "Committee to visit the Female Department of the African Free School in New York": The Female Department of the New York African Free School instructed young persons on reading, writing, arithmetic, and needlework. Charles C. Andrews, in *The History of the New-York African Free-Schools, from Their Establishment in 1787, to the Present Time; Embracing a Period of More Than Forty Years: Also a Brief Account of the Successful Labors, of the New-York Manumission Society: With an Appendix* (New York: Mahlon Day, 1830), specifies that an instructor was hired in 1791 to teach the female students needlework (16). For selections from Andrews's *History of the New-York African Free-Schools*, see appendix B. Abigail Field Mott's name appears (among others) in the extant visitors' records of the African Free School on 135 Mulberry Street for January 3, 1822. See New-York African Free School Records, 1817–1832, vol. 2, New-York Historical Society Digital Collections.

Preface: "tickets": Trustees of New York African Free Schools implemented a ticket system that both rewarded students for good behavior and punished them for bad behavior. The ticket system may be understood as a part of the Lancasterian system of education created by the British pedagogue Joseph Lancaster (1778–1838). Reacting to a growing student population in his free school in England, Lancaster created a monitorial system in which more advanced students, or monitors, supervised by an adult, assisted in the education of younger students. Thus, Lancaster created an educational system that decreased costs; he also regularly boasted about its effectiveness. As *Manual of the Lancasterian System, of Teaching Reading, Writing, and Arithmetic, and Needle-Work, as Practised in the Schools of the Free-School Society, of New-York* (New York: Samuel Wood and Sons, 1820) makes clear, "every [student] is rewarded who distinguishes himself in performing his lesson, or by his attention and orderly conduct in the school" (61). However, under the Lancasterian model, according to the *Manual of the Lancasterian System*, the "forfeiture of tickets" (62) was one of the ways pedagogues punished students. According to *An Address to the Parents and Guardians of the Children Belonging to the New-York African Free-School, By the Trustees of the Institution* (New York: Samuel Wood and Sons, 1818), the most serious punishments resulted in students paying forty tickets for "playing truant, second time" along with "scratching or cutting the desks, &c. or defacing the walls" (20). Students forfeited fewer tickets for what trustees viewed as more minor acts of disobedience. For instance, students paid two tickets for "staring at persons who may come into the school" (19) and four tickets for being "disobedient, or saucy to a monitor" (19), a more advanced peer of African descent. For the *Address*, see appendix B.

Preface: "6th mo. 1825": This date indicates that Mott likely completed *Life and Adventures* four years before the Woods printed the book.

5: "Embrenche": In Durell's edition, vol. 1, Equiano writes the following:

> This mark is conferred on the person entitled to it, by cutting the skin across at the top of the forehead, and drawing it down to the eye-brows: and while it is in this situation applying a warm hand, and rubbing it until it shrinks up into a think *weal* across the lower part of the forehead. Most of the judges and senators were thus marked; my father had long borne it: I had seen it conferred on one of my brothers,

Explanatory Notes

and I also was *destined* to receive it by my parents. Those Embrenche[,] or chief men, decided disputes and punished crimes; for which purpose they always assembled together. (4–5; emphases in original)

6: "We are all habituated to labour from our earliest years . . . ": Africans in the province of Essaka, where Equiano was born, according to his autobiography, were not the only individuals who labored. Acknowledging that his people kept prisoners of war, Equiano writes the following in Durell's edition, vol. 1:

> Those prisoners which were not sold or redeemed we kept as slaves: but how different was their condition from that of the slaves in the West Indies! With us they do no more work than other members of the community, even their master; their food, clothing[,] and lodging were nearly the same as theirs, (except that they were not permitted to eat with those who were free-born;) and there was scarce any other difference between them, than a superior degree of importance which the head of a family possesses in our state, and that authority which, as such, he exercises over every part of his household. Some of these slaves have even slaves under them as their own property, and for their own use. (19)

6: "eddas": According to the *Oxford English Dictionary*, this word may be understood as "[t]he tuberous stems of various araceous plants."

6: "We believe there is one Creator . . . ": In Durell's edition, vol. 1, Equiano offers the following commentary on a monotheistic religious tradition in his African nation:

> As to religion, the natives believe that there is one Creator of all things, and that he lives in the sun, and is girted round with a belt that he may never eat or drink; but, according to some[,] he smokes a pipe, which is our own favourite luxury. They believe he governs events, especially our deaths or captivity; but, as for the doctrine of eternity I do not remember to have ever heard of it: some[,] however[,] believe in the transmigration of souls in a certain degree. (19–20)

7. Illustrations: In *Alexander Anderson*, vol. 2, Jane Pomeroy specifies that the New York visual artist signed the upper and lower and images on page 7 (1408). In the upper image, the signature "AA" may be seen under the individual seated holding what appears to be a spear and to the left of the stooped individual holding a spear and carrying a heavy load of produce. This signature also appears in the lower left corner of the lower image. Mott's and the Woods' placement of "Page 5." under the upper image and "Page 6." under the lower image indicates that they invited New York African Free School students to identify prose passages from these pages that aligned with the visual images. Therefore, Mott's adaptation may be understood as a text that consistently tested and honed African American children's reading comprehension skills. Pomeroy characterizes the images in *Life and Adventures* as "typical of Anderson's work for Samuel Wood. They show the sturdy lines, warm handling of human figures, and uncluttered drawing" (1409).

8: " . . . particularly the first wife, who was some [*sic*] like my mother": The final part of this sentence contains a printing error. This part should read "who was somewhat like my mother," "who was something like my mother," or "who was like my mother."

8: "bellows": According to the *Oxford English Dictionary*, this term may be understood as "[a]n instrument or machine constructed to furnish a strong blast of air" (788). Furthermore, this instrument "may be portable, as the common hand-bellows, or fixed, as a smith's

43

bellows." Samuel Johnson, in his 1755 *Dictionary*, vol. 1, defines the word as "[t]he instrument used to blow fire."

8: " . . . I got into one of these thickets . . . ": Equiano pinpoints, in Durell's edition, vol. 1, the reason why he concealed himself in this space, a point Mott eliminates: "I used to be sometimes employed in assisting an elderly woman slave, to cook and take care of the poultry: and one morning, while I was feeding some chickens, I happened to toss a small pebble at one of them, which hit it on the middle, and directly killed it" (38). Having confessed to the elderly slave that he killed the chicken, Equiano observes that

> she flew into a violent passion, threatened that I should suffer for it; and, my master being out, she immediately went and told her mistress what I had done. This alarmed me very much, and I expected an instant flogging, which to me was uncommonly dreadful; for I had seldom been beaten at home. I[,] therefore[,] resolved to fly; and accordingly I ran into a thicket that was hard by, and hid myself in the bushes. (38)

9: "I remembered the happiness we had enjoyed together . . . ": Equiano, in Durell's edition, vol. 1, offers additional insights on the permanent separation from his young sister:

> To that Heaven which protects the weak from the strong, I commit the care of your innocence and virtues, if they have not already received their full reward, and if your youth and delicacy have not long since fallen victims to the violence of the African trader, the pestilential stench of a guinea ship, the seasoning in the European colonies, or the lash and lust of a brutal and unrelenting overseer. (43–44)

10: "At length understanding . . . ": Mott excises from whom Equiano learns this knowledge. Equiano notes, in Durell's edition, vol. 1, that "some [male slaves] of my own nation" (52) informed him that they "were to be carried to these white people's country to work for them" (53).

10: "After enduring more hardships than I can now relate . . . ": Mott preserves the site of Equiano's first encounter with the Americas, Barbados, but she significantly reduces the life writer's graphic descriptions of the Middle Passage. Notwithstanding the controversy over the autobiographer's African origins, Equiano's recollection of the Middle Passage is the most comprehensive account written in English by an individual of African descent. In Durell's edition, vol. 1, Equiano recalls when slavers brought him onboard a slave ship:

> I was immediately handled, and tossed up to see if I were sound, by some of the crew; and I was now persuaded that I had gotten into a world of bad spirits, and that they were going to kill me. Their complexions too differing so much from ours, their long hair, and the language they spoke (which was very different from any I had ever heard) united to confirm me in this belief. Indeed[,] such were the horrors of my views and fears at the moment, that, if ten thousand worlds had been my own, I would have freely parted with them all to have exchanged my condition with that of the meanest slave in my own country. When I looked round the ship too and saw a large furnace or copper-boiling, and a multitude of black people of every description chained together, every one of their countenances expressing dejection and sorrow, I no longer doubted of my fate; and, quite overpowered with horror and anguish, I fell motionless on the deck and fainted. (50)

Mott likely thought that these graphic descriptions (among others) would be excessive for New York African Free School students. In doing so, she reduces the representation of white people as cruel and inhumane in Equiano's life story.

11: Illustrations: Pomeroy, in *Alexander Anderson*, vol. 2, specifies that the New York visual artist signed the upper and lower and images on page 11 (1408). In the upper image, Anderson's signature appears at the bottom below the child on the right. This signature appears, as well, at the bottom of the lower image, below the slave with outstretched arms who will be struck by a white person holding a walking stick. Mott's and the Woods' placement of "Page 8." below the upper image and "Page 15." below the lower image continues to test New York African Free School students' reading comprehension skills. The cue "Page 15." invites African American children to turn to a part in *Life and Adventures* they have not yet read.

12: "my master": Equiano provides, in Durell's edition, vol. 1, the name of this Virginia master: Mr. Campbell (66).

12: "a watch": Equiano refers to a clock. Reflecting on the moment of his life when he was young, displaced, and traumatized, Equiano offers an additional point on the material object in vol. 1 of Durell's edition: he was "afraid it would tell the gentleman [Mr. Campbell] any thing I might do amiss" (65). Thus, Equiano reads the clock as an instrument of surveillance.

12: "the pictures": In Mr. Campbell's room, Equiano observes painted portraits.

12: "a large iron": Equiano observes a domestic slave wearing an instrument designed to punish disobedience. The broadside, *Injured Humanity; Being a Representation of What the [U]nhappy Children of Africa [E]ndure from [T]hose [W]ho [C]all [T]hemselves Christians* (New York: Samuel Wood, 1805), contains information on this instrument of torture. The author clarifies that the device, also called an iron muzzle, contains a "Head-frame" and "Mouth-piece," which prevented the slave from speaking, eating, and drinking. In *Life and Adventures*, the Woods use three images from *Injured Humanity*: the lower image on page 22, signed by Anderson, and the upper and lower images on page 33.

12: "...when some of the people made me believe I was going to my native country...": Crew members of the *Industrious Bee* play a cruel joke on Equiano regarding their destination, which was never Africa. Mott eliminates another joke played on Equiano by the captain of the *Industrious Bee*, Michael Henry Pascal, the enslaver. According to Durell's edition, vol. 1, Pascal informs Richard Baker, Equiano's friend and teacher, that he "would kill and eat me" (70). Equiano recalls, too, that Pascal boasts that "he would kill Dick (as he always called him) first, and afterwards me" (70). Pascal's comments on cannibalism grow from the fact that the transatlantic trip from Virginia to England was "very long" and "on that account we had very short allowance of provisions" (68).

12: "... on board this ship I received my name of Gustavus Vassa ... ": Pascal plays another cruel joke on Equiano by renaming him after a Swedish king. Vincent Carretta, editor of Olaudah Equiano, *The Interesting Narrative and Other Writings*, rev. ed. (New York: Penguin, 2003), observes that

> [s]laves were often given ironically inappropriate names of powerful historical figures like Caesar and Pompey to emphasize their subjugation to their masters' wills. Equiano probably expected his readers to recognize the parallel between the Swedish

freedom fighter and the modern leader of his people's struggle against the slave trade, as well as the irony of his initial resistance to his new name. (252–53n130)

Mott does not retain Equiano's reaction to Pascal renaming him Gustavus Vassa. According to Durell's edition, vol. 1, Equiano writes that, once his English language skills began to improve, he at first "refused to be called" (68) Gustavus. Equiano also recollects that Pascal physically abused him when he "refused to answer to my new name" (68). Nor does Mott include Equiano's observation that, before he was owned by Pascal, he was "called" (66) Michael.

12: "Richard Baker": Baker, a slave owner from North America who served in the British Royal Navy alongside Equiano, plays a pivotal role in the autobiographer's life. In Durell's edition, vol. 1, Equiano refers to Baker as his "constant companion and instructor" for a period of two years, during which the two were "inseparable" (69). When Equiano unexpectedly hears about Baker's death in 1759, the life writer refers to him as a "friend, whom I loved, and grieved for, as a brother" (98). Mott does not incorporate Equiano's use of familial rhetoric in relation to Baker. Mott excises, too, Equiano's remark that he and Baker had "many nights laid in each other's bosoms when we were in great distress" (69). For this point, I am indebted to Connie King.

13: "... I often took up a book and talked to it ...": Equiano outlines his frustrations with attempting to hear a printed book speak to him. In other words, the adult Equiano reflects on when he was a displaced African child who had not yet been introduced to the dynamics of print culture and the ways he might decipher the codes in the printed text. Equiano was not the first individual of African descent to comment upon a talking book (or nontalking book). Before Equiano, James Albert Ukawsaw Gronniosaw, John Marrant, and Ottobah Cugoano orally related or wrote about their or others' experiences with a nontalking book. Following Gronniosaw, Marrant, Cugoano, and Equiano, John Jea wrote about his experiences with a nontalking book. For these nontalking book scenes, consult *A Narrative of the Most Remarkable Particulars in the Life of James Albert Ukawsaw Gronniosaw, An African Prince, As Related by Himself* (Bath: William Gye, 1772), 10; *A Narrative of the Lord's Wonderful Dealings with John Marrant, A Black, (Now Going to Preach the Gospel in Nova-Scotia) Born in New-York, in North America. Taken Down from His Own Relation, Arranged, Corrected, and Published by the Rev. Mr. Aldridge*, unauthorized 1st ed. (London: Gilbert and Plummer, 1785), 27; *Thoughts and Sentiments on the Evil and Wicked Traffic of the Slavery and Commerce of the Human Species, Humbly Submitted to the Inhabitants of Great-Britain, by Ottobah Cugoano, A Native of Africa*, authorized 1st ed. (London: unknown publisher, 1787), 80; *The Interesting Narrative of the Life of Olaudah Equiano, or Gustavus Vassa, the African. Written by Himself*, vol. 1 (New York: William Durell, 1791), 75; and *The Life, History, and Unparalleled Sufferings of John Jea, the African Preacher. Compiled and Written by Himself* (Portsea[?]: J. Williams[?], 1815/1816[?]), 33.

13: "a press gang": According to the *Oxford English Dictionary*, this term may be understood as "[a] body of men employed, under the command of an officer, to press men for service in the navy or army." Samuel Johnson, in his 1755 *Dictionary*, vol. 2, defines the term as a "crew that strolls about the streets to force men into naval service." According to Denver Brunsman, in *The Evil Necessity: British Naval Impressment in the Eighteenth-Century Atlantic World* (Charlottesville: University of Virginia Press, 2013), "approximately 250,000 British seamen were impressed during the long eighteenth century—many more than once" (6).

13: "chilblains": According to the *Oxford English Dictionary*, this term may be understood as "[a]n inflammatory swelling produced by exposure to cold, affecting the hands and feet, accompanied with heat and itching, and in severe cases leading to ulceration." Samuel Johnson, in his 1755 *Dictionary*, vol. 1, defines the term as "[s]ores made by frost."

13: " . . . many engagements with the French . . . ": Equiano references his service in the British Royal Navy during the Seven Years' War (1756–1763), a global conflict between Great Britain and France. Mott includes few of Equiano's reflections on this war. For instance, in Durell's edition, vol. 1, Equiano writes that he longed "to have an opportunity of being gratified with a sea-fight" (84), and, during one engagement with the French at sea, he was "a witness of the dreadful fate of many of my companions, who, in the twinkling of an eye, were dashed in pieces, and launched into eternity" (105).

13: "During my stay here . . . ": Mott glosses over a passage in which Equiano writes about discovering different skin complexions while he and Richard Baker lodged with one of Pascal's colleagues in Guernsey:

> This mate had a little daughter, aged about five or six years, with whom I used to be much delighted. I had often observed that when her mother washed her face it looked very rosy; but when she washed mine it did not look so: I therefore tried oftentimes myself if I could not by washing make my face of the same colour as my little play-mate (Mary)[,] but it was all in vain; and I now began to be mortified at the difference in our complexions. (77)

13: "The [*Namur*] being again ready . . . ": Mott eliminates the scene in which Equiano reflects on his baptism in Saint Margaret's Church in London, which occurs before the autobiographer sails to the Mediterranean onboard the *Namur*. The parish record from this church indicates that "Gustavus Vassa" or Olaudah Equiano was born in "Carolina," that is, the North American colonies, instead of Africa. For this document, consult Vincent Carretta, *Equiano, the African: Biography of a Self-Made Man* (New York: Penguin, 2006), 89.

13: "a sober man": Equiano references Daniel Queen, though Mott eliminates his name. Queen, like Baker, was an individual who served alongside Equiano in the British Royal Navy. Equiano writes in Durell's edition, vol. 1, that Queen "taught me to shave and dress hair a little, and also to read in the Bible, explaining many passages to me, which I did not comprehend" (121). Queen also posits that Equiano, following his commitment to the Royal Navy, was "as free as himself or any other man on board" (122). Equiano submits that Queen "was like a father to me" and the life writer "almost loved him with the affection of a son" (122). Mott eliminates Equiano's use of familial rhetoric in describing his relationship with Queen.

13: " . . . but he was offended, for he had determined to send me to the West-Indies": In Durell's edition, vol. 1, Equiano provides additional context for Pascal's selling of him to Captain James Doran. According to Equiano, a disagreement with an unnamed lady with whom Pascal was "once very intimate" (131), who also trusted the autobiographer "to sell and take care of a great deal of property for her" (131), motivated the Royal Navy captain to sell him after years of committed service. As Equiano writes,

> unfortunately for me, a disagreement soon afterwards took place between them; and she was succeeded in my master's good graces by another lady, who appeared sole mistress of the *[Ae]tna* [the ship], and mostly lodged on board. I was not so great a favourite with this lady as with the former; she had conceived a pique against me on some occasion when she was on board, and she did not fail to instigate my master to treat me in the manner he did. (132)

Equiano adds, in a note, that Pascal's new acquaintance "felt her pride alarmed at the superiority of her rival in being attended by a black servant: it was not less to prevent this than to be revenged on me, that she caused the captain to treat me thus cruelly" (132).

14: "The Captain, whose name was Doran . . . ": Mott eliminates a conversation between Equiano and Doran in which the individual of African descent questions the grounds on which he was purchased. Equiano claims that Pascal, his former owner, cannot sell him because of his committed service, loss of prize money, and baptism. In response to these arguments, Equiano writes, in Durell's edition, vol. 1, that "Captain Doran said I talked too much English; and if I did not behave myself well, and be quiet, he had a method on board to make me" (125-26).

14: "eight guineas": Samuel Johnson, in his 1755 *Dictionary*, vol. 1, specifies that the name of this currency derives from "*Guinea*, a country in *Africa* abounding with gold" (emphases in original). Johnson defines this currency as "[a] gold coin valued at one and twenty shillings." For Equiano's explanation, in *Life and Adventures*, of Guinea, consult the second paragraph on page 5.

14: "Rule of Three": Michael Walsh, in *A New System of Mercantile Arithmetic, Adapted to the Commerce of the United States, in its Domestic and Foreign Relations; With Forms of Accounts, and Other Writings Usually Occurring in Trade*, 2nd ed. (Newburyport, MA: Edmund M. Blunt, 1803), defines the rule of three as a principle that "teaches, from three numbers given, to find a fourth, that shall be in the same proportion to the third as the second is to the first" (64). Walsh provides examples using the rule of three to purchase cloth, corn, wheat, rice, sugar, iron, wine, beef, coffee, butter, among others, and to calculate interest rates for loans, rations for a given number of individuals embarking on sea travel, as well as taxes on land and property (64-70). In Durell's edition, vol. 1, Equiano observes that, on board the *Aetna*, Pascal's clerk "taught me to write, and gave me a smattering of arithmetic as far as the rule of three" (121). William Gordon, in *The History of the Rise, Progress, and Establishment of the Independence of the United States of America: Including an Account of the Late War, and of the Thirteen Colonies, from Their Origin to that Period*, vol. 1, 3rd ed. (New York: John Woods, 1801), argues that the rule of three was one way in which an individual may "[pass] for a man of learning" (172). New York African Free School students completed exercises involving the rule of three. Consult New-York African Free School Records, 1817-1832, vol. 4, New-York Historical Society Digital Collections, along with *"Hope Is the First Great Blessing": Leaves from the African Free School Presentation Book, 1812-1816*, annotated by Anna Mae Duane and Thomas Thurston (New York: New-York Historical Society, 2008), 30, 38, and 47.

15: "In my passing about the Island . . . ": Mott does not include important comments Equiano makes about working for Robert King, a Quaker, throughout the West Indies. For instance, in Durell's edition, vol. 1, Equiano writes:

> While I was thus employed by my master[,] I was often a witness to cruelties of every kind, which were exercised on my unhappy fellow slaves. I used frequently to have different cargoes of new negroes in my care for sale; and it was almost a constant practice with our clerks, and other whites, to commit violent depredations on the chastity of the female slaves; and these I was, though with reluctance, obliged to submit to at all times, being unable to help them. (145-46)

15: "three pence": Samuel Johnson, in his 1755 *Dictionary*, vol. 2, defines this currency as "[t]he plural of penny," which he refers to as "[a] small coin, of which twelve make a shilling" and "the radical denomination from which English coin is numbered." Mott wrote a children's book, *The Mother and Her Children, or Twilight Conversation* (New York: Mahlon Day, 1828), in which she structures the first nocturnal discussion around Equiano's three pence. For this conversation, see appendix C.

15: "'Guide to the Indians'": According to Vincent Carretta, in his revised edition of *Interesting Narrative and Other Writings*, Equiano likely refers to *The Knowledge and Practice of Christianity Made Easy to the Meanest Capacities: or, An Essay Towards an Instruction for the Indians*, written by Thomas Wilson, Lord Bishop of Sodor and Man (261n199). Eighteenth-century printers in London disseminated numerous editions of this best-selling book. In Durell's edition, vol. 1, Equiano states that he first became acquainted with this book because, following his baptism, the "clergyman . . . gave me a book, called a Guide to the Indians, written by the Bishop of Sodor and Man" (95). However, Equiano leaves this copy of the book on the *Aetna* after Pascal abruptly sells him to Doran.

15: "tierce": According to the *Oxford English Dictionary*, this term may be understood as "[a]n old measure of capacity equivalent to one third of a pipe (usually 42 gallons old wine measure, but varying for different commodities)," along with "a cask or vessel holding this quantity."

16: Illustrations: Pomeroy, in *Alexander Anderson*, vol. 2, specifies that the New York visual artist signed the upper image, depicting a shipwreck (1408). Anderson's signature appears below the floating barrel. Pomeroy notes that the lower image, a polar scene, appears in a larger form on the title page of the Hon. D. Barrington's *The Possibility of Approaching the North Pole Asserted* (New York: James Eastburn, 1818). Mott's and the Woods' placement of "Page 18." below the upper image and "Page 20." below the lower image continues to test New York African Free School students' reading comprehension skills.

17: "my captain" and "the captain": Equiano refers to Captain Thomas Farmer, employed by Robert King. In Durell's edition, vol. 1, Equiano describes Farmer as "an Englishman, a very [a]lert and active man, who gained my master [King] a great deal of money by his good management in carrying passengers from one island to another" (164).

17: " . . . I recovered so us [*sic*] to get out of bed . . . ": The compositor uses the word "us" for "as."

18: "uncurrent": According to the *Oxford English Dictionary*, this term may be understood as "[n]ot current; not in circulation." Samuel Johnson, in his 1755 *Dictionary*, vol. 2, defines this term as "not passing in current payment."

18: " . . . and I loved him as a father": Mott retains Equiano's use of familial rhetoric when describing his relationship with Farmer. In Durell's edition, vol. 2, Equiano writes:

> Every man on board loved him, and regretted his death; but I was exceedingly affected at it, and found that I did not know, till he was gone, the strength of my regard for him. Indeed[,] I had every reason in the world to be attached to him; for, besides that he was in general mild, affable, generous, faithful, benevolent, and just, he was to me a friend and father; and had it pleased Providence, that he had died about five months before, I verily believe I should not have obtained my freedom when I did; and it is not improbable that I might not have been able to get it at any rate afterwards. (25)

18: " ... I consented to go [*sic*] one more voyage to Georgia ... ": The compositor neglects to include the word "on" before the phrase "one more voyage to Georgia."

18: "When we came near the shore we saw several flamingoes on the beach ... ": Mott includes, in the first nocturnal discussion from *The Mother and Her Children*, Equiano's commentary on the crew mistaking flamingoes for cannibals. For this conversation, see appendix C.

18: " ... and we were taken (but not without experiencing a severe gale) to New Providence": The compositor neglects to include a period after the word "Providence."

19: " ... although he would gladly have kept [*sic*] in his service, he gave me the following certificate": The compositor neglects to include the word "me" after the phrase "have kept."

19: "He was surprised to see me, and asked me [*sic*]": The compositor neglects to include a comma after the phrase "asked me."

19: " ... but not to any satisfaction": In Durell's edition, vol. 2, Equiano writes about this encounter with Pascal:

> I met Capt. Pascal at Miss Guerin's house, and asked him for my prize-money. He said there was none due to me; for, if my prize-money had been [£]10,000[,] he had a right to it all. I told him I was informed otherwise: on which he bade me [defiance]; and in a bantering tone, desired me to commence a lawsuit against him for it: "There are lawyers enough," said he, "that will take the cause in hand, and you had better try it." I told him then that I would try it, which enraged him very much; however, out of regard to the ladies, I remained still, and never made any f[u]rther demand of my right. (62)

19: "Dr. Charles Irving": Ann Savours (Mrs. Shirley), in "'A [V]ery [I]nteresting [P]oint in [G]eography': The 1773 Phipps Exhibition towards the North Pole," *Arctic* 37, no. 4 (1984), observes that Parliamentary members awarded, in 1772, a prize of five thousand pounds to Irving for a distilling method that produced fresh water from sea water (424). Nevertheless, Savours indicates that Irving was by no means the first individual to attempt this process. For this source, I am indebted to Paul Lovejoy.

20: "An expedition was now fitting out to explore a North-east passage to India [*sic*] ... ": The compositor inserts an unnecessary space after the word "India." The comma should immediately follow the word "India."

20: "the [*Race Horse*]": The muster list from the *Racehorse* indicates that the place of birth for "Gustavus Weston" or Olaudah Equiano was South Carolina instead of Africa. For this document, consult Carretta, *Equiano, the African*, 149.

20: "While here we killed manys [*sic*] different kind [*sic*] of animals ... ": The compositor misspells the word "many" and neglects to make the word "kind" plural.

21: " ... 'No new thing happeneth under the sun' ... ": Equiano quotes part of Ecclesiastes 1:9.

21: " ... 'no murderer hath eternal life abiding in him' ... ": Equiano quotes part of 1 John 3:15.

22: Illustrations: Pomeroy, in *Alexander Anderson*, vol. 2, lists the upper image, depicting eleven men in a boat, as being signed by the New York visual artist (1408). Anderson's signature appears below the first cresting wave on the left-hand side. Anderson's signature also appears in the lower image under the right foot of the female slave whom the child embraces. Pomeroy indicates, in *Alexander Anderson*, vol. 1, that the lower image on this page first appeared in *Remarks on the Methods of Procuring Slaves with a Short Account of Their Treatment in the West-Indies, &c.* (London: Printed for Darton and Harvey, 1793), 212. The prose in *Remarks* indicates that these three individuals of African descent constitute a family. The caption under this image, figure V, reads, "The Husband and Wife, after being sold to different purchasers, violently separated—probably never to see each other more!" Wood printed this image before *Life and Adventures*. Consult, for instance, the broadside *Injured Humanity*, published in 1805; *Mirror of Misery*, 15, first published in 1807; and *The Method of Procuring Slaves on the Coast of Africa; With an Account of Their Sufferings on the Voyage, and Cruel Punishment in the West-Indies*, 267, bound with the "enlarged" second edition of *Penitential Tyrant*. Mott's and the Woods' placement of "Page 23." below the upper image and "Page 29." below the lower image continues to test New York African Free School students' reading comprehension skills.

23: "Thus I saw verified what was written in the 107th Psalm": In Durell's edition, vol. 2, Equiano quotes extensively Psalm 107:

> O give thanks unto the Lord, for he is good, for his mercy endureth for ever. Hungry and thirsty, their souls fainted in them. They cried unto the Lord in their trouble, and he delivered them out of their distresses. And he led them forth by the right way, that they might go to a city of habitation. O that men would praise the Lord for his goodness and for his wonderful works to the children of men! For he satisfieth the longing soul, and filleth the hungry soul with goodness.

> Such as sit in darkness and in the shadow of death:

> Then they cried unto the Lord in their trouble, and he saved them out of their distresses. They that go down to the sea in ships; that do business in great waters: these see the works of the Lord, and his wonders in the deep. Whoso is wise and will observe these things, even they shall understand the loving kindness of the Lord. (128–29)

23: "We went soon to the Musqueto shore and began to cultivate the land": In Durell's edition, vol. 2, Equiano recollects that he and Dr. Charles Irving "purchase[d] some slaves" to bring to the Mosquito Shore in order to "cultivate a plantation" (134). Further, Equiano claims that "[a]ll my poor countrymen, the slaves, when they heard of my leaving them, were very sorry, as I had always treated them with care and affection, and did every thing I could to comfort the poor creatures, and render their condition easy" (146). Mott excises Equiano's unsuccessful attempt at converting a Mosquito to Christianity. Like his contemporaries, Equiano spelled the name of this shore, located on the eastern coast of what is now Honduras and Nicaragua, as both "Mosqueto" and "Mosquito." Mott endorses this flexible eighteenth-century spelling.

23: "I once had a proposition made [*sic*] me to go as a missionary to Africa . . . ": The compositor likely neglects to include the word "to" after the words "proposition made."

23: " . . . I feared they would serve me worse than Alexander the coppersmith did St. Paul . . . ": Equiano references 2 Timothy 4:14.

24: "the Free School": Nancy Slocum Hornick, in "Anthony Benezet and the Africans' School: Toward a Theory of Full Equality," *Pennsylvania Magazine of History and Biography* 99, no. 4 (1975), notes that the abolitionist Anthony Benezet (1713–1784) successfully proposed the establishing of a school for African Americans to Philadelphia Monthly Meeting in January 1770 (404), seventeen years before the first African Free School opened in New York. Hornick adds that instruction began on June 28, 1770, and by December 1773, due to an increasing study body, Philadelphia Quakers organized the construction of a schoolhouse (405). Maurice Jackson, in *Let This Voice Be Heard: Anthony Benezet, Father of Atlantic Abolitionism* (Philadelphia: University of Pennsylvania Press, 2009), writes that "[a]lthough the exact number of students who attended the school between 1770 and 1775 is not known, at least 250 young blacks attended. Several students who attended the school later became leaders of Philadelphia's black community" (22). At this African Free School, Equiano may have orally related his life story (or parts of it) to African American children years before he started writing in London the authorized first edition of the *Interesting Narrative*.

24: " . . . a settlement on the coast of Africa, and that vessels were engaged to carry them to Sierra Leona": Christopher Fyfe, in *A History of Sierra Leone* (Oxford: Oxford University Press, 1962), describes the origins of the Sierra Leone resettlement project:

> At the end of the War of American Independence[,] some of the former slaves who had left Republican or Loyalist masters in response to proclamations offering them freedom if they served against the rebels, found their way to London. Sailors stranded at the end of a voyage also swelled the African population. Unlike those in service[,] they lacked employers to protect them. Friendless, often destitute, they wandered the streets, distressing the kind-hearted, alarming the timorous and propertied. (14)

Fyfe notes that, at first, members of the Committee for the Black Poor distributed food and opened a hospital. However, committee members eventually accepted a proposal that highlighted the "commercial advantages of a settlement" in Sierra Leone and secured financial backing from the British government. Additionally, Mott eliminates Equiano's commentary on the potential benefits of transatlantic commerce between Britain and Africa along with his critique of the project. In Durell's edition, vol. 2, Equiano classifies the project as "humane and politic in its design, nor was its failure owing to government: every thing was done on their part; but there was evidently sufficient mismanagement attending the conduct and execution of it to defeat its success" (180). After discovering the mismanagement of goods, Equiano resigns as commissary.

24: "After much difficulty and delay we set sail with 426 persons on board . . . ": In Durell's edition, vol. 2, Equiano writes on his participation in the project: "Thus provided, they proceeded on their voyage; and at last, worn out by treatment, perhaps not the most mild, and wasted by sickness, brought on by want of medicine, cloaths, bedding, &c. they reached Sierra Leona just at the commencement of the rains" (180). That is, according to Durell's edition, Equiano does not return to Africa. This point applies to all authorized editions as well.

25: "In a work that has lately come into my hands . . . ": Mott refers to Henri Grégoire's *An Enquiry Concerning the Intellectual and Moral Faculties, and Literature of Negroes; Followed with an Account of the Life and Works of Fifteen Negroes and Mulattoes, Distinguished in Science, Literature and the Arts*, trans. D. B. Warden (Brooklyn: Thomas Kirk, 1810), 226–27. Grégoire's point on Equiano having a son named Sancho who worked for Sir Joseph Banks

Explanatory Notes

has not been confirmed by any twentieth-century or twenty-first-century scholars. Equiano and his wife, Susanna Cullen, had two daughters, Ann Mary and Joanna.

25: "'guilty of a skin not coloured like their own'": This line comes from Book II, "The Time-Piece," of William Cowper's *The Task, A Poem, in Six Books* (London: Printed for J. Johnson, 1785), 46. James G. Basker, editor of *Amazing Grace: An Anthology of Poems about Slavery, 1660–1810* (New Haven: Yale University Press, 2002), writes that Cowper was "one of the most prolific and influential antislavery poets of the eighteenth century" (294). Marcus Wood, editor of *The Poetry of Slavery: An Anglo-American Anthology, 1764–1865* (Oxford: Oxford University Press, 2003), claims that Cowper "was more frequently reprinted by American abolitionists than any other poet with the exception of [William] Wordsworth" (83).

25: "R[emarks] [on] [the] S[lave] T[rade]": Like other parts from *Life and Adventures*, "Remarks" circulated, in various forms, throughout the Atlantic world before appearing in Mott's adaptation. Some of the prose may be found in the broadside "Plan of an A[frican] S[hip's] [L]ower [D]eck with N[egroes] in the [P]roportion of [O]nly One to a [T]on," created and published in 1788 by William Elford and the Plymouth chapter of the Society for Effecting the Abolition of the Slave Trade. Matthew Carey (1760–1839), a Philadelphia printer and bookseller, published only the prose of "Remarks" in the May 1789 issue of *The American Museum: or Repository of Ancient and Modern Fugitive Pieces, &c. Prose and Poetical*. In this year, Carey published, for members of the Philadelphia Society for Promoting the Abolition of Slavery, "Remarks," containing an illustration of the slave ship *Brooks*. In 1807, before *Life and Adventures*, Wood printed "Remarks" on a broadside titled "Plan of an African Ship's [L]ower Deck, with Negroes in the [P]roportion of [N]ot [Q]uite [O]ne to a [T]on," under an illustration of the *Brooks*. Wood also included "Remarks" in *Mirror of Misery*, 9–14, and *Method of Procuring Slaves*, 261–66.

25: "plate": According to the *Oxford English Dictionary*, this term may be understood as "[a] polished sheet of brass, copper, etc., engraved or etched to print from."

26: "Plan of a Slave Ship's [L]ower [D]eck, with Negroes in the [P]roportion of [N]ot [Q]uite [O]ne to a [T]on": Marcus Rediker, in *The Slave Ship: A Human History* (New York: Viking, 2007), provides a succinct explanation of the significance of this image of a slave ship:

> The best known of these [images of slave ships], in its own day and since, was the slave ship *Brooks*, first drawn and illustrated by William Elford and the Plymouth chapter of the Society for Effecting the Abolition of the Slave Trade in November 1788. The *Brooks* would be redrawn and republished many times around the Atlantic in the years that followed, and indeed it would come to epitomize the cruelties of the Atlantic slave trade in the eighteenth and nineteenth centuries, as well as the many-sided struggle against it. (308–9)

Rediker notes as well that captains used the *Brooks* for ten slaving voyages in which they "purchased an estimated total of 5,163 Africans, 4,559 of whom they delivered alive, giving the ship a mortality rate of 11.7 percent, close to the average for ships over the four centuries of the slave trade (12.1 percent), but high for its own day (average for British ships between 1775 and 1800 was 7.95 percent)" (311). Pomeroy, in *Alexander Anderson*, vol. 2, writes that this image of the slave ship "may be . . . [the] work" (1408) of the New York visual artist. In 1807, before *Life and Adventures*, Wood published the broadside

"Plan of an African Ship's [L]ower Deck," which contained an illustration of the *Brooks*. Wood also included "Plan" in *Mirror of Misery*, 10-11, and *Method of Procuring Slaves*, 262-63. Note the designation of a "B[oy's] R[oom]" and "G[irl's] R[oom]" in a book designed for African American children.

29: "A S[ubject] [for] C[onversation] and R[eflection] [at] [the] T[ea]-T[able]": See the note on "C[omplaint]" for information on the circulation of "A S[ubject]." Before *Life and Adventures*, Wood printed another version of "A S[ubject]" in *Mirror of Misery*, 37-48, and the "enlarged" second edition of *Penitential Tyrant*, 243-51.

29: "Mr. Cowper": The author of "A S[ubject] for C[onversation] and R[eflection] [at] [the] T[ea]-T[able]" refers to William Cowper (1731-1800), a British poet. The Woods included in *Life and Adventures* some of Cowper's poetry on the slave trade and the institution of slavery. However, Mott clearly valued Cowper's poetry. The Quaker elder uses four lines from *Tirocinium: or, a Review of Schools* (London: Printed for J. Johnson, 1785) as one of the epigraphs for *Observations*: "From education, as the leading cause, / The public character its colour draws; / Thence the prevailing manners take their cast, / Extravagant or sober, loose or chaste." Mott also included Cowper's "Morning Dream" in *Biographical Sketches* (175-76). According to the chapter "A[frican] F[ree] S[chools] in N[ew]-Y[ork]" from *Biographical Sketches*, one student, on an examination day in 1824, recited "thirteen lines from Cowper, in favour of liberty" (154). Examination days were public events designed to draw attention to the New York African Free Schools and their students. Trustees publicized these events in New York newspapers. Attendees at an examination day held in May 1824 experienced, for instance, "exhibitions in spelling, reading, writing, arithmetic, geography, elocution, and needlework," according to an article titled "African Free School," published in the May 13, 1824, issue of the *Evening Post*. Furthermore, according to *Memoir of Purchase Monthly Meeting, Concerning Abigail Mott* (New York: James Egbert, 1852), Mott recited, near the end of her life, the following lines from Book II from Cowper's *The Task* (London: Printed for J. Johnson, 1785): "'I would not have a slave to till my ground, / To carry me, to fan me while I sleep, / And tremble when I wake, for all the wealth / That sinews bought and sold have ever earned'" (16). (These lines appear in the poem "R[eflections]" in *Life and Adventures* [30]). After reciting these lines, Mott then "spoke encouragingly to those friends, to bear their testimony against slavery, by declining the use of articles produced by the unrequited labor of the poor slaves, who are as much the objects of Redeeming love as ourselves" (16). For the *Memoir*, see appendix C.

30: "R[eflections]": This verse comprises part of Book II, "The Time-Piece," from Cowper's *The Task, a Poem, in Six Books* (London: Printed for J. Johnson, 1785), 45-47. Slight differences exist in the version of the poem that appears in the London book and the one in *Life and Adventures*. Furthermore, the Woods, in the excerpted portion in *Life and Adventures*, did not include the following lines: "Lands intersected by a narrow frith / Abhor each other. Mountains interposed, / Make enemies of nations who had else / Like kindred drops been mingled into one. / Thus man devotes his brother, and destroys" (46). These lines appear after the line that begins, "Dooms and devotes," and before the line that begins, "And worse than all." Prior to *Life and Adventures*, Wood printed this part of Cowper's poem in *Mirror of Misery*, 39-40, and "A S[ubject] for C[onversation] and R[eflection] [at] [the] T[ea]-T[able]," 245-46, bound with the "enlarged" second edition of *Penitential Tyrant*.

30: "We have no slaves at home—then why abroad?": Slaves certainly resided in Britain at the time Cowper published *The Task* in 1785. The transatlantic slave trade was prohibited by law in Britain in 1807. However, as James Walvin observes in *Questioning Slavery* (New York and London: Routledge, 1996), approximately six hundred thousand slaves remained in the West Indies after the eradication of the transatlantic slave trade (164). The institution of slavery was prohibited by law in Britain and its colonies in 1838. In the lines that follow the claim "We have no slaves at home—then why abroad?," Cowper may have referenced Lord Chief Justice Mansfield's June 1772 ruling on the status of the slave James Somerset. Somerset escaped from his Scottish master, Charles Stewart, but was discovered and, against his will, put on board a ship, the *Ann and Mary*, sailing for Jamaica. Somerset's court case began in February 1772. As James Walvin clarifies in *Britain's Slave Empire* (Stroud: Tempus, 2007),

> The Somerset Case ended only with the judgment that slaves could not be removed from England against their wishes. Mansfield had *not* resolved that slavery in England was illegal, though this last point was repeated in various newspaper reports and, more recently, by modern scholars. Slavery survived—legally—in England (though assailed by a changing political and social climate). But to remove slaves against their wishes *was* illegal. (90; emphases in original)

30: "That part us, are emancipate [*sic*] and loos'd": The compositor did not include the letter "d" after the word "emancipate" to ensure that both verbs have the same tense. Samuel Johnson, in his 1755 *Dictionary*, vol. 2, defines the verb "loose" as "[t]o free from imprisonment."

31: "C[omplaint]": The full title of this poem is "The Negro's Complaint," written by Cowper and first published in 1788. Thomas Clarkson, a British abolitionist, provides important information on the circulation of Cowper's poem in late eighteenth-century England. In *The History of the Rise, Progress, and Accomplishment of the Abolition of the African Slave-Trade by the British Parliament*, vol. 2 (London: R. Taylor, 1808), Clarkson writes,

> This little piece, Cowper presented in manuscript to some of his friends in London; and these, conceiving it to contain a powerful appeal in behalf of the injured Africans, joined in printing it. Having ordered it on the finest hot-pressed paper, and folded it up in a small and neat form, they gave it the printed title of "A Subject for Conversation at the Tea-table." After this, they sent many thousand copies of it in franks into the country. From one it spread to another, till it traveled almost over the whole island. Falling at length into the hands of the musician, it was set to music; and it then found its way into the streets, both of the metropolis and of the country, where it was sung as a ballad; and where it gave a plain account of the subject, with an appropriate feeling, to those who heard it. (190–91)

John O'Brien observes, in *Literature Incorporated: The Cultural Unconscious of the Business Corporation, 1650–1850* (Chicago: University of Chicago Press, 2015), that "The Negro's Complaint" was "being sung at Vauxhall Gardens in the summer of 1788," and editors of the *Public Advertiser* printed it in the April 2, 1789, issue to ensure that the poem aligned with the publication of the first authorized edition of Equiano's *Interesting Narrative* (170). Before *Life and Adventures*, Wood printed the poem in *Mirror of Misery*, 41–42, and "A S[ubject] for C[onversation] and R[eflection] at the T[ea]-T[able]," 247–48.

33: Illustrations: Pomeroy, in *Alexander Anderson*, vol. 1, notes that both images not signed by Anderson first appeared in *Remarks on the Methods of Procuring Slaves* (212). The caption under the upper image, figure VI, reads, "When Slaves are purchased by the dealers[,] they are generally marked on the breast with a red hot iron." The caption under the lower image, figure XII, reads, "Another method of fixing the poor victims on a ladder to be flogged, which is also occasionally laid flat on the ground for severer punishments." Before

Life and Adventures, Wood printed these images on the broadside *Injured Humanity*, as well as in *Mirror of Misery*, 21, 22, and *Method of Procuring Slaves*, 273, 274. Mott's and the Woods' placement of "Page 29." below the upper image and "Page 29." below the lower image continues to test New York African Free School students' reading comprehension skills.

34: "'H[elp]! Oh, help! thou God of Christians!'": Philip Gould, in *Barbaric Traffic: Commerce and Antislavery in the Eighteenth-Century Atlantic World* (Cambridge: Harvard University Press, 2003), identifies the author of the poem, likely first published in the *American Museum* in 1789, as Theodore Dwight (73). Editors of children's books and newspapers for children regularly republished the poem, occasionally with a different title. Consult, for instance, the October 23, 1813, issue of *The Juvenile Port-Folio, and Literary Miscellany. Devoted to the Instruction, and Amusement of Youth* (Philadelphia); *The Child's Own Book. New Series* (London: Houlston and Stoneman, 1851), 84; and Reverend J. L. Blake, *The Juvenile Companion and Fireside Reader, Consisting of Historical and Biographical Anecdotes, and Selections in Poetry* (New York: Harper and Brothers, 1855), 153–54.

35: "T[he] N[egro] B[oy]": Peter C. Hogg, in *The African Slave Trade and Its Suppression: A Classified and Annotated Bibliography of Books, Pamphlets and Periodical Articles* (London and New York: Routledge, 2013), specifies that editors of *The Britannic Magazine; or [E]ntertaining Repository of Heroic Adventures and Memorable Exploits* (London), vol. 3, printed the poem in 1795 (330). Hogg also notes that editors of *The Monthly Magazine, and British Register* (London), vol. 2, published the poem, written by "Anti-Doulos," in 1796. (*Doulos* is the Greek word for "slave.") Mott includes this poem in her anthology, *Biographical Sketches*, 184–85. She acknowledges that she consulted "an English publication" for the poem, which was written "some years ago" (184). Furthermore, students at New York African Free Schools may have read this poem before 1829, the year the Woods published *Life and Adventures*. Editors of *Freedom's Journal*, the first African American newspaper, published "The Negro Boy" in the November 2, 1827, issue. Charles C. Andrews, teacher at African Free School no. 2 and historian of the educational system, acknowledges in a letter addressed to John Russwurm, an editor of *Freedom's Journal*, that the latter sent the "regular weekly numbers" of the newspaper "for the benefit of the Library in the School in Mulberry-street." Editors of *Freedom's Journal* published Andrews's letter in the November 9, 1827, issue. For this letter, see appendix B. "The Negro Boy" continued to appear, albeit in slightly different forms, in children's books. Consult, for instance, Joseph Payne, ed., *Select Poetry for Children: With Brief Explanatory Notes. Arranged for the Use of Schools and Families* (London: Relfe and Fletcher, 1839), 21–22, and *The Youth's Poetical Instructor, Part II, A Selection from Modern Poets, British and American* (Belfast: Alexander Mayne, 1851), 63. Joseph Payne, editor of *Select Poetry for Children*, identifies "Samwell" as author of "The Negro Boy" (22), whereas editors of *The Youth's Poetical Instructor* claim that Cowper wrote this poem (63).

36: "T[he] N[egro's] P[rayer]": James G. Basker, editor of *Amazing Grace*, writes that this poem was the third in a series of antislavery texts, written by different authors and published in the *Baltimore Weekly Magazine* in 1800–1801 (553). Basker posits that "[i]f this poem's prefatory stanza is true, it may have been written or adapted by the editor of the magazine, John B. Colvin." The version of the poem the Woods include in *Life and Adventures* contains different stanza breaks and six fewer lines than the one published in the *Baltimore Weekly Magazine*. Also, this poem, titled "The N[egroe's] P[rayer]" and lacking the stanza breaks in *Life and Adventures*, appears in *A Selection of Miscellaneous Pieces, in Verse and Prose. Respectfully Dedicated to the Youth of Both Sexes. Part 1* (Philadelphia: Daniel Lawrence, 1792), 44–45.

Explanatory Notes

36: "When will Jehovah hear onr [*sic*] cries?": The compositor misspelled the word "our."

36: Illustration: Martha J. Cutter, in "The Child's Illustrated Antislavery Talking Book: Abigail Field Mott's Abridgement of Olaudah Equiano's *Interesting Narrative* for African American Children," in *Who Writes for Black Children? African American Children's Literature before 1900*, ed. Katharine Capshaw and Anna Mae Duane (Minneapolis: University of Minnesota Press, 2017), interprets this illustration as one that "sarcastically reworks the famous Wedgwood antislavery medallion, with its kneeling, supplicant slave, by suggesting that unless slavery was abolished, liberation would be discovered exclusively 'in the grave'" (119).

Back Cover: "Juvenile Books": To maximize space allocated to advertising children's books, the Woods abbreviated many titles from this series. The full titles of books listed in this advertisement, published by Wood and Sons unless otherwise noted, with first known publication dates, include *Rural Scenes, or, A Peep into the Country, For Children* (1823); *The Infant's Cabinet* (Wood, 1814); *Choice Emblems, Natural, Historical, Fabulous, Moral and Divine, For The Instruction and Amusement of Youth; Displaying The Beauties and Morals of The Ancient Fabulists* (1818); *The Hedge of Thorns* (1820); *The History of Alexander Selkirk, the Real Robinson Crusoe. To Which Are Added Sketches of Natural History* (1815); *The Rational Dame; or, Hints Towards Supplying Prattle for Children* (1821); *The Daisy, or, Cautionary Stories, in Verse* (around 1820); *Alice, the Negro Girl; and the Good Old Indian: To Which Are Added A Memoir of Ann Watson, and The Advice of Thomas Gwin, &c.* (1817); *The Cries of New-York* (1818); *Songs, Divine and Moral, for the Use of Children* (between 1817 and 1820); *Garden Amusements, For Improving The Minds Of Little Children* (1815); *Pictures of English History, In Miniature, Designed by Alfred Mills: With Descriptions* (1817); *The Rose Bush, or, Stories in Verse* (likely before 1824); *Giddy Gertrude; A Story for Little Girls* (likely between 1816 and 1830); *Æsop's Fables* (1818); *The School of Good Manners* (1822); *Franklin's Way to Wealth; or, "Poor Richard Improved"* (1820); *Original and Select Juvenile Hymns. Adapted To the Use of Free Schools; More Particularly to Those Called Sunday or Sabbath Schools* (1817); *The Olio* (1816); and *The Decoy; or, An Agreeable Method of Teaching Children the Elementary Parts Of English Grammar, By Conversations and Familiar Examples* (1816).

Back Cover: "&c. &c. &c.": For additional "Juvenile Books" printed and sold by the Woods, see the advertisements in *The Seven Wonders of the World; and Other Magnificent Buildings, &c.* (1816), *The Hedge of Thorns* (1820), and *A Father's Gift to His Son, on His Becoming an Apprentice. To Which Is Added Dr. Franklin's Way to Wealth* (1821).

Appendix A

Rethinking Textual Paradigms in Early Black Atlantic Studies

Texts orally related or written in English by individuals of African descent, predominantly those first published before 1800, constitute the early Black Atlantic literary canon. Early Black Atlantic orators and writers utilized genres such as the captivity narrative, conversion narrative, slave narrative, criminal confession, elegy, petition, epistle, almanac, and jeremiad for a variety of reasons. They attempted to convince readers that individuals of African descent were full members of the human family; establish that Africans possessed meaningful cultural, religious, and linguistic traditions; demonstrate that individuals of African descent possessed intellectual curiosity along with the capacity to produce literature; secure basic rights for individuals of African descent in various pockets of the Atlantic world; create religious, political, and literary networks in order to gain power and authority in personal and social spaces; and dismantle the transatlantic slave trade and institution of slavery. Most of these texts were addressed to Euro-American readers who had the power to remedy the ills of the slave system, yet some carried messages to Black people about means of defying racism and enslavement. As captives, converts, castaways, preachers, sailors, merchants, explorers, musicians, slaves, and free persons, many pre-1800 Black orators and writers also navigated multiple parts of the Atlantic world, whether it was because of the slave trade, evangelism, commerce, adventure, war, pursuit of better health, publication of a book, or resettlement. Thus, several early Black Atlantic orators and writers experienced, at different points in their lives, Africa, the West Indies, the North American colonies, and Great Britain. Movement also punctuated the life spans of several early Black Atlantic texts. The transatlantic, transnational circulation of early Black Atlantic literature established the textual foundation upon which other individuals of African descent with more permanent connections to the United States developed the African American literary tradition.

Yet this architectural metaphor offers misleading notions of stability in analyzing early Black Atlantic literature. Like a plethora of texts published in the eighteenth and nineteenth centuries, nearly all early Black Atlantic literature experienced the same textual fate. Authorial and nonauthorial agents revised, in specific ways and for specific ends, captivity narratives, conversion narratives, slave narratives, criminal confessions, elegies, petitions, epistles, almanacs, and jeremiads, resulting in the creation of different versions of these texts. In numerous instances, early Black Atlantic literature may be classified as what John Bryant calls a fluid text, which he defines as "any literary work that exists in more than one version," whether in "early manuscript forms, subsequent print editions, or even adaptations in other media with or without the author's consent." Bryant classifies the fluid text as an "inescapable [element] of the literary phenomenon."[1] Unfortunately, early Black Atlantic scholars have not fully realized the significance of textual fluidity. Instead of pinpointing textual fluidity along with authorial and nonauthorial revision practices as fundamental characteristics of the print contexts from which early Black Atlantic literature emerged, critics have largely ignored the unstable nature of these texts. Rather than dismiss the presence of textual fluidity or relegate this apparently tedious work to a conscientious editor or bibliographer, it is time for scholars to attend to the manifestations of textual fluidity in authorized, unauthorized, abridged, and posthumous editions of early Black Atlantic literature. An examination of a multitude of revision practices, ones made by early Black Atlantic orators and writers along with those made by nonauthorial subjects, yields a number of heretofore unexplored narratives concerning the lives and texts of pre-1800 individuals of African descent.

THE STATE OF EARLY BLACK ATLANTIC STUDIES

In taking stock of the state of early Black Atlantic studies during the second decade of the twenty-first century, one may claim that the field sits at an important crossroads, a critical impasse concerning textuality. On one hand, some scholars have contributed important studies by employing methodologies from book history, which have produced sophisticated understandings of the production, circulation, and consumption of early Black Atlantic literature.[2] On the other hand, Leon Jackson's point on scholars' limited understandings of early Black Atlantic texts still rings true. As he observes, "we know very little about the production, dissemination, or consumption of the books that deployed [the nontalking book] trope, and still less of the books that were begged, borrowed, stolen, owned, or encountered by the authors who wrote them."[3] Jackson's comment must be extended to represent another shortcoming in the field: early Black Atlantic scholars know relatively little about the transatlantic, transnational publishing and reception histories of certain texts, nor do they know much about the print networks responsible for the continued circulation of this literature *after* 1800. In other words, scholars have not adequately addressed where selected early Black Atlantic texts with transatlantic, transnational publishing histories surfaced, in what forms they appeared as material artifacts and marketable commodities, who produced, marketed, and sold them, who read them, how these individuals responded to them, and what factors contributed to the preservation of them. In the case of Olaudah Equiano, the production, distribution, and consumption of his life story in the United States has been dismissed by several scholars because they align him closely with a given nation. Equiano's bestselling *Interesting Narrative* has been fused, for decades, with anti-slave-trade and antislavery agitation in late eighteenth-century Great Britain, even though this autobiography appeared in various forms in the United States and Europe during his lifetime and following his death.[4] As a result, an understanding of the publishing and reception histories of this autobiography have remained mostly stagnant.

Attending to the phenomenon of textual fluidity in the early Black Atlantic literary canon first requires interrogating the current textual paradigm to which numerous editors and scholars subscribe. A textual paradigm impacts a given field in far-reaching ways: it dictates what copy-texts editors choose for scholarly editions and anthologies, it influences what editions and anthologies pedagogues use in their undergraduate and graduate classrooms, and it determines what texts members of a discourse community routinely cite in peer-reviewed scholarship. A transatlantic, transnational approach to the production, dissemination, and consumption of early Black Atlantic books will not transpire if scholars do not take seriously unauthorized, posthumous, and abridged editions. At present, practitioners in the field overwhelmingly subscribe to a textual paradigm, one created by mid-twentieth-century bibliographers, that does not value multiple versions of literary works, especially the content found in unauthorized, posthumous, and abridged editions. The neglect of these editions derives from a firm allegiance to authorized editions, that is, ones that highlight early Black Atlantic orators' and writers' attempts to control their lives, texts, and selves via oversight, revision, sales, or copyright.

There is absolutely no question that several editions underscore important agential acts of early Black Atlantic orators and writers. For example, the authorized fourth edition of John Marrant's conversion-captivity narrative, the authorized second edition of Quobna Ottobah Cugoano's jeremiad, and nine authorized editions of Equiano's autobiography illuminate how an early Black Atlantic orator and two early Black Atlantic writers exerted control over their books. For Marrant, control over his life story meant adding—and likely writing—material to the authorized fourth edition, from which he economically benefited. William Aldridge, a white minister who subscribed to Equiano's *Interesting Narrative*, wrote and sold several unauthorized editions of Marrant's autobiographical narrative after attending the Black minister's ordination ceremony. The majority of this material did not appear in several editions printed in London before the authorized fourth edition, so Marrant likely viewed these unauthorized editions as incomplete ones that failed to document all the significant events from his life. In the authorized fourth edition, he reflects on preaching to slaves on a South Carolina plantation, witnessing the beating of these individuals by a white mistress, and converting individuals of African descent, among others. For Cugoano, control over the authorized second edition of his jeremiad included selling the book along with significantly condensing the text in order to redirect his argumentation to "Sons of Africa" instead of the "Inhabitants of Great Britain," the audience for the authorized first edition. This revision pertaining to audience indicates that he attempted to groom the next generation of literate Afro Britons who would continue to engage in anti-slave-trade and antislavery agitation. For Equiano, control over his life story occurred on multiple levels: securing the copyright to his book, revising his autobiography, and marketing the book, which included a book tour.[5] Without a doubt, scholars should continue discussing these unique editions and teaching them in relevant pedagogical contexts; notably, though, Marrant's authorized fourth edition and some of Equiano's authorized editions are more frequently taught than Cugoano's authorized second edition.

Traditionally, editors of anthologies containing early Black Atlantic literature, including Adam Potkay, Sandra Burr, Vincent Carretta, Joanna Brooks, and John Saillant, have utilized authorized editions as copy-texts. If there is no textual evidence justifying this classification, editors have selected as copy-text the first extant edition, which allegedly aligns more fully with the orator's or writer's intentions compared with subsequent print editions that may contain traces of nonauthorial intervention. This point means that authorized and first editions structure the most commonly used anthologies: Potkay and Burr's *Black Atlantic Writers of the Eighteenth Century: Living the New Exodus in England and the Americas*, Carretta's *Unchained Voices: An Anthology of Black Authors in the English-Speaking World of the Eighteenth Century*, and Brooks and Saillant's

"Face Zion Forward": First Writers of the Black Atlantic, 1785–1798. These editors deserve credit for excavating what D. C. Greetham has referred to as the "archaeology of the text" by documenting in endnotes, bibliographies, introductions, or elsewhere the ways authorial and nonauthorial agents revised early Black Atlantic texts.[6] Judging by the few studies on textual fluidity and early Black Atlantic literature, one may claim that most readers have not given adequate attention to this commentary or, worse yet, have glossed over it. In many cases, though, it is difficult to determine the extent to which an early Black Atlantic orator or writer exerted control over a text. Editions with indeterminable degrees of control and authority far outweigh authorized ones. This point means that scholars have endorsed a paradigm that automatically excludes dozens of editions from serious study, including ones produced by and for individuals of African descent. A new field can be built from the ground up if scholars examine a wider variety of texts printed in the eighteenth and nineteenth centuries.

Early Black Atlantic literary scholars' dedication to this textual paradigm is inconsistent and at times baffling. For instance, Equiano writes in numerous authorized editions that he was "glad" that unauthorized editions of his life story circulated in Germany, Holland, and New York.[7] Knowing that he would never see money from sales of these books, Equiano praises the transatlantic, transnational print networks that enabled more readers in the Atlantic world to access his anti-slave-trade and antislavery arguments. The early Black Atlantic writer's comment on unauthorized editions of his life story undermines twenty-first-century scholars' commitment to a paradigm that cannot account for the transatlantic, transnational circulation of his text and several others from this literary canon. Additionally, little attention has been paid to authorial revision practices in extant manuscripts, even though these documents conform to the present criteria for what constitutes a legitimate text. Important authorial revision practices, as documented in the nine authorized editions of Equiano's autobiographical narrative and the authorized second edition of Cugoano's jeremiad, have also been overlooked. Further, scholars have rigorously studied some authorized editions but ignored others, especially those that were commercial failures. Thus, scholars have not yet identified all the factors determining why some early Black Atlantic texts continued to circulate while others experienced brief life spans or textual death.

A textual paradigm valuing only a select number of authorized editions ultimately divorces the literature from the principal contexts from which it emerged: the unstable textual worlds of eighteenth-century transatlantic and transnational print networks. That is, the current textual paradigm ignores one of the most fundamental dynamics of eighteenth-century print culture that shaped how and why different versions of early Black Atlantic texts appeared in print. As Eve Tavor Bannet writes, "various forms of textual editing and paratextual rewriting" were commonplace in the eighteenth century. Bannet adds that printed texts such as autobiographical narratives and novels were routinely "altered, reworded, epitomized, re-compiled, renamed, adapted, repositioned, reinterpreted, re-contextualized[,] or reframed." In doing so, nonauthorial subjects (e.g., editors, compositors, book binders) did not necessarily corrupt the text, as proponents of the current paradigm maintain. Rather, Bannet holds that these individuals functioned as "cultural brokers" who "acted as purveyors and translators . . . [as] they left traces of their readings . . . in the text or paratext."[8] Consequently, the current paradigm too easily dismisses the social nature of textual production and the cultural work performed by nonauthorial subjects who altered linguistic and bibliographic codes of authorized and first editions. The forces of print culture modulated early Black Atlantic literature, as they did with many other eighteenth-century and nineteenth-century texts. Rather than sever the relationship between early Black Atlantic literature and the fundamental print contexts from which it emerged, a book history and print culture approach attends to the unstable nature of eighteenth-century print culture by teasing out the ways texts mutated, situating them in relevant contexts, and historicizing the forces driving diverse sets of revision practices. Indeed, Marrant's reflection on his life as a freewheeling musician in Charlestown being "[u]nstable as water" provides the most productive way to approach early Black Atlantic literature.[9]

Equally concerning is the fact that a dismissal of transatlantic publishing and reception histories runs counter to practitioners' consistent subscription to Paul Gilroy's influential thinking on the Black Atlantic. Taking a cue from Gilroy, scholars have insisted time and time again that the crossing (even crisscrossing) of the Atlantic Ocean positions early Black Atlantic orators and writers as individuals whose lives included pertinent experiences in multiple geographical points. Oddly enough, while scholars uniformly embrace the Gilroy-inspired premise that early Black Atlantic *lives* are transatlantic phenomena, a large portion of them ignore the fact that early Black Atlantic *texts* are also transatlantic phenomena. Outlining the chronotype of the ship that encapsulates Black Atlantic culture, Gilroy observes that this space assisted in the "movement of key cultural and political artefacts: tracts, books, gramophone records, and choirs."[10] In other words, Gilroy's theorizing of the Black Atlantic has not been adequately extended to the transatlantic publishing and reception histories of early Black Atlantic texts. What is most alarming about this point is that transatlantic print networks ensured that African American readers, including children, accessed unauthorized, posthumous, and abridged editions. Therefore, scholars endorse a textual paradigm unable and unwilling to account for Black readers. At this juncture, it is no longer adequate to accept, on one hand, the transatlantic nature of early Black Atlantic lives as a fundamental disciplinary premise and to refuse, on the other hand, to attend to the transatlantic publishing and reception histories of early Black Atlantic texts. To put this matter another way, recognizing the transatlantic nature only of early Black Atlantic lives prohibits generating more sophisticated understandings of the production, circulation, and consumption of early Black Atlantic texts. Necessary discoveries on early Black Atlantic lives and texts grow from repositioning authorized and first editions as not the only texts worthy of serious study but ones in a larger, more complex network involving authorial and nonauthorial agents.

ABIGAIL FIELD MOTT AND *Life and Adventures of Olaudah Equiano*

In what follows, I offer the most thorough discussion to date on Abigail Field Mott's life along with the books she coauthored, wrote, and edited; establish essential historical information relating to the curriculum and politics of the New York African Free Schools in the late 1820s when the Woods printed Mott's adaptation of Equiano's life story; identify a number of key differences between William Durell's unauthorized 1791 New York edition of Equiano's life story, the base text from which Mott structured her abridgment, *Life and Adventures of Olaudah Equiano*; and interpret one of the most significant instances of Mott rewriting Equiano's life story that connects to early nineteenth-century resettlement schemes. The commentary in this section functions as a model to examine the publishing histories of other early Black Atlantic texts.

Like her adaptation of Equiano's autobiography, Abigail Field Mott, a white Quaker, remains an understudied subject (figure 1).[11] Historians and literary critics likely recognize one part of this Quaker elder's name because she was related through marriage to well-known abolitionist and women's rights activist Lucretia Coffin Mott, who occasionally corresponded with Abigail's sister, Lydia. The Mott sisters were cousins of Lucretia's husband, James Mott. However, the significance of Abigail Field Mott must be understood beyond her affiliation with her famous relative. Mott committed, for instance, a good portion of her life to antislavery politics. Abigail and Lydia subscribed to Frederick Douglass's paper, *The North Star*.[12] In Albany, where she lived with her sister during one part of her life, Abigail sold copies of Douglass's first autobiography, *Narrative of the Life of Frederick Douglass, an American Slave. Written by Himself*, published in Boston in 1845, which she positively reviewed in the June 6, 1845, issue of William Lloyd Garrison's antislavery paper, *The Liberator*.[13] Douglass knew and

Fig. 1. Photograph of Abigail Field Mott, Richard Mott Papers (MC 961), Quaker and Special Collections, Haverford College, Haverford, PA. Used by permission.

trusted the Motts to the extent that he felt comfortable with his seven-year-old daughter, Rosetta, living with them from 1845 to 1848, when she attended school in Albany while he traveled to Great Britain.[14] This transatlantic voyage was necessary for Douglass because it protected the Black fugitive life writer from being recaptured by his owners, especially after his first autobiography became more popular in certain areas of the United States.[15]

The relationship between Abigail Field Mott and Douglass, especially in the 1840s, may be best understood by the African American autobiographer's inscription in the two-volume *Poems by Alfred Tennyson*, published by Edward Moxon in London in 1846. Douglass purchased the two-volume set while he was in Manchester in the winter of 1846 and sent the inscribed books to Abigail Field Mott. Douglass wrote the following inscription in vol. 1: "From her sincere, and grateful Friend, Frederick Douglass. Manchester—Eng. 3d Dec—1846." At some point, women's rights activist Susan B. Anthony acquired Mott's two-volume set and wrote the following inscription in volume 1: "In memory of my dear friend <u>Abigail Mott</u>—and my longer and still more dear & helpful friend—<u>Lydia Mott</u>—of Albany—N.Y." [16] In volume 2, Anthony's inscription reads as follows: "These volumes were sent to Abigail Mott—when Frederick Douglass was for the first time visiting England—The miss[es] Mott—Abigail and Lydia[—]had earned his gratitude by teaching him to read—[and] talk correctly—and being all that mortals could be to him—as friends." [17] Douglass and Abigail Field Mott also corresponded, and, on at least one occasion, the African American editor published one of her letters in *The North Star*.[18] Furthermore, in Douglass's third and final autobiography, *Life and Times of Frederick Douglass*, first published in 1881, years after his relationship with Abigail Field Mott ended and years after her death, the African American life writer names the "Misses Motts" as "forwarders" in Albany for the Underground Railroad and lists "the Motts" among those who "welcome[d] me to my newly found heritage of freedom." [19]

As residents of Albany, New York—a location that was a key site of the Underground Railroad—the Motts, according to William J. Switala, were also entrepreneurs who owned "a linen goods store, boardinghouse, and clothing store that they operated at 524 Broadway." [20] The Motts used this property to lodge a wide variety of individuals, including fugitive slaves, abolitionists, and women's rights advocates.[21] As active participants in the Eastern Network of the Underground Railroad, the Motts "regularly aided fugitives passing through the city from the late 1820s onward" and assisted in forming the Ladies' Anti-Slavery Society of Albany.[22] In 1847, for instance, the Motts assisted fugitive slave George Lewis, who had escaped north from Virginia. Eventually, individuals learned about Lewis, and Austin Bearse, a member of the Boston Vigilance

Committee, assisted by sailing to Albany on his yacht, *Moby Dick*, and bringing the fugitive slave to Boston, where he was reunited with his daughter.[23]

Beyond her relationship with Douglass and involvement in antislavery circles, Abigail Field Mott coauthored, wrote, and edited a variety of books, including several for children. Prior to *Life and Adventures*, Mott coauthored, with her husband, Richard, her first book, *A Short Account of the Last Sickness and Death of Maria Mott, Daughter of Richard and Abigail Mott, of Mamaroneck, in the [S]tate of New-York*, published by Samuel Wood and Sons in 1817. Maria was born in 1799 and died in 1817.[24] *A Short Account* stands as Abigail Field Mott's first foray into writing for children. The Motts articulate that they hoped the book would be "useful and instructive to some of [Maria's] young acquaintances," among other readers.[25] For the Motts, writing about their deceased daughter offered a therapeutic outlet to process their loss along with the opportunity to continue to mold young persons as pious, socially conscious, and intellectually curious Christians. Abigail Field Mott further memorialized Maria by working with Mahlon Day, a New York printer, bookseller, and visitor to New York African Free Schools, on the book *The Juvenile Album, Being a Collection of Poetical Pieces, Selected by M. M.[,] A Little Girl About Ten Years of Age*, published in 1826.[26]

In 1825 Day published another of Mott's books, *Observations on the Importance of Female Education, and Maternal Instruction, with Their Beneficial Influence on Society. By A Mother*. The Quaker elder includes individuals' reflections on education and indicates that she wrote the book for the "proper cultivation of the youthful mind." Drawing upon knowledge of ancient and modern histories, she correlates "darkness and superstition" with "debas[ing]" the "female character" as well as "enlighten[ment]" with "cultivating" the "female mind." Thus, Mott positions the education of young women as a national priority: "It is often asserted, and with great propriety, that on a proper education, the safety and happiness of a nation very materially depend." Mott insists, as well, that there is no other place in the world where women had a better opportunity to receive education than the United States. Further, she highlights the significance of extending education to a wide variety of individuals, including the "poor little African." She advises, "And seeing the great Parent of the Universe, has not made any distinction in the distribution of his blessings, on account of colour, let us follow his example, by not making any, in the distribution of our care."[27]

Following these publications on her daughter and women's education, Mott consistently edited Equiano's autobiography and wrote about him. By November 1825 Mott likely completed the compiling of life stories of Diasporic Africans, African Americans, and Indigenous persons for her anthology,

Biographical Sketches and Interesting Anecdotes of Persons of Colour. To Which Is Added, A Selection of Pieces in Poetry, published by Day in 1826. Mott articulates in the preface that she wished "to show the baneful effects of that degradation to which the children of Africa have, in [a special] manner, been subjected by the Slave Trade; and to exhibit for encouragement and imitation, the salutary and cheering influence of the Christian religion, on such as have faithfully followed its dictates, though some of them have been held in a state of bondage."[28] Mott utilized the sketch of Equiano (or Gustavus Vassa, as the white Quaker editor refers to him) found in this anthology to structure most of *Life and Adventures*.[29] Additionally, *Biographical Sketches* is likely the first book on which Mott collaborated with trustees of the New York African Free Schools and edited specifically for Black children. The trustees patronized the volume and recommended that the book be divided into reading sections "with a view to have the volume introduced into Schools, as a Class Book." Likely based on suggestions from the trustees, Day and Mott numbered each paragraph in the anthology to make the book appropriate for New York African Free School students and teachers "who may use it in their Schools."[30] Extant records do not indicate whether the trustees adopted this book, but there is a possibility that Black students had access to it, given their support of the publication. Plus, Mott may have donated *Biographical Sketches* to one of the libraries at the New York African Free Schools, meaning African American children could have read the abridged version of Equiano's *Interesting Narrative* in *Biographical Sketches* before Wood and Sons printed *Life and Adventures*. Charles C. Andrews, historian of New York African Free Schools and educator at one of them, writes that "many individuals, both in and out of the society, have generously contributed towards [the libraries] in books."[31] As of 1830, the year Day published Andrews's *The History of the New-York African Free-Schools, from Their Establishment in 1787, to the Present Time; Embracing a Period of More Than Forty Years: Also a Brief Account of the Successful Labors, of the New-York Manumission Society: With an Appendix* and one year after Wood and Sons published *Life and Adventures*, the library at the New York African Free School on Mulberry Street held 450 volumes, and the library at the New York African Free School on Williams Street held two hundred.[32] Importantly, Mott's anthology contains a wide range of information on Diasporic African and African American lives, including Equiano's global travels, Paul Cuffe's voyages to Sierra Leone, Solomon Bayley's letter articulating his desire to visit Haiti and Sierra Leone, Serena M. Baldwin's letters from Haiti, and John Mosely's obituary, which indicates that he willed two hundred dollars to the American Colonization Society, among others.[33] These selections underscore that Mott conceptualized the emigration to Haiti and colonization of Liberia as appropriate ways for individuals of African descent to experience more fulfilling lives outside the United States.[34]

Two years after the release of *Biographical Sketches*, Day published Mott's children's book, *The Mother and Her Children, or Twilight Conversation*. In an advertisement in the enlarged third edition of the book, dated May 1837, Mott articulates her goal in completing this volume. She hoped "to show the advantages, and to stimulate mothers who have young children under their care to embrace opportunities of free and social conversation with them, and encourage them in a frank and generous expression of ideas."[35] The names of the children Mott uses indicate, nevertheless, that she did not necessarily rely on fiction to create nocturnal dialogues between a "Mother" and "Children." By 1828, the year the first edition of *Mother and Her Children* appeared in print, the majority of Richard and Abigail Field Mott's children were dead. Four of five children died young: their daughter Maria, born in 1799, died in 1817; their sons, both named William, born in 1790 and 1796, died in infancy; and their son Robert, born in 1794, died in 1826.[36] Their son Richard, born in 1825, lived at least until 1890. This information indicates that nearly all the "Children" who participate in the twilight conversations with "Mother" correspond with the names of Richard and Abigail's children: Maria, William, and Richard.[37] Therefore, Mott likely wrote *Mother and Her Children* to revisit conversations she had with some of her children before they died or to outline imagined conversations she wished she had with her deceased children.[38]

In the first conversation in *Mother and Her Children*, Mott writes about Gustavus Vassa, the name given to Equiano by his master, Michael Henry Pascal.[39] This dialogue containing young persons' commentary on Equiano's life and life story has been entirely overlooked by scholars. After William suggests that the familial group begin their discussion with Vassa and his three pence, the amount with which he commences trade to acquire his freedom, Maria asks, "What can we make of that? I never have heard anything about it; who is Gustavus Vassa?"[40] William, Maria's sibling and a young person who self-identifies as a reader of Equiano's autobiography, responds to her inquiry:

> He was an African, and stolen from his parents when he was about seven years old, carried to the West Indies, and sold several times, like a great many of his country folks; but he at last had a kind master, who told Gustavus when he could get as much money as had been given for him, and would let him have it, he should be free. The three pence, I suppose, was given to him for something he had done. By trading with that little, he got

more, and so on, until by great industry and prudence, he got money enough, paid it to his master, and became free.⁴¹

Building upon William's commentary, Mother drives home the pedagogical lesson for children on Vassa's three pence: "Here we have one striking instance already, of what a small beginning will do." After Eliza poses a question concerning what happened to Vassa after he acquired freedom, William adds that "[h]e went to sea for many years, and suffered a great deal, in many ways. When he was about forty years old, he gave that up, and wrote a history of his life, which was printed; and by reading that, I learned what I have just told you." ⁴² William's commentary propels the familial unit to discuss flamingos, cannibals, and shipwrecks, including Equiano's experience with one onboard the *Nancy*. With its linkage of children, Equiano's life story, and moral lessons, one part from *Mother and Her Children* may now be recognized as containing significant commentary on the publishing history of the *Interesting Narrative* in the United States.

These books prepared Mott to complete *Life and Adventures*. In the majority of the slim body of scholarship on Mott's adaptation, critics most often mention in passing the existence of the 1829 book, though there are recent exceptions to this point.⁴³ Samuel Wood and Sons, a major publisher of children's books in the early nineteenth-century United States, printed Mott's little-known and seldom-referenced adaptation thirty-two years after Equiano's death in London.⁴⁴ Thus, Equiano never had the opportunity to evaluate the adaptation. Wood and Sons included Mott's book in their Juvenile Series.⁴⁵ When it is contextualized appropriately as a product of transatlantic, transnational print networks, this book productively disrupts foundational understandings of Equiano and his autobiographical narrative.

Importantly, Mott edited the thirty-six-page adaptation for African American children studying at New York African Free Schools, an educational system first created in 1787 by members of the New York Manumission Society.⁴⁶ The trustees of the New York African Free Schools adopted the British pedagogue Joseph Lancaster's model of education in which more advanced students would teach those at lower levels. Though Lancaster's methods were eventually adopted around the world in the nineteenth century, including in the education of African Americans and Native Americans, this system grew from a localized pedagogical context in Great Britain stemming from what the pedagogue called "the sheer offspring of necessity." Lacking a suitable income from teaching and unable to pay an assistant to attend to a growing student body, Lancaster had "to make use of the services of his pupils, to teach each other, as monitors." For Lancaster, the power in this pedagogical system stemmed from the ability of "one master to teach hundreds, by means of juvenile and economical auxiliaries."[47] Anna Mae Duane has referred to the employment of the Lancasterian model in the New York African Free Schools as "liberatory," for Black students were "not expected to inhabit the affective and cognitive register represented by a white schoolmaster."[48] However, despite the revolutionary act of more advanced African American students teaching younger ones, especially the way this pedagogical space likely intellectually groomed a number of graduates who later comprised the Black elite in nineteenth-century New York, many scholars (including Duane) have been critical of these schools. Carla L. Peterson, for instance, argues that the "trustees promised to produce 'men of distinction,' but the school trained its graduates for places that were hardly distinguished. Boys were taught to be mechanics and artisans, and in the African Free School for girls, the female students learned skills such as sewing and knitting. An employment service sought to place the graduates in trades by means of indenture."[49]

Unfortunately, at this point, it is difficult to point to concrete evidence that trustees of the New York African Free Schools adopted Mott's book for libraries or classrooms. And, had the text been deemed acceptable by the trustees, it is difficult to judge exactly how African American children processed Mott's adaptation because no extant records provide direct access to these responses. Nonetheless, Mott's editing of Equiano's *Interesting Narrative* for Black children raises at least four questions. First, what exactly did Mott keep from Equiano's late eighteenth-century life story? Second, what did Mott excise from the autobiographical narrative? Third, what are the implications of Mott's editorial decisions? And fourth, how can we best explain her editorial work, including the rewriting of certain parts of the life story, in relation to early nineteenth-century New York culture along with the curricula at African Free Schools, given that, as Peterson writes, "[s]ome boys had close ties to slavery," while others "enjoyed origins with deeper roots in freedom?"[50]

Peterson's comment alludes to the changing status of Black New Yorkers in the early nineteenth century. By 1829, the year *Life and Adventures* appeared in print, two laws had already initiated the gradual emancipation of the institution of slavery in the state. The first abolition law of 1799 affected the status of Black New Yorkers born after July 4, 1799; the second abolition law of 1817 shaped the status of enslaved Black New Yorkers born before July 4, 1799. As Shane White writes,

> Under the terms of the [1799] act, all children born to slave women after July 4, 1799, were to be free, but males were to remain in a form of indentured servitude until they reached the age of twenty-eight, and females

were to be so bound until they were twenty-five. Those who were still slaves on July 4, 1799, were abandoned to their fate; not until 1817 would the legislature finally agree to free such persons and even then that was not to occur for another decade, until July 4, 1827.[51]

Hence, White names the pace at which gradual emancipation occurred in New York as "glacial."[52] In a similar vein, Patrick Rael observes that the 1817 legislation also decreased the indenture period to twenty-one years for African American men and women. Further, Rael points out that the "apprenticeship of those emancipated under the 1799 law was likely to end more quickly than slavery" and "bound black labor" in New York lasted until the 1860s.[53] When Wood and Sons published *Life and Adventures*, key questions about the status of African Americans circulated in New York. Many individuals experienced the first opportunity to negotiate their identities as free persons, while others looked forward to eventually obtaining this important status.

Mott's adaptation may be best understood as the end product forged from a chain of textual mutations, one that reveals the unstable nature of Equiano's *Interesting Narrative*. The adaptation grew from the authorized second edition published in London in 1789 and the unauthorized New York edition published in 1791 by William Durell. According to Paul Edwards and Vincent Carretta, Durell used the authorized second edition to structure his unauthorized edition.[54] To create the "First American Edition," as the title page indicates, Durell made significant changes to the authorized second edition. First, the New York printer and bookseller eliminated the frontispiece and replaced it with another visual text created by Cornelius Tiebout, a New York "copper-plate engraver," as he is identified in the list of subscribers.[55] Second, Durell's list of subscribers does not include any names found in the one that appeared in the authorized second edition. Instead, the New York printer identifies readers from Connecticut, New Jersey, New York, Massachusetts, Pennsylvania, and Antigua who economically supported him in printing the autobiographical narrative. Third, unlike the title page from the authorized second edition, which indicates that the book was "Printed and [S]old for the Author,"[56] the title page from the New York edition reads, "Printed and Sold By W. Durell, at his Book-Store and Printing-Office," altogether eliminating Equiano in the production and distribution processes. Durell also did not print Equiano's petition to British parliamentary members. These nonauthorial revisions reveal that Durell minimized Equiano's connection to Great Britain and his status as an Afro-British subject.

Durell's list of subscribers provides additional information on the textual chain leading to Mott's adaptation. Unlike the subscribers identified in authorized editions printed in Britain, which included numerous noble persons, the subscribers named in Durell's book were mostly artisans, including bakers, grocers, cabinetmakers, carpenters, tailors, tanners, and masons, who likely read Equiano's autobiography to learn more about geography, traveling, sailing, and survival. As Akiyo Ito observes, "[i]ndeed, we must rid ourselves of the misunderstanding that Equiano was received in America in the same manner as in England, and by the same kind of audience."[57] Mott knew at least four individuals identified on the list of subscribers in Durell's edition: the merchants Melancton Smith and John Murray Jr., trustees of the New York African Free Schools; Cornelius Davis, a teacher at one of the African Free Schools; and Robert Mott, Abigail's brother-in-law, who purchased two copies of Durell's edition. James Green observes that one of Robert Mott's copies likely "came into [Abigail Field Mott's] hands, and that she used it to prepare her *Biographical Sketches* [thirty-five] years later."[58]

Smith's, Murray's, and Davis's names on the list of subscribers are meaningful because Mott establishes in the preface to the adaptation her connection to New York African Free Schools. She writes:

> Having, for several years, been one of the Committee to visit the Female Department of the African Free School in New York; and having also been occasionally at that for boys, I have observed that the tickets given to the pupils, as rewards for attention to their studies, have a very favourable tendency. A specific value being given to those tickets, they become a sort of currency in the schools, and are received by the teachers in payment for toys and other articles which are provided as premiums for the scholars. Similar observation induces me to believe that there is scarcely any thing which can be given to a child as a premium for good behaviour which has a better tendency than a book. This belief prompted me to attempt an abridgement of the Memoirs of Gustavus Vassa, the African; which, as they contain many interesting circumstances, may not be thought unsuitable for distribution in those schools.
>
> Whether or not the design of these extracts meet[s] the approbation of the Trustees of the African Schools, I think it will be an interesting little work for children of any class, and I have therefore placed it in the hands of the publisher.[59]

Mott's remarks allow scholars to classify *Life and Adventures* as African American children's literature since she designed it for New York African Free School students. Drawing upon the work of Donnarae MacCann and W. Nikola-Lisa who define African American children's literature in inclusive ways, Michelle Martin classifies "texts written by African American authors and illustrators . . . but also [ones] . . . about the Black experience and/or the image of the Black child written by non-African Americans"[60] as ones that comprise this literary canon. Likewise, Giselle Liza Anatol observes that "[s]cholars may hesitate to name [Abigail Field Mott] as an originator of a Black literary tradition for children when people of African descent have so long been denied agency and voice in US society. This perspective fails to address the agency of the child reader, however, in choosing and using texts that serve their needs."[61] Andrews, historian of New York African Free Schools, identifies that the ages of students attending this system ranged from seven to fifteen years.[62] In 1818 trustees of African Free Schools specified that they would not extend admission to any "child under six years of age, nor girls above the age of fourteen and boys of fifteen."[63] These ages align with the more flexibly conceived category of childhood in the nineteenth-century United States. As Karen Sánchez-Eppler writes, "for the nineteenth century, childhood is better understood as a status or idea associated with innocence and dependency than as a specific developmental or biological period."[64] Even though Equiano's and New York African Free School students' lives differed on many levels, Mott utilizes the life writer's commentary on his youth to minimize these disparities. She employs the adaptation of Equiano's life story to assist African Free School students in acquiring a more comprehensive understanding of their selves in relation to other individuals of African descent and to the dynamics of the slave trade and slavery beyond the confines of New York and the United States. *Life and Adventures*, then, may also be understood as comprising a story of freedom for New York African Free School students, as Mott, following the trajectory of authorized editions, traces Equiano's path from freedom to slavery to freedom.[65]

Mott's statement about her creating the adaptation for New York African Free School students places the book in a unique category. This point does not apply to Durell's 1791 edition, nor does it offer an adequate description of Isaac Knapp's 1837 edition. Therefore, Mott's book occupies a unique place in the publishing history of the *Interesting Narrative* in the nineteenth-century United States as the only edition designed for African American children.[66] Additionally, Mott reveals that she obtained firsthand knowledge of African Free Schools along with students enrolled in this system based on numerous visits to these educational institutions. Extant visitors' records indicate that Mott (and others) evaluated African Free School no. 2, located at 135 Mulberry Street, on January 3, 1822. In a brief, collaboratively written report, the visitors note they found the female students "here as in the other school comfortably clad and diligently employed."[67] Mott's interest in the Female School, where educators taught Black youth how to read, write, and sew, grew at least in part from her advocacy for educating young girls in the United States.[68] For Mott, part of educating young girls included the ability "to make and repair most articles of their dress."[69] Furthermore, Mott acknowledges her long-term familiarity with African Free Schools by underscoring that she has been associated with the educational institution for a number of years. Mott observes, as well, that educators at New York African Free Schools rewarded well-behaved students with tickets that "become a sort of currency for toys and other articles," including, as Mott hoped, her adaptation.[70] Andrews clarifies, in his *History of the New-York African Free-Schools*, that school tickets had "nominal value," but with consent from teachers, students could use them "in purchasing books for the Library."[71] In the Lancasterian system, the most advanced students in the eighth class read the Bible and "other books as may be selected by the board of trustees." At the end of each month, students at schools run by the Lancasterian system could claim prizes by exchanging tickets for "small books."[72] Mott's book may have been considered a "small" one; it contains thirty-six pages and measures about seven inches by four inches.[73] It is a possibility, too, that African Free School students had access to Mott's *Life and Adventures* before Wood and Sons printed it in 1829.[74] Mott includes in the preface the date "6th mo. 1825" after her point on "plac[ing] [the book] in the hands of the publisher," meaning that she finished editing Equiano's life story four years before the Woods published the adaptation.[75] Besides, Mott indicates in the preface to *Biographical Sketches* that she completed her editing of this anthology, one containing language from Equiano's autobiography, as early as November 1825.[76]

Given her connections to individuals associated with New York African Free Schools along with her frequent visits to them, Mott may have attended one of the examination days at which members of the public (and those outside New York City) heard students' oral recitations, including poems written by themselves or trustees, and viewed the needlework and other material objects they produced. Announcements of upcoming examination days and evaluations of them regularly appeared in New York periodicals.[77] In *History of the New-York African Free-Schools*, Andrews quotes an article from the *Commercial Advertiser*, a New York periodical, containing information on a "goodly number of those people ... called Quakers" who attended an examination day in May 1824.[78] As an advocate for the "proper cultivation of the youthful mind," Mott would have been eager to attend a New York African Free School Fair, an event held every three months, rotating between the boys' and girls' schools. At the fair, attendees could view students' "little works of art," such as the boys' wagons, carts, wheelbarrows, chairs, benches, candle stands, boats, brigs, anchors, and hammers as well as the girls' dresses, hats, shirts, cushions, and patchwork. According to the poem "Lines on the School Fair," written by student Andrew R. Smith, he and his colleagues took the event seriously: "'I' excel we all will work and strive, / Till to perfection we arrive; / Many will work and strive in vain, / The fifty tickets to obtain."[79] Smith references the fifty-ticket prize a qualified student would obtain for the most impressive "little [work] of art."

Based on Mott's multiple visits to New York African Free Schools and her familiarity with individuals on the list of subscribers in Durell's edition, it is safe to conclude that she utilized the unauthorized 1791 New York edition of Equiano's life story as the base text from which to assemble *Life and Adventures*.[80] Though Mott almost certainly consulted Durell's edition for her book, she and the Woods altered numerous parts from this New York edition, continuing a chain of mutations concerning the publishing history of the *Interesting Narrative*. For instance, they eliminated Durell's list of subscribers, who of course were not Mott's intended audience. However, this editorial decision was likely motivated by the fact that a multipage subscriber list like the one in the New York edition would have overwhelmed the New York African Free School students and occupied an unnecessary amount of space in the adaptation.

Additionally, the Woods did not reproduce Tiebout's frontispiece from Durell's edition; instead, they printed a frontispiece by another artist from the United States. The signature under the frontispiece in Mott's book reads "AA," indicating that the New York woodcut artist Alexander Anderson created this visual representation of Equiano. He also created a number of the visual illustrations in the book. Jane R. Pomeroy refers to Anderson as "the first skilled relief engraver in America," and he was known to individuals in the nineteenth-century United States as "the Father of American Wood Engraving," according to the inscription on his tombstone in Brooklyn's Green-Wood Cemetery.[81] Harry B. Weiss notes that Anderson "made many wood engravings for the juvenile library of Samuel Wood."[82] Anderson's visual representation of Equiano aligns with components found in frontispieces from authorized editions and Durell's edition: the author sits confidently, wears the clothes of a gentleman, locks eyes with the reader, and holds a Bible turned to Acts. The language under Anderson's frontispiece, however, reads only, "Gustavus Vassa," thus eliminating the life writer's African name, Olaudah Equiano, and the designation "the African," which appear under visual representations of the autobiographer in numerous authorized editions and Durell's unauthorized edition. Although the name Olaudah Equiano appears in the title of Mott's adaptation, the elimination of this information indicates another departure from Durell's edition.[83]

Another alteration may be found in the number of pages Mott excised from

Durell's edition. Even though the total number of pages in *Life and Adventures* is thirty-six, Equiano's prose (including alterations thereof) occupies pages five through twenty-five. Nonetheless, this information needs to be qualified because illustrations, ones mainly created by Anderson, occupy pages 7, 11, 16, and 22.[84] This visual art reinforces Wood's argument in *The New-York Preceptor; or, Third Book*, a school book published in 1828, that "[o]bjections have been made to the admission of pictures into the school-books of children, from a belief that they too much divert the attention from the lessons; but the publisher is decidedly of [the] opinion, that the reverse is the case, when those representations are introduced with judgment." [85] In Wood's estimation, "when the child is made to understand that the lesson connect[s] with the picture, [it] will furnish him with satisfactory information respecting it[;] his attention, it is presumed, will be prompted by an impulse which would not probably be so well supplied by other means." [86]

Mott and Wood included page numbers under all images in the section devoted to Equiano's life story to sharpen New York African Free School students' critical reading skills.[87] This interplay between images and page numbers can be read as complementing what the students were learning in reading classes. At times, the page number under the image requires students to make connections between the image and language on an earlier page, whereas in other instances the page number under the image invites students to turn to a page they had not previously read. For instance, on page 11 of *Life and Adventures*, the second page on which one image appears above another, young readers would have viewed the top image, signed by Anderson, capturing the moment in which three Black adults, two of whom hold spears, forcibly separate two Black children. All parties are surrounded by a lush environment filled with trees and bushes. The children's attempt to remain connected via outreached hands has been undermined by the Black adults pulling them in opposite directions. The Black adult on the left-hand side of the scene pulls at the left arm of one of the children, while one of the Black adults on the right-hand side has picked up the other child to ensure that the youths no longer remained physically connected to one another. The bottom image on this page, signed by Anderson, depicts a scene outside a slave cabin in another lush environment, populated by a single palm tree, with a white slave owner posed to strike with his cane a barefoot slave, as two other slaves—one seated outside of the cabin and one smoking a pipe in the doorway of the cabin—witness the evitable physical violence. "Page 8" appears under the first image, whereas "Page 15" appears under the more violent scene.[88]

This visual-verbal interplay hones New York African Free School students' interpretive skills. To comprehend the first image on page 11, students needed to turn to page 8 and locate an appropriate passage they had already read that aligns with the illustration. On page 8, students would have discovered Equiano's description of the separation in Africa between himself and his unnamed sister: "The next day proved to be one of great sorrow indeed, for my sister and myself were separated, while we lay clasped in each other's arms. It was in vain that we besought them not to part us—She was torn from me and carried away, while I was left in a state not to be described. I grieved continually, and for several days did not eat any thing but what they forced into my mouth." To make sense of the lower illustration on page 11, students needed to turn to page 15 and locate an appropriate passage they had likely not yet read. On page 15, students would have discovered Equiano's description of what he witnessed while trading goods on the island of Montserrat: "In my passing about the Island I had great opportunity of seeing the wretched situation, and dreadful usage of the poor slaves. This reconciled me to my own condition, and made me thankful for falling into the hands of such a kind master."[89] These images and page numbers underneath them aid students to draw what Wood identifies as "satisfactory information" relating to the "lesson[s]" Equiano establishes in his life story: the autobiographer's enslavement begins by Africans on the continent on which he was born, according to the life story; the institution of slavery permanently severs relationships among African siblings; and varieties of slavery exist in the West Indies. Additionally, the illustrations help twenty-first-century readers understand the extent to which Mott abridged Equiano's *Interesting Narrative*. By taking into consideration the pages with illustrations, Equiano's prose (occasionally rewritten by Mott) fills approximately sixteen and a quarter pages of *Life and Adventures*. To put it another way, Mott preserves in her adaptation less than 6 percent of the language found in Durell's edition.

Pages 25–36 continue the departure from Durell's edition, for they do not contain language written by Equiano. Wood and Sons added content beginning with the heading "R[emarks] [on] [the] S[lave] T[rade]." After the final sentence from Equiano's autobiographical narrative and Mott's "Note," Wood inserted the following language: "The publishers have thought proper to enlarge this small work by adding the following Remarks upon the Slave Trade: not with a view to excite the indignation of any, but to give the young and the uninformed a correct idea of what the poor inhabitants of Africa suffer; for which their oppressors can give no better excuse, than that they are 'guilty of a skin not coloured like their own.'" Wood pinpoints the intended readers of *Life and Adventures* as the "young," particularly ones who do not know about abuses Africans experienced via the slave trade and institution of slavery. Following this observation, the Woods added "R[emarks] [on] [the] S[lave] T[rade]," containing an illustration of the lower deck of the slave ship *Brooks*, "A S[ubject] [for] C[onversation] and R[eflection] [at] [the] T[ea]-T[able]," which contains one part from British poet William Cowper's *The Task*, along with his poem "The Negro's Complaint." This part contains, as well, two illustrations documenting slave abuse, likely created but not signed by Anderson, and the poems "The Negro Boy" and "The Negro's Prayer." Whereas a dialogue involving an African prince inspired "The Negro Boy," "a Black man, a slave, in the lower part of Virginia" wrote "The Negro's Prayer." Before publishing *Life and Adventures*, Wood printed much of this material on a broadside and in a handful of books.[90]

Though Wood expresses that he does not wish for the added content to illicit "indignation" from child readers, he likely added material after Equiano's abridged life story because he thought Mott's adaptation lacked important content on the life writer's and others' experiences with slavery.[91] After all, Mott does not include many of Equiano's graphic depictions of slavery, including his detailed reflections on surviving the Middle Passage, and she does not retain his multiple reflections on interacting with slaves in the Atlantic world.[92] Wood likely hoped that child readers, armed with more information on "what the poor inhabitants of Africa suffer," would then agree with him that the institution of slavery was "the greatest evil under the sun," and that children (among others) would "make the case your own," as he articulates in a book he published in 1807.[93] The designation of a "G[irl's] R[oom]" and "B[oy's] R[oom]" in the illustration of the slave ship *Brooks* included in "Remarks" provides evidence that Wood established clear connections between New York African Free School students and slaves based on the category of age.[94] The Woods' supplementing of Mott's adaptation aligns with what Paula T. Connolly has identified as one goal of radical abolitionist literature written for children: "to politicize children as young abolitionists."[95] Thus, *Life and Adventures* aligns with several children's books printed by the Woods in which an author or publisher makes this directive explicit. For instance, in "An Address to Children," included in a book printed by the Woods around 1829, Amelia Opie, a British novelist, poet, and author of children's books, reminds young readers that "it is one of your Christian duties to abolish the cruelties practised on poor Negro Slaves in the West India islands, and to try, by every means possible, to put a stop to them when you grow up."[96]

The Woods' intervention in designing the final eleven pages of *Life and Adventures* also positions the adaptation in a wider field of transatlantic, transnational discourse on the slave trade and slavery. Whereas several of Mott's revisions to the life story either minimize or altogether eliminate Equiano's association with Great Britain, most of the material added by the Woods reestablishes a connection between Equiano, his autobiography, and British culture. In other words, it would be too sweeping to claim that Mott along with Wood and Sons eliminate all references and connections to Great Britain. Consequently, the Woods' participation in shaping the book results in an adaptation that moves even further away from Durell's edition. In the abridgment, Mott, the Woods, and Anderson contributed parts they thought were important for New York African Free School students. Mott's adaptation contains, then, a wider range of collaboration than Durell's edition. Up to this point, many Equiano scholars have submitted that, if the life writer was not born in Africa, then he most likely constructed the African origins section from oral narratives spoken to him by individuals of African descent who experienced life as both free persons and slaves in Africa, survived the Middle Passage, and resided as slaves in various parts of the Atlantic world. In other words, Equiano certainly read about Africa, but he likely utilized his extensive travel throughout the Atlantic world by internalizing oral narratives he heard from Diasporic Africans. He then probably transformed these narratives from the realm of oral history or testimony to print when he wrote the first section of his autobiography. In this regard, even the authorized editions of the *Interesting Narrative* may be considered collaborative autobiographies. That is, the authorized editions not only map the life of Equiano but also contain interesting narratives about Diasporic Africans in the Atlantic world collected and written down by the author/amanuensis named Olaudah Equiano or Gustavus Vassa. If readers of the *Interesting Narrative* are willing to recognize the collaborative nature of authorized editions published in Great Britain, then they should also acknowledge that a different, equally meaningful type of collaboration exists in unauthorized, posthumous, and abridged editions of the autobiography published in the United States.

A cursory glance at the full title of Mott's adaptation, *The Life and Adventures of Olaudah Equiano; or, Gustavus Vassa, the African. From an Account Written by Himself. Abridged by A. Mott. To Which Is Added Some Remarks on the Slave Trade*, reveals additional departures from Durell's edition. As the title indicates, Mott emphasizes the presence of adventures to draw New York African Free School students in to her book. In fact, several portions of the text reflect Mott's editorial choice to preserve Equiano's adventures. Mott includes Equiano's extensive travels as a slave throughout the Atlantic world as well as his adventures as a free person in Italy, Turkey, Portugal, the West Indies, and the North Pole, along with travels to Spain, participation in Dr. Irving's plantation scheme in Central America, and (reimagined) involvement with the Sierra Leone resettlement project. By editing Equiano's life story in this way, Mott ensures that New York African Free School students read an autobiographical account filled with travels and adventures. Mott's retaining of Equiano's transatlantic, transnational travels reinforces the trustees' goal of "alert[ing] [the students] to a world larger than the neighborhood or city they inhabited," according to Carla L. Peterson. Likewise, Mott's book aligns with the curricula at New York African Free Schools by providing students with "a broader cosmopolitan outlook" through students' engagement with the autobiographer's travels and adventures.[97] This pedagogical vision may be understood through the trustees' educational initiative that encouraged individuals to bring material objects from parts of the world to the New York African Free School on Mulberry Street. As early as August 1828, for instance, New York African Free School students could examine a variety of objects displayed in a "cabinet of Natural Curiosities and Minerals," containing art, shells, and reptiles from "different quarters" of the world. The trustees invited "travellers, masters of vessels, and all persons visiting foreign places"[98] to contribute objects to the cabinet they acquired during their global travels.

Mott likely utilized Equiano's travels and adventures to reinforce another part of the curricula at New York African Free Schools: the teaching of "practical knowledge."[99] In one part of *History of the New-York African Free-Schools*, Andrews includes a letter from three individuals—Alderman Seymour, Mr. St. John, and Mr. Cowdry—who visited a New York African Free School in May 1824. Accounts of visitors observing and interacting with students routinely appeared in nineteenth-century newspapers printed in New York in the hopes of securing attention as well as funding for the educational system. Seymour, St. John, and Cowdry's observations highlight the emphasis placed on the students' acquisition of practical skills. According to the testimonies of the epistle writers delivered at a New York City Common Council meeting, students displayed knowledge of "Spelling, Reading, Writing, Arithmetic, Grammar, Geography, and Elocution, and of Needlework in addition to these, on the part of the females." The visitors were pleased with the "answers of both boys and girls to questions in the important and useful branches of simple and compound Arithmetic, of Grammar, and of general and local Geography." By 1828, one year before the Woods published *Life and Adventures*, the trustees expanded the curricula to include astronomy, the use of globes, map and linear drawing, and navigation. The inclusion of these new subjects in New York African Free Schools likely grew from Andrews's point that "a large portion of the most intelligent lads go to sea, after leaving school." For Andrews, "a knowledge of practical navigation [must] certainly contribute greatly to [students'] interest and their usefulness."[100]

In several parts of the adaptation, Mott calls attention to the benefits of Equiano obtaining an education and practical knowledge. Mott focuses on Equiano's learning during his maritime adventures and other relevant educational experiences obtained on land. These scenes—ones also found in authorized editions—underscore not only Equiano's development as a young person but also that increased knowledge largely results from his interactions with whites on either ships or land, mostly through his position as Michael Henry Pascal's and Robert King's slave. Aligning her adaptation with the curricula at New York African Free Schools in the late 1820s, Mott retains Equiano's comments to King that he knew how to "shave and dress hair pretty well," "refine wines," "write," and understand "arithmetic as far as the Rule of Three." Equiano also observes that, in the West Indies, he learned how to "load and unload vessels."[101] Equiano's reflections on learning as a young person underscore for New York African Free School students the importance of acquiring practical knowledge. As Equiano makes clear, King purchases him not only because of his "good" character, as Captain Doran attests, but his acquisition of these skills.[102] Equiano consistently uses these skills in the capacity of clerk for the Quaker merchant in the West Indies. Thus, Equiano's acquisition of relevant knowledge aligns with increased exposure to areas outside what eventually became the United States and learning from a variety of white people. In this way, Mott frames Equiano's recollections of his youth as a developmental blueprint for Black child readers. Through Mott's adaptation, New York African Free School students learn about the significance and benefits of practical knowledge, albeit in the form of a book instead of on various ships. Mott consistently highlights the positive consequences resulting from Equiano's intellectual curiosity and drive for additional education.

Nonetheless, Mott does not gloss over problems Equiano encounters in the North American colonies, ones also included in authorized editions and Durell's unauthorized edition. For instance, Equiano comments on receiving different forms of abuse from individuals in Georgia. He recollects, "This time, being in a yard one evening with some negroes, whose master coming home drunk, he, and a very rough white man with him, beat me almost to death; though I gave him a good account of myself, and he knew my captain." On his first trip to Georgia as a free person, Equiano remembers being "met as usual with poor treatment, receiving uncurrent money for my goods, and some other abuses hard for human nature to bear." Due to this treatment in North America (among other factors), Equiano submits that he "set [his] heart again on going to England."[103] Mott reinforces to New York African Free School students the idea that Equiano receives harsh treatment both as a slave and free person in North America; that is, geographical places outside the North American colonies and later the United States consistently provide safer spaces for him. Compared with Georgia, the various ships on which Equiano travels the world offer more conducive environments for safety as well as development.

Following these negative remarks on Georgia, Equiano offers positive commentary concerning his penultimate trip to the United States. During a May 1785 trip to Philadelphia, Equiano notes that he visited an African Free School created in 1770 by abolitionist Anthony Benezet: "it rejoiced my heart when one of those people [a Quaker] took me to the Free School where I saw the children of my colour instructed, and their minds cultivated to fit them for usefulness." At this Philadelphia school, Equiano may have orally related his life story (or parts of it) to African American children, years before he started writing in London the authorized first edition. Nonetheless, Mott employs this commentary on Equiano's penultimate trip to the United States to form an additional link between the autobiographer and New York African Free School students. If Mott presents Equiano's life as a type of developmental blueprint for African Free School students, then the life writer's praise of the African Free School in Philadelphia translates into an endorsement of the educational system in New York. After his visit to the school, Equiano recollects that he took a transatlantic voyage from the United States to England.[104] Therefore, the life writer establishes a link between an African Free School and transatlantic travel.

Strikingly, Andrews uses the word "usefulness" to describe the origins of the African Free Schools in New York; Equiano also employs this word to describe why pedagogues at the African Free School in Philadelphia educated African American children. Andrews outlines the founding of the New York Manumission Society and quotes an act passed on February 19, 1808. According to this act, members of the Manumission Society "established a free school in the city of New-York, for the education of the children of such persons as have been liberated from bondage, that they may hereafter become useful members of the community."[105] Like Equiano's commentary on the African Free School in Philadelphia, Andrews's language indicates that trustees of African Free Schools in New York designed curricula to ensure that Black children became "useful members" of the city. Nonetheless, the pedagogical approach at New York African Free Schools regarding how to ensure that Black children would become "useful" members of society shifted in the 1820s. As early as the mid-1820s, members of the New York Manumission Society began "to support the American Colonization Society's programs for sending free blacks to Africa." As Leslie M. Harris writes, "The Colonization Society publicized free blacks' difficulties with poverty, crime, and white racism to demonstrate that blacks could not survive in the United States and that blacks' true home was in Africa." Harris also observes that "[m]embers of the Manumission Society founded the New York City Colonization Society in 1817 and were instrumental in founding the New York State Colonization Society in 1829." As a result, Harris notes, "African Free Schools began to train blacks for emigration to Liberia."[106] Plus, as early as

February 1828, trustees of New York African Free Schools were sending samples of students' work to the Washington, D.C. chapter of the American Colonization Society.[107] Furthermore, articles in two early nineteenth-century periodicals indicate that Andrews sent *History of the New-York African Free-Schools* to editors of *The African Repository, and Colonial Journal*, the official newspaper of the American Colonization Society, and *Freedom's Journal*, the first African American newspaper.[108] John Russwurm, an editor of *Freedom's Journal*, shared the white African Free School teacher's views on colonization and corresponded with him.[109] These points mean that the year in which the Woods printed *Life and Adventures* aligns with an important change in the politics of many responsible for and associated with New York African Free Schools.

Despite a substantial amount of scholarship linking New York African Free Schools with colonizationists, twenty-first-century readers of *Life and Adventures* have been skeptical regarding any connections between Mott and this resettlement scheme.[110] It was not uncommon for nineteenth-century Quakers to support Liberian colonization.[111] Plus, evidence certainly exists indicating that Mott supported the American Colonization Society. In *Biographical Sketches*, an anthology containing accounts of Diasporic African, African American, and Indigenous lives, Mott includes a brief sketch of John Mosely, an African American who finically supported colonizationist schemes. Utilizing an article from the *Hartford Courant*, Mott describes Mosely as "an aged coloured man, well known for his industry, prudence, and integrity," who willed the American Colonization Society two hundred dollars. Importantly, Mosely gave twice as much money to the American Colonization Society as he did to the Hartford Female Beneficent Society, Connecticut Bible Society, and American Education Society. As noted, Mott designed *Biographical Sketches* for New York African Free Schools, and trustees of this educational system "liberally patronized the work."[112] Mott's inclusion of the sketch on Mosely indicates that she supported individuals of African descent donating money to the American Colonization Society and, in turn, this organization's efforts to convince free African Americans to abandon the United States and move to Liberia. The sketch of Mosely also reinforces to New York African Free School students, the intended audience of the anthology, that when they reached a certain age and acquired a certain income, they could follow this "coloured man" and donate to this organization, which many African Americans rejected.

Most importantly, nearly all readers of *Life and Adventures* have missed Mott's most significant nonauthorial revision, which provides additional evidence on her views regarding the American Colonization Society.[113] Near the end of the adaptation, Mott rewrites Equiano's commentary on the Sierra Leone resettlement project, an initiative orchestrated by the British government in the mid-1780s to help transplanted Black Loyalists and lascars who struggled to find adequate food, housing, and employment in England.[114] Mott likely altered in her adaptation (and elsewhere) Equiano's commentary on the Sierra Leone resettlement project to offer an endorsement for African Americans' colonization of Liberia. Mott's repurposing of Equiano's commentary on the Sierra Leone resettlement project may be best understood by Bryant's description of the fluid text. He remarks that some instances of textual fluidity "attest not simply to localized fine-tunings but to new conceptualizations of the entire work."[115] In fact, Mott's blatant rewriting of one event from Equiano's life story reinforces G. Thomas Couser's observation on the "not always clear lines between making, taking, and faking the life of another person in print."[116]

In numerous authorized editions, Equiano offers commentary on the Sierra Leone resettlement project in the final chapter of his autobiography. He reflects,

> On my return to London in August [1786], I was very agreeably surprised to find, that the benevolence of government adopted the plan of some philanthropic individuals, to send the Africans from hence to their native quarter, and that some vessels were then engaged to carry them to Sierra Leona; an act which redounded to the honour of all concerned in its promotion, and filled me with prayers and much rejoicing.[117]

At this point in authorized editions, Equiano outlines what he sees as the potential in the resettlement project. However, following his appointment as "Commissary of Provisions and Stores for the Black Poor to Sierra Leona," a position that charged him with handling supplies and serving the British government in interactions with African authorities, he notes that white authorities dismissed him after he exposed the mismanagement of goods. Therefore, instead of going back to Africa, as he hoped, Equiano watched the ships sail to Sierra Leone: "Thus provided, *they* proceeded on *their* voyage; and at last, worn out by treatment, perhaps, not the most mild, and wasted by sickness, brought on by want of medicine, clothes, bedding, &c. *they* reached Sierra Leona just at the commencement of the rains." Here Equiano clearly distances himself from participants in the resettlement project who traveled to Sierra Leone through the use of "they" and "their." Despite the corruption he discovered in this project, he adds that the "expedition . . . was humane and politic in its design, nor was its failure owing to government; every thing was done on their part; but there was evidently sufficient mismanagement attending the conduct and execution of it to defeat its success." The autobiographer writes that theory and practice did not merge in this case.[118] According to all twentieth-century and twenty-first-century accounts, Equiano never returned to Africa.

In the adaptation, Mott remains, at first, loyal to Equiano's observations on the resettlement project. That is, language from *Life and Adventures* indicates that Equiano heard about the initiative after returning to London in 1786. The autobiographer also expresses concern, as he does in authorized editions, that the transatlantic slave trade could undermine the resettlement project. The consistency in documenting this part of Equiano's life ends, however, with Mott's handling of the sentence describing the autobiographer's reflection of the moment at which members of the resettlement project sailed for Sierra Leone. According to *Life and Adventures*, Equiano observes, "After much difficulty and delay[,] *we* set sail with 426 persons on board, and reached *our* destined port in June, just as the rainy season commenced. Having been closely confined for several months[,] *we* were unprepared for such a season, and many of them died. Thus was the benevolent intention frustrated for that time, and *I* returned to England."[119] The rewriting from "they" and "their," as seen in authorized editions, to "we," "our," and "I," as seen in the adaptation, places Equiano in a radically different position in relation to the Sierra Leone resettlement project. Instead of a detached observer who praises the potential of the project yet publicly denounces the corruption within the initiative, the life writer, according to Mott's book, becomes an active participant and actually revisits the continent from which he was forcibly removed as a child, as he claims in the life story.

How should readers make sense of Mott's reimagining of the relationship between Equiano and Africa, one that reveals the presence of what may be referred to as the edited "I," a term signifying instances in which a nonauthorial subject has manipulated the autobiographical text without permission or acknowledgment from the autobiographical subject? One response to this query is simply to dismiss this part of Mott's adaptation because the white Quaker does not remain faithful to Equiano's account of the Sierra Leone resettlement project found in authorized editions. That is, Mott's rewriting of this episode from Equiano's life may be regarded as an extreme fabrication and misrepresentation. Certainly, truth value matters in life writing, especially when it is produced by individuals from marginalized populations. Nevertheless, it is important, at this point, to acknowledge the friction present in *Life and Adventures*: on one hand, Mott condenses for Black child readers the life story of Equiano, a literate, politically active individual of African descent, who exercises agency in various ways in the Atlantic world to earn his freedom, and, on the other hand, she propagandizes the life story through her unauthorized alterations.

A number of reasons may explain why Mott repurposed the Sierra Leone resettlement scene. Perhaps Mott recreated this episode for the sake of increasing the probability that New York African Free School students would understand the autobiography. In other words, by beginning her adaptation in Africa and inserting Equiano's alleged travel back to Africa near the end of the text, Mott may have constructed a largely circular narrative that provided Black child readers with an understandable life story. Another possible explanation may be that this refashioning ensures that Equiano's travel back to Africa aligns with the title of Mott's adaptation, which promises to showcase the "[a]dventures" of the life writer. However, the Sierra Leone resettlement scene found in the first and second editions of *Biographical Sketches*, published by Mahlon Day in 1826 and 1837, parallels the one in *Life and Adventures*; Equiano travels back to Africa.[120] That is, Mott remains consistent in three books designed for New York African Free School students by repurposing Equiano's travel to Africa with the Sierra Leone resettlement project. Another interesting point regarding Mott's handling of the resettlement project is that Durell's edition remains faithful to authorized editions published in Great Britain. In Durell's edition, the base text from which Mott likely constructed *Life and Adventures*, Equiano observes that he did not sail with the resettlement project: "Thus provided, *they* proceeded on *their* voyage; and at last, worn out by treatment, perhaps not the most mild, and wasted by sickness, brought on by want of medicine, cloaths, bedding, &c. *they* reached Sierra Leona just at the commencement of the rains."[121] Equiano draws a clear line between himself and the individuals who sailed to Sierra Leone. This portion from Mott's adaptation devoted to Equiano's commentary on the resettlement project reveals, then, another departure from Durell's edition.

Given the consistency regarding Equiano's relationship with Africa in Mott's books, her rewriting of the resettlement scene was likely motivated by problems identified by individuals associated with New York African Free Schools. In 1819 Reuben Leggett, a white trustee, wrote a valedictory speech for student James Fields, who delivered it at a public examination.[122] Unlike other Free School students, who offer in speeches lavish praise for trustees, teachers, and the Lancasterian system, Fields declares:

> Why should I strive hard, and acquire all the constituents of a man, if the prevailing genius of the land admit me not as such, or but in an inferior degree! Pardon me if I feel insignificant and weak. Pardon me if I feel discouragement to oppress me to the very earth. Am I arrived at the end of my education, just on the eve of setting out into the world, of commencing some honest pursuit, by which to earn a comfortable subsistence? What are my prospects? To what shall I turn my hand? Shall I be a mechanic? No

one will employ me; white boys won't work with me. Shall I be a merchant? No one will have me in his office; white clerks won't associate with me. Drudgery and servitude, then, are my prospective portion.[123]

Certainly, this speech underscores what Duane has identified as the "tension between the white scriptwriter and the black child." The extent to which Fields subscribed to Leggett's opinions in 1819 may be unknown, but it is crucial to note that years later the graduate served as secretary at the Fourth Annual Convention of the Free People of Colour of the United States at which African American attendees opposed Liberian colonization.[124] In the speech delivered by Fields, Leggett acknowledges the dire prospects of the Black child attempting to enter the workforce after graduation. In fact, Leggett frames Fields as "insignificant" and "weak" because he will not be able to perform an acceptable form of masculinity, as "[d]rudgery" and "servitude" are the grim guarantees in this Black child's future. Leggett's take on the problematic nature of nineteenth-century New York even prompts him to have Fields question the point of becoming an educated individual of African descent and exercising industry in light of the circumstances he is sure to meet after graduation.[125]

Following Leggett, Andrews identifies, near the end of *History of the New-York African Free-Schools*, a problem that mirrors the one Leggett addresses. After an observation that only a small portion of African American children attend New York African Free Schools, Andrews comments on "poor Isaac," a "young man, 17 years of age, who about two and a half years ago, left this school with a respectable education, and an irreproachable character." Isaac, according to Andrews, apprenticed with a New York blacksmith, but his master had to let him go because of "[d]epression of business." Even though the master released Isaac from the apprenticeship, Andrews writes that "every place that appeared suitable to his object, was closed against him, *because he was black!*"[126] After moving to Philadelphia to labor in a friend's factory, Isaac learned that whites refused to work alongside him. While readers of *History* do not learn about what happened to Fields after his valedictory address, Andrews informs readers about Isaac's whereabouts: "When the lad was informed of this, so far from uttering a word of angry disappointment, he resolved to leave the country and go to the Colony of Liberia." Andrews frames Isaac's move to Liberia as a productive way for young African Americans to handle the hostile nineteenth-century New York marketplace; that is, the white teacher and historian does not advocate for New York African Free School students to voice publicly frustrations, as Fields did. For Andrews, Isaac will be remembered for his "good character, but also several highly credible specimens of his abilities as a scholar."[127] In the early

1830s, Andrews was dismissed from a New York African Free School because he supported the American Colonization Society.[128]

Both Fields's speech and Andrews's narrative of Isaac underscore the problems New York African Free School students faced around the time when Mott adapted Equiano's life story and the Woods published *Life and Adventures*. Given her knowledge of New York African Free Schools and the Black children who attended this educational system, Mott's alteration of Equiano's commentary on the Sierra Leone resettlement project would have provided an answer to students' difficulties securing work in cities like New York and Philadelphia. Of course, Mott's reframing of Equiano's involvement with the resettlement project does not encourage New York African Free School students to relocate to Sierra Leone. Such a location was not pertinent to resettlement plans circulating in nineteenth-century New York, the "epicenter of colonization sentiment" in the North.[129] Yet, Equiano's observation in *Life and Adventures* that the Sierra Leone resettlement project was "frustrated for that time" suggests that a door had been opened by late eighteenth-century Britons for a future and allegedly more successful project in Africa.[130] To put it another way, Mott's repurposing of the Sierra Leone resettlement project scene may be read as an endorsement of the project familiar to all parties involved with New York African Free Schools: members of the American Colonization Society attempting to convince African Americans, including children, to move to Liberia. For colonizationists like Andrews, Fields's and Isaac's problems would not exist if they participated in colonizing Liberia. Thus, Mott's reframing of Equiano's commentary on Sierra Leone may be read as encouraging New York African Free School students to return to Africa.[131] In *Life and Adventures*, New York African Free School students would have also read about the trick played on Equiano by his colleagues onboard Michael Henry Pascal's *Industrious Bee*; they convince him that they were sailing to Africa instead of England. Granted, Mott includes this scene to punctuate Equiano's innocence as a displaced child, but she also preserves the life writer's observation that "the thought that I should have so many wonderful things to tell of when I got home [to Eboeland], made me very happy."[132] Equiano's hope to orally relate to Eboes an interesting narrative about his adventures, years before he even started to imagine the authorized first edition of his life story, stands as another positive endorsement for African American children to travel to Africa. By offering Equiano's life as a blueprint from which New York African Free School students should model their own, Mott marries in *Life and Adventures* liberation and empowerment via education and the acquisition of literacy along with subordination via expatriation.

Countering selected methodological, canonical, and pedagogical problems in the field of early Black Atlantic studies, this approach to an unauthorized, posthumous adaptation of Equiano's *Interesting Narrative* investigates the transatlantic, transnational travel of a late eighteenth-century life story as well as the textual fluidity that accompanied it. Further, it demonstrates that pertinent questions about the publishing, circulation, and consumption of early Black Atlantic books are just beginning to be posed and answered. Mott's *Life and Adventures* stands as an important example concerning when, how, and for what complicated purposes Equiano's life story entered the United States and African American canons. In other words, some of the foundational tenets of early Black Atlantic studies, especially a preference for selected authorized editions, have taken the field only so far. A textual paradigm that more fully accounts for the production, circulation, and consumption of editions of early Black Atlantic texts, including those produced by and for individuals of African descent, promises to take the field in new directions for years to come.

Notes

1. John Bryant, *The Fluid Text: A Theory of Revision and Editing for Book and Screen* (Ann Arbor: University of Michigan Press, 2002), 1.
2. Consult, for instance, Akiyo Ito, "Olaudah Equiano and the New York Artisans: The First American Edition of *The Interesting Narrative of the Life of Olaudah Equiano, or Gustavus Vassa, the African*," *Early American Literature* 32, no. 1 (1997): 82–101; Vincent Carretta, "'Property of Author': Olaudah Equiano's Place in the History of the Book," in *Genius in Bondage: Literature of the Early Black Atlantic*, ed. Vincent Carretta and Philip Gould (Lexington: University Press of Kentucky, 2001), 130–50; Joseph Rezek, "The Orations on the Abolition of the Slave Trade and the Uses of Print in the Early Black Atlantic," *Early American Literature* 45, no. 3 (2010): 655–82; Joanna Brooks, "The Unfortunates: What the Life Spans of Early Black Books Tell Us about Book History," in *Early African American Print Culture*, ed. Lara Langer Cohen and Jordan Alexander Stein (Philadelphia: University of Pennsylvania Press, 2012), 40–52; Joseph Rezek, "The Print Atlantic: Phillis Wheatley, Ignatius Sancho, and the Cultural Significance of the Book," in Cohen and Stein, *Early African American Print Culture*, 19–39; and Eric D. Lamore, "Olaudah Equiano in the United States: Abigail Mott's Abridged Edition of the *Interesting Narrative*," in *Reading African American Autobiography: Twenty-First-Century Contexts and Criticism*, ed. Eric D. Lamore (Madison: University of Wisconsin Press, 2017), 66–88.
3. Leon Jackson, "The Talking Book and the Talking Book Historian: African American Cultures of Print—The State of the Discipline," *Book History* 13 (2010): 252.
4. Like many Equiano scholars, I refer to the author of the *Interesting Narrative* as Olaudah Equiano even though he used and embraced throughout his lifetime the name Gustavus Vassa, given to him by his master, Michael Henry Pascal. For more information on this topic, consult Paul E. Lovejoy, "Olaudah Equiano or Gustavus Vassa—What's in a Name?," *Atlantic Studies* 9, no. 2 (2012): 165–84. Lovejoy maintains that critics should use the name Gustavus Vassa because the author referred to himself by

this name for most of his life and, at one point, reacted strongly when individuals referred to him as Olaudah Equiano (166).
5. On Equiano's book tour, see John Bugg, "The Other Interesting Narrative: Olaudah Equiano's Public Book Tour," *Publications of the Modern Language Association of America* 121, no. 5 (2006): 1424–42.
6. D. C. Greetham, introduction to D. C. Greetham, ed., *Scholarly Editing: A Guide to Research* (New York: Modern Language Association of America, 1995), 2.
7. Olaudah Equiano, *The Interesting Narrative and Other Writings*, ed. Vincent Carretta, rev. ed. (New York: Penguin, 2003), 235.
8. Eve Tavor Bannet, *Transatlantic Stories and the History of Reading, 1720–1810: Migrant Fictions* (Cambridge: Cambridge University Press, 2011), 6, 3, 7. For Bannet's commentary on early Black Atlantic literature, consult 139–57. She does not analyze the transatlantic publishing histories of early Black Atlantic texts.
9. William Aldridge and John Marrant, *A Narrative of the Lord's Most Wonderful Dealings with John Marrant, A Black*, [authorized] 4th ed. (London: R. Hawes, 1785), 9.
10. Paul Gilroy, *The Black Atlantic: Modernity and Double Consciousness* (Cambridge, MA: Harvard University Press, 1993), 4. Rezek, in "The Orations on the Abolition of the Slave Trade," observes that Gilroy's theory includes the "movement and dissemination of texts" (656).
11. For brief commentary on Mott, see A. Day Bradley, "Abigail Mott of Mamaroneck," *Westchester Historian* 53 (1977): 88–89; Mary Finn and Christopher Densmore, "Quaker Educators and Authors," in *Quaker Crosscurrents: Three Hundred Years of Friends in the New York Yearly Meetings*, ed. Hugh Barbour, Christopher Densmore, Elizabeth H. Moger, Nancy C. Sorel, Alson D. Van Wagner, and Arthur J. Worrall (Syracuse: Syracuse University Press, 1995), 163; Mary Ellen Snodgrass, *The Underground Railroad: An Encyclopedia of People, Places, and Operations*, vol. 1 (Armonk, NY: Sharpe Reference, 2008), 375–76; Carol Faulkner, *Lucretia Mott's Heresy: Abolition and Women's Rights in Nineteenth-Century America* (Philadelphia: University of Pennsylvania Press, 2011), 31; and Beth Ann Rothermel, "Prophets, Friends, Conversationalists: Quaker Rhetorical Culture, Women's Commonplace Books, and the Art of Invention, 1775–1840," *Rhetoric Society Quarterly* 43, no. 1 (2013): 88.
12. William S. McFeely, *Frederick Douglass* (New York: W. W. Norton, 1991), 154, 152.
13. Robert K. Wallace, *Douglass and Melville: Anchored Together in Neighborly Style* (New Bedford: Spinner, 2005), 26, 28. For Mott's review of Douglass's first autobiography, see appendix C.
14. For Douglass's reflections on this time abroad, see Frederick Douglass, "Twenty-One Months in Great Britain," in *My Bondage and My Freedom*, ed. David W. Blight (New Haven: Yale University Press, 2014), 292–313. On the Dublin editions of Douglass's autobiography, see Patricia J. Ferreira, "Frederick Douglass in Ireland: The Dublin Edition of His *Narrative*," *New Hibernia Review* 5, no. 1 (2001): 53–67; and Robert S. Levine, *The Lives of Frederick Douglass* (Cambridge, MA: Harvard University Press, 2016), 75–118. Writing on why Anna Murray, Douglass's wife, wanted Rosetta to stay with the Motts, Leigh Fought, in *Women in the World of Frederick Douglass* (New York: Oxford University Press, 2017), offers the following points:

> Sacrificing her desire to keep her daughter with her by sending Rosetta to the Motts meant that Rosetta could acquire the sort of refinement and education that would ensure that she would never have to clean other people's homes, take in other people's laundry, or bind shoes for pennies a piece as Anna had. Furthermore, the choice of two abolitionist Quakers meant that Rosetta would be insulated from the harsh racial prejudice that permeated even the integrated schools while also being inculcated in abolitionist ideology. (64–65)

Fought posits that Douglass first met the Motts in 1842 in Albany (64). For Rosetta's comments on living with the Motts, see Dorothy Sterling, ed., *We Are Your Sisters: Black Women in the Nineteenth Century* (New York: W. W. Norton, 1984), 134.
15. For a study on this period of Douglass's life, see Alan J. Rice and Martin Crawford, eds., *Liberating Sojourn: Frederick Douglass and Transatlantic Reform* (Athens: University of Georgia Press, 1999).
16. Alfred Tennyson, *Poems by Alfred Tennyson* (London: Edward Moxon, 1846). This copy of Tennyson's *Poems* may be viewed at the Library of Congress. Anthony likely acquired Abigail Field Mott's copy of *Poems by Alfred Tennyson* via her friendship with Lydia. According to Ann D. Gordon, Lydia taught Anthony in Philadelphia. See Ann D. Gordon, ed., *The Selected Papers of Elizabeth Cady Stanton and Susan B. Anthony*, vol. 1 (New Brunswick: Rutgers University Press, 1997), 28n10. For Anthony's correspondence to Lydia, consult Gordon, 475. For Lydia's correspondence to Anthony, see 450–51.
17. Tennyson, *Poems*.
18. For the correspondence between Douglass and the Motts, consult "Frederick Douglass to Abigail Mott," in Frederick Douglass, *The Frederick Douglass Papers, Series 3: Correspondence*, ed. John R. McKivigan, vol. 1 (New Haven: Yale University Press, 2009), 111–15; and "Frederick Douglass to Abigail and Lydia Mott," in *The Frederick Douglass Papers*, 297–98. See, as well, the letter written by "A.M." (Abigail Field Mott) to "Mr. Douglass," *North Star* (Rochester, NY), April 5, 1850, wherein she outlines how African American communities in Albany "obtained the idea of the advantage of sending their children to the several District Schools" and then learned that their children were "expelled."
19. Frederick Douglass, *The Frederick Douglass Papers, Series 2: Autobiographical Writings, Life and Times of Frederick Douglass*, edited by John R. McKivigan (New Haven: Yale University Press, 2012), 208, 369–70.
20. William J. Switala, *Underground Railroad in New Jersey and New York* (Mechanicsburg, PA: Stackpole, 2006), 100. Switala estimates that Albany "had more than two dozen sites and agents active in its Underground Railroad system" (100).
21. Dorothy Sterling, *Ahead of Her Time: Abby Kelley and the Politics of Antislavery* (New York: W. W. Norton, 1991), 159; Miriam Gurko, *The Ladies of Seneca Falls: The Birth of the Woman's Rights Movement* (New York: Schocken, 1976), 114; and Julie Roy Jeffrey, *The Great Silent Army of Abolitionism: Ordinary Women in the Antislavery Movement* (Chapel Hill: University of North Carolina Press, 1998), 179.
22. Switala, *Underground Railroad*, 100. For a report written by members of this antislavery society, published in 1845, see appendix C.
23. Tom Calarco, with Cynthia Vogel, Kathryn Grover, Rae Hallstrom, Sharron L. Pope, and Melissa Waddy-Thibodeaux, *Places of the Underground Railroad: A Geographical Guide* (Santa Barbara: Greenwood, 2011), 8.
24. Thomas Clapp Cornell, *Adam and Anne Mott: Their Ancestors and Descendants* (Poughkeepsie, NY: A. V. Haight, 1890), 213.
25. Abigail Field Mott and Richard Mott, *A Short Account of the Last Sickness and Death of Maria Mott, Daughter of Richard and Abigail Mott, of Mamaroneck, in the [S]tate of New-York* (New York: Samuel Wood and Sons, 1817), 3. For *A Short Account*, see appendix C.
26. Day was active in a variety of ways with New York African Free Schools. In a March 7, 1828, article titled "New-York African Free School," published in *Freedom's Journal*, an anonymous author identifies Day as a trustee; the printer and bookseller, located at 376 Pearl Street, also worked in conjunction with the African Dorcas Society, an organization comprised of African American women who collected second-hand clothing for indigent students. In a December 19, 1828, article titled "American Convention,"

also published in *Freedom's Journal*, another anonymous writer specifies that Day attended an antislavery convention and presented New York African Free School students' work. Day collected, as well, material objects for the "Cabinet of Minerals and Natural Curiosities," a part of the New York African Free School on Mulberry Street. See Charles C. Andrews, *The History of the New-York African Free-Schools, from Their Establishment in 1787, to the Present Time; Embracing a Period of More Than Forty Years: Also a Brief Account of the Successful Labors, of the New-York Manumission Society: With an Appendix* (New York: Mahlon Day, 1830), 59. Consult *"Hope Is the First Great Blessing": Leaves from the African Free School Presentation Book, 1812–1816*, annotated by Anna Mae Duane and Thomas Thurston (New York: New-York Historical Society, 2008), 29–78, for a range of work completed by New York African Free School students. See, too, the digitized records of the African Free Schools from 1817–1832 on the New York Heritage Digital Collections website at https://cdm16694.contentdm.oclc.org/digital/collection/p15052coll5/id/28553.

27. Abigail Field Mott, *Observations on the Importance of Female Education, and Maternal Instruction, with Their Beneficial Influence on Society. By A Mother* (New York: Mahlon Day, 1825), 3, 5, 13, 65, 64. For one part from *Observations*, see appendix C.
28. Abigail Field Mott, *Biographical Sketches and Interesting Anecdotes of Persons of Colour. To Which Is Added, A Selection of Pieces in Poetry. Compiled by A. Mott* (New York: Mahlon Day, 1826), iii. For selections from *Biographical Sketches*, see appendix C.
29. *The Life and Adventures of Olaudah Equiano; or, Gustavus Vassa, the African. From an Account Written by Himself. Abridged by A. Mott. To Which Is Added Some Remarks on the Slave Trade* (New York: Samuel Wood and Sons, 1829) may be understood as a richer account compared with the one devoted to Equiano's life in Mott's *Biographical Sketches*. In *Life and Adventures*, Mott includes more of Equiano's commentary on the events that shaped his life.
30. Mott, *Biographical Sketches*, ii.
31. Andrews, *History of the New-York African Free-Schools*, 103. On donations of books to the New York African Free Schools, see, for instance, the article on the New-York Bible Society in the March 13, 1830, issue of the *New-York Observer*. Members of the Committee on Prisons, Penitentiaries, and Humane Institutions donated twelve Bibles and twelve Testaments to African Free School no. 2, located on Mulberry Street between Hester and Grant Streets. Andrews observes that monetary donations were made to African Free Schools as well. In the late 1820s, following the disbanding of the New-York Association for Educating Coloured Male Adults, members donated one hundred sixty-three dollars and sixty-nine cents (103). Also, "A Friend to Humanity," author of *Condemnation of the Slave-Trade; Being an Investigation of the Origin and Continuation of that Inhuman Traffic* (New York: Printed for the Author, 1794), indicates, in a note, that "one-third of the profits arising from this pamphlet" were to be "donation[s] to the African Free School in this city" (ii).
32. Andrews, *History of the New-York African Free-Schools*, 103.
33. Mott, *Biographical Sketches*, 55–64, 26–31, 31–43, 156–58, and 141.
34. In *Against Wind and Tide: The African American Struggle against the Colonization Movement* (New York: New York University Press, 2014), Ousmane K. Power-Greene differentiates emigration from colonization. He employs the terms "*colonization, colonizationist*, and *colonizationism*" to refer to "people and ideas of those who associated themselves with the [American Colonization Society] and Liberia" and "*[e]migrationist, emigrationism*, and *emigration movements*" to refer to "black-led movements that paralleled the colonization movement" (xix; emphases in original). That is, he names individuals who "promoted emigration to Haiti, Canada, and West Africa (except for Liberia) as *emigrationists* and those aligned with the [American Colonization Society] as *colonizationists*" (xix; emphases in original).

35. Abigail Field Mott, *The Mother and Her Children, or Twilight Conversation*, enlarged 3rd ed. (Mahlon Day: New York, 1841), 68. For selections from the first edition of *Mother and Her Children*, see appendix C.
36. Cornell, *Adam and Anne Mott*, 213.
37. Mott includes "Eliza" in the conversations, but Cornell does not mention in *Adam and Anne Mott* a daughter with this name.
38. According to *Memoir of Purchase Monthly Meeting, Concerning Abigail Mott* (New York: James Egbert, 1852), which contains a rare, biographical sketch of the Quaker's life, written partly by her daughter-in-law, Hannah B. Smith, Mott valued these nocturnal conversations with her children: "The twilight of the evening was a favorite season with her, for collecting her little ones around her, to enter into free and cheerful conversation with them, on subjects suited to their capacity, and calculated while enlivening their feelings to enlarge their sphere of useful knowledge" (8). According to the same book, Mott, shortly before passing, expressed, "It is a great comfort to believe that we have four dear children in heaven" (18). For the *Memoir*, see appendix C.
39. In *Equiano, the African*, Carretta writes that "British audiences associated the name Gustavus Vasa with eighteenth-century arguments over political freedom in Britain" (41). In the sixteenth century, Vasa became King of Sweden.
40. Mott, *Mother and Her Children*, 2–3.
41. Mott, 3.
42. Mott, 5.
43. See, for instance, Vernon Loggins, *The Negro Author: His Development in America to 1900* (Port Washington, NY: Kennikat, 1964), 30; Paul Edwards, introduction to Olaudah Equiano, *The Life of Olaudah Equiano, or, Gustavus Vassa[,] the African*, ed. Paul Edwards, vol. 1 (London: Dawsons, 1969), viii; Angelo Costanzo, *Surprising Narrative: Olaudah Equiano and the Beginnings of Black Autobiography* (New York: Greenwood, 1987), 119; Sidney Kaplan and Emma Nogrady Kaplan, *The Black Presence in the Era of the American Revolution*, rev. ed. (Amherst: University of Massachusetts Press, 1989), 215–17n; Henry Louis Gates Jr., introduction to Henry Louis Gates Jr. and William L. Andrews, eds., *Pioneers of the Black Atlantic: Five Slave Narratives from the Enlightenment, 1772–1815* (Washington, D.C.: Civitas, 1998), 19n7; Robert J. Allison, introduction to Olaudah Equiano, *The Interesting Narrative of the Life of Olaudah Equiano[,] Written by Himself with Related Documents*, ed. Robert J. Allison, 2nd ed. (Boston: Bedford/St. Martin's, 2007), 32; Werner Sollors, introduction to Olaudah Equiano, *The Interesting Narrative of the Life of Olaudah Equiano, or Gustavus Vassa, the African[,] Written by Himself*, ed. Werner Sollors (New York: W. W. Norton, 2001), xxviii; and Angelo Costanzo, "A Note on the Text," in Olaudah Equiano, *The Interesting Narrative of the Life of Olaudah Equiano*, ed. Angelo Costanzo (Peterborough, Ontario: Broadview, 2001), 38. For more thorough treatments of Mott's *Life and Adventures*, see Nazera Sadiq Wright, *Black Girlhood in the Nineteenth Century* (Urbana: University of Illinois Press, 2016), 41–45; Lamore, "Olaudah Equiano in the United States," 66–88; Valentina K. Tikoff, "A Role Model for African American Children: Abigail Field Mott's *Life and Adventures of Olaudah Equiano* and White Northern Abolitionism," in *Who Writes for Black Children? African American Children's Literature before 1900*, ed. Katharine Capshaw and Anna Mae Duane (Minneapolis: University of Minnesota Press, 2017), 94–116; and Martha J. Cutter, "The Child's Illustrated Antislavery Talking Book: Abigail Field Mott's Abridgement of Olaudah Equiano's *Interesting Narrative* for African American Children," in Capshaw and Duane, *Who Writes for Black Children?*, 117–44. In "Nuggets from the Field: The Roots of African American Children's Literature, 1780–1866," also included in *Who Writes for Black Children?*, Laura Wasowicz comments on Mott's 1829 *Life and Adventures*, 208–9.
44. Marketing initiatives in Wood's (and Wood and Sons') books offer some of the best

clues on the extent to which this publishing house impacted New York culture. On the back cover of *Arithmetical Tables, For the Use of Schools* (New York: Samuel Wood and Sons, 1824), for instance, Wood marketed products such as "a great Variety of School-Books, Writing and Ciphering Books, Copies, Drawing-Books, Pen and Pocket Knives, Slates and Pencils, Lead Pencils, India Rubber, Grammars, Spelling-Books, School Testaments, &c."

45. As early as 1811, Wood included advertisements in books he published for and sold at his Juvenile Book-Store. In *The History of Insects* (New York: Samuel Wood, 1811), for example, Wood included the following paragraph:

> Samuel Wood hereby informs the good little Boys and Girls, both of city and country, who love to read better than to play, that if they will please to call at his Juvenile Book-Store, No. 357, Pearl-Street, New-York, it will be his pleasure to furnish them with a great variety of pretty little books, with neat cuts, calculated to afford to the young mind pleasing and useful information. Besides many from Philadelphia, New-Haven, and elsewhere, he has twenty kinds of his own printing, and proposes to enlarge the number. (29)

46. By the early 1830s, several African Free Schools were open in New York City, most of which William Hooker identifies in *Hooker's New Pocket Plan of the City of New York* (New York: W. Hooker, 1835). According to the creators of the map "Black New York City, 1785–1835" (https://www.nyhistory.org/web/africanfreeschool/map/map-print.html), New York African Free School no. 1 was located on 245 Williams Street near Duane; African Free Schools nos. 2 and 4 were located on 135 Mulberry Street between Hester and Grant; African Free School no. 3 was located on 120 Amity Street near Sixth Avenue; African Free School no. 5 was located on 161 Duane Street; and African Free School no. 6 was located on 108 Columbia Street.

47. Joseph Lancaster, *Epitome of Some of the Chief Events and Transactions in the Life of Joseph Lancaster, Containing an Account of the Rise and Progress of the Lancasterian System of Education; And the Author's Future Prospects of Usefulness to Mankind; Written by Himself, and Published to Promote the Education of His Family* (New Haven: Baldwin and Peck, 1833), 6.

48. Anna Mae Duane, "'Can You Be Surprised at My Discouragement?': Global Emulation and the Logic of Colonization at the New York African Free School," in *Warring for America: Cultural Contests in the Age of 1812*, ed. Nicole Eustace and Fredrika J. Teute (Williamsburg, VA, and Chapel Hill: Omohundro Institute of Early American History and Culture and University of North Carolina Press, 2017), 351.

49. Carla L. Peterson, "Black Life in Freedom: Creating an Elite Culture," in *Slavery in New York*, ed. Ira Berlin and Leslie M. Harris (New York: The New Press, 2005), 190.

50. Peterson, "Black Life in Freedom," 184.

51. Shane White, *Stories of Freedom in Black New York* (Cambridge, MA: Harvard University Press, 2002), 13.

52. White, *Stories of Freedom in Black New York*, 13.

53. Patrick Rael, "The Long Death of Slavery," in Berlin and Harris, *Slavery in New York*, 132.

54. Edwards, introduction to Equiano, *The Life of Olaudah Equiano, or, Gustavus Vassa[,] the African*, ix; Vincent Carretta, "A Note on the Text," in Equiano, *The Interesting Narrative and Other Writings*, xxxi.

55. Olaudah Equiano, *The Interesting Narrative of the Life of Olaudah Equiano, or Gustavus Vassa, the African. Written by Himself*, vol. 1 (New York: W. Durell, 1791).

56. Olaudah Equiano, *The Interesting Narrative of the Life of Olaudah Equiano, or Gustavus Vassa, the African. Written by Himself*, authorized 2nd ed., vol. 1 (London: Printed and [S]old for the Author, 1789).

57. Ito, "Olaudah Equiano and the New York Artisans," 89–90, 85.
58. Ito, 87; and James Green, "The Publishing History of Olaudah Equiano's *Interesting Narrative*," *Slavery and Abolition: A Journal of Slave and Post-Slave Studies* 16, no. 3 (1995): 372.
59. Olaudah Equiano, *The Life and Adventures of Olaudah Equiano; or, Gustavus Vassa, the African. From an Account Written by Himself. Abridged by A. Mott. To Which Is Added Some Remarks on the Slave Trade* (New York: Samuel Wood and Sons, 1829), 4.
60. Michelle Martin, "African American," in *Keywords for Children's Literature*, ed. Philip Nel and Lissa Paul (New York: New York University Press, 2011), 10.
61. Giselle Liza Anatol, "Life Writing for Black Children and Youth," in *A History of African American Autobiography*, ed. Joycelyn K. Moody (Cambridge: Cambridge University Press, 2021), 347.
62. Andrews, *History of the New-York African Free-Schools*, 44, 118. For selections from *History*, see appendix B.
63. *An Address to the Parents and Guardians of the Children Belonging to the New-York African Free-School, By the Trustees of the Institution* (New York: Samuel Wood and Sons, 1818), 16. For the *Address*, see appendix B.
64. Karen Sánchez-Eppler, *Dependent States: The Child's Part in Nineteenth-Century American Culture* (Chicago: University of Chicago Press, 2005), xxi. Relying on the work of Howard Chudacoff, Sánchez-Eppler adds, "age only became a meaningful form of classification at the end of the nineteenth century."
65. Shane White uses a version of this phrase in the title of his book, *Stories of Freedom in Black New York*.
66. For additional insights on the packaging of the *Interesting Narrative* for young readers in the United States, consult Karen Kennerly, *The Slave Who Bought His Freedom: Equiano's Story* (New York: Dutton, 1971); and Ann Cameron, *The Kidnapped Prince: The Life of Olaudah Equiano* (New York: Yearling, 1995).
67. New-York African Free School Records, 1817–1832, vol. 2, New-York Historical Society Digital Collections, https://digitalcollections.nyhistory.org/islandora/object/islandora:139453#page/14/. The names of the New York publishers Samuel Wood and Mahlon Day appear in these records as well.
68. On the logistics of a "Female Department" run by the educational methods of Joseph Lancaster, see *Manual of the Lancasterian System, of Teaching Reading, Writing, Arithmetic, and Needle-Work, as Practiced in the Schools of the Free-School Society, of New-York* (New York: Samuel Wood and Sons, 1820), 38–45. This section provides descriptions of the types of student work Mott likely evaluated during her visits to the Female Department of the New York African Free School.
69. Mott, *Observations*, 59.
70. Equiano, *Life and Adventures*, 4.
71. Andrews, *History of the New-York African Free-Schools*, 82. For additional information on the ticket system, a part of the Lancasterian method, see *Address to the Parents and Guardians*, 17–20; and *Manual of the Lancasterian System*, 61–63.
72. *Manual of the Lancasterian System*, 20, 63.
73. Jane R. Pomeroy, *Alexander Anderson (1775–1870): Wood Engraver and Illustrator: An Annotated Bibliography*, vol. 2 (New Castle, DE: Oak Knoll, 2005), 1407.
74. Tikoff, "A Role Model for African American Children," 98.
75. Equiano, *Life and Adventures*, 4.
76. Mott, *Biographical Sketches*, iv.
77. For an announcement of an upcoming examination day, see the advertisement page, *New-York Gazette*, May 5, 1820. For a sampling of reviews of examination days, consult "To the Editors of the *Mercantile Advertiser*," *Mercantile Advertiser* (New York), April 13, 1819; "African Free School," *New-York Daily Advertiser*, May 9, 1820; "African

Free School," *Evening Post* (New York), May 13, 1824; "African Free School," *Spectator* (New York), May 14, 1824; "African Free School," *New-York Observer*, May 15, 1824; "Report," *The Statesman* (New York), May 21, 1824; and "General La Fayette," *Evening Post* (New York), September 11, 1824.

78. Andrews, *History of the New-York African Free-Schools*, 39.
79. Mott, *Observations*, 3; Andrews, *History of the New-York African Free-Schools*, 109, 109–10, 148. For Smith's poem, see appendix B.
80. Mott's note at the end of Equiano's narrative in *Life and Adventures* provides another relevant point relating to Durell's edition. Here she admits consulting "a work that has lately come into my hands" (25), which refers to Henri Grégoire's *An Enquiry Concerning the Intellectual and Moral Faculties, and Literature of Negroes; Followed with an Account of the Life and Works of Fifteen Negroes and Mulattoes, Distinguished in Science, Literature and the Arts*, trans. D. B. Warden (Brooklyn: Thomas Kirk, 1810). It would have been impossible for Mott to construct her adaptation based solely on Grégoire's *Enquiry* because he provides a biographical sketch of Equiano or Vassa instead of quoting extensively from the life writer's autobiography. Language written by Equiano comprises Durell's edition, which does contain the autobiographer's prose.
81. "A New Bibliography of the Work of Wood Engraver and Illustrator Alexander Anderson," *Proceedings of the American Antiquarian Society* 115, no. 2 (2005): 322. For more information on Anderson's work for and connections with nineteenth-century book publishers in New York, including Samuel Wood, Wood and Sons, and Mahlon Day, consult Pomeroy's *Alexander Anderson (1775–1870)*. See, as well, Pomeroy's *Alexander Anderson's New York City Diary, 1793 to 1799* (New Castle: Oak Knoll, 2014). Many of the illustrations from Mott's adaptation appear in Alexander Anderson's Scrapbooks, a part of the New York Public Library Digital Collections (https://digitalcollections.nypl.org/collections/alexander-anderson-scrapbooks). This digital archive showcases Anderson's representations of slaves, among other subjects. I thank Joycelyn K. Moody for drawing my attention to this digital archive. The frontispiece from Mott's adaptation differs from the visual representations of Equiano in authorized and other unauthorized editions. For a preliminary discussion of frontispieces in editions of the *Interesting Narrative* published in Great Britain and the United States, consult Srinivas Aravamudan, *Tropicopolitans: Colonialism and Agency, 1688–1804* (Durham: Duke University Press, 1999), 247. A comprehensive analysis of these frontispieces has not been completed.
82. "Samuel Wood and Sons, Early New York Publishers of Children's Books," *Bulletin of the New York Public Library* 46, no. 9 (1942): 759. In *One Hundred Years of Publishing [1804–1904]: A Brief Historical Account of the House of William Wood and Company* (New York: William Wood, 1904), William C. Wood solidifies this connection: Samuel Wood's children's books were "illustrated with copper-plate engravings, both plain and hand-colored, and a little later with wood-engravings by Dr. Alexander Anderson . . . whose earliest work is found in these little books" (7). Anderson earned his medical degree at Columbia College in the spring of 1796.
83. In the adaptation, Mott more frequently refers to the author as Gustavus Vassa instead of Olaudah Equiano.
84. In *Alexander Anderson*, vol. 2, Pomeroy identifies illustrations in *Life and Adventures* signed by Anderson. These images include the frontispiece; upper and lower images on page 7; upper and lower images on page 11; upper image on page 16; and upper image on page 22 (1407–8). In "The Child's Illustrated Antislavery Talking Book," Cutter acknowledges that Anderson "remodel[ed]" some images (133). For more commentary on Anderson's visual work, see Martha J. Cutter, *The Illustrated Slave:*

Empathy, Graphic Narrative, and the Visual Culture of the Transatlantic Abolition Movement, 1800–1852 (Athens: University of Georgia Press, 2017), 51–54.

85. Samuel Wood, *The New-York Preceptor; or, Third Book* (New York: Samuel Wood and Sons, 1828), iii. For a list of Wood and Sons' "School Books" available in 1829, consult the final page of *The New-York Reader, No. 1: Adapted to the Capacities of the Younger Class of Learners; Being Selections of Easy Lessons, Calculated to Inculcate Morality and Piety* (New York: Samuel Wood and Sons, 1829).

86. Wood, *The New-York Preceptor*, iii–iv.

87. The Woods used this technique merging the visual and verbal in other children's books on the institution of slavery. Consult, for instance, the frontispiece from *The Negro Boy's Tale; A Poem, By Amelia Opie. To Which are Added, The Morning Dream, By Cowper, and Other Poems* (New York: Samuel Wood and Sons, c. 1829). "See page 19" appears under the frontispiece.

88. For broadsides and books published by Wood or Wood and Sons containing narratives about, visual representations of, dialogues concerning/involving, and orations by individuals of African descent, consult, for instance, *Injured Humanity; Being a Representation of What the [U]nhappy Children of Africa [E]ndure from [T]hose [W]ho [C]all [T]hemselves Christians* (1805); "enlarged" 2nd ed. of Thomas Branagan's *The Penitential Tyrant; or, Slave Trader Reformed: A Pathetic Poem, in Four Cantos* (1807); *An Oration on the Abolition of the Slave Trade; Delivered in the African Church, in the City of New-York, January 1, 1808* (1808); "A Family Conversation on the Slavery of the Negroes," in *The New-York Reader, No. 2: Being, Selections in Prose and Poetry, for the Use of Schools* (1813), 190–99; *The Cries of New-York* (1816), 18–20, 24–25, 27, 38; *Alice, the Negro; and the Good Old Indian: To Which are Added a Memoir of Ann Watson, and the Advice of Thomas Gwin* (1817); "Master and Slave," in *The New-York Reader, No. 3: Being, Selections in Prose and Poetry, from the Best Writers: Designed for the Use of Schools, and Calculated to Assist the Scholar in Acquiring the Art of Reading, and at the Same Time to Fix His Principles, and Inspire Him with a Love of Virtue* (1819), 194–97; *False Stories Corrected* (1822), 15–17; *The Tawny Girl; or the History of Margaret Russel, Illustrating the Benefits of Education on the Most Degraded Classes of Society* (1823); and *The Negro Boy's Tale*. For "A Family Conversation on the Slavery of the Negroes" and "Master and Slave," see appendix D. For another early Black Atlantic text published by Samuel Wood, see Jupiter Hammon, *An Address to the Negroes in the State of New-York* (New York: Samuel Wood, 1806). According to the advertisement on the back cover of Hammon's *Address*, Wood also sold—but did not print—Joseph Lavallée's *The Negro Equalled by Few Europeans*, which contained "the Poems of Phillis Wheatley, of Boston, in N. Engl'd."

89. Equiano, *Life and Adventures*, 8, 15. Mott condenses Equiano's extensive trade and travel throughout the West Indies to mostly the island of Montserrat.

90. Equiano, 25, 36. In 1807 Wood published "Remarks" on a broadside, containing an illustration of the slave ship *Brooks*. For other texts in which Wood used "Remarks," consult *The Mirror of Misery; or, Tyranny Exposed. Extracted from Authentic Documents, and [E]xemplified by Engravings* (1807, 1811, and 1814), 9–14; and *The Method of Procuring Slaves on the Coast of Africa; With an Account of Their Sufferings on the Voyage, and Cruel Punishment in the West-Indies*, 261–66, bound with the "enlarged" second edition of *Penitential Tyrant*; for illustrations on page 33 in *Life and Adventures*, see the broadside *Injured Humanity*, *Mirror of Misery* (1807, 1811, and 1814), 21 and 22, and *Method of Procuring Slaves*, 273 and 274; and for "A S[ubject] [for] C[onversation] and R[eflection] [at] [the] T[ea]-T[able]," see *Mirror of Misery* (1807, 1811, and 1814), 37–45, and the "enlarged" second edition of *Penitential Tyrant*, 242–51.

91. Nevertheless, at least one early nineteenth-century book printed by Wood indicates that the publisher and bookseller attempted to mobilize young children as antislavery activists through the employment of "indignation." According to "A Family Conversation on the Slavery of the Negroes," a dialogue Wood included in (and may have written for) *The New-York Reader, No. 2*, Charles, a child, exclaims, "My indignation rises at the recital" of his father narrating how slaves "fall into the hands of their cruel oppressors" and experience "a life of laborious servitude" (196–97). Following Charles's emotional reaction, all children in this familial conversation—Augusta, Sophia, Henry, and Charles—commit to antislavery activism by agreeing with their sister, Cecilia, that they should "forgo any indulgences to alleviate [slaves'] sufferings" (198). Thus, the children agree not to purchase items produced from slave labor.
92. Tikoff, "A Role Model for African American Children," 101.
93. "To the Reader," *Penitential Tyrant*, v, vii. For "To the Reader," see appendix D. This essay does not appear in the 1805 edition of *Penitential Tyrant*, printed in Philadelphia, so one may conclude that Wood wrote this essay. It was not uncommon for Wood to write introductory essays for books printed or sold by him or ones printed by him and his sons. See, for instance, the preface to *The New-York Expositor; or, Fifth Book: Being a Collection of the Most Useful Words in the English Language. By Richard Wiggins. To Which Is Added, A Vocabulary of Scientific Terms. By John Griscom* (New York: Samuel Wood and Sons, 1818), iii–iv.
94. Equiano, *Life and Adventures*, 26.
95. Paula T. Connolly, *Slavery in American Children's Literature, 1790–2010* (Iowa City: University of Iowa Press, 2013), 16.
96. *The Negro Boy's Tale*, v–vi.
97. Peterson, "Black Life in Freedom," 187–88.
98. *New-York Advertiser*, August 12, 1828.
99. Peterson, "Black Life in Freedom," 187.
100. Quoted in Andrews, *History of the New-York African Free-Schools*, 36, 54, 68, 86.
101. Equiano, *Life and Adventures*, 14. Numerous authors of nineteenth-century books define the rule of three, or simple proportion. According to the author of *Mathematics, Compiled from the Best Authors and Intended to be the Text-Book of the Course of Private Lectures on These Sciences in the University of Cambridge*, vol. 1 (Boston: Thomas and Andrews, 1801), for instance, the "*Rule of Three* is that, by which a number is found, having to a given number the same ratio, which is between two other given numbers. For this reason[,] it is sometimes named the *Rule of Proportion*. It is called the *Rule of Three*, because in each of its questions there are given *three numbers* at least. And because of its excellent and extensive use, it is often named the *Golden Rule*" (105; emphases in original). For exercises involving the rule of three in extant records of New York African Free Schools, consult Duane and Thurston, *"Hope Is the First Great Blessing,"* 30, 38, and 47. According to *Manual of the Lancasterian System*, published by the Woods, students would have learned the rule of three in the tenth class of arithmetic (21). Students "being promoted to the rule of three" (62) received twenty-four tickets.
102. Equiano, *Life and Adventures*, 14.
103. Equiano, 15–18.
104. Equiano, 24.
105. Quoted in Andrews, *History of the New-York African Free-Schools*, 11.
106. Leslie M. Harris, *In the Shadow of Slavery: African Americans in New York City, 1626–1863* (Chicago: University of Chicago Press, 2003), 134.
107. "[R]esolution," *Commercial Advertiser* (New York), February 7, 1828. For the entire article, see appendix B.
108. *The African Repository, and Colonial Journal* (Washington, D.C.), December 1830; *Freedom's Journal* (New York), August 7, 1829.

109. For Andrews's missive to Russwurm, published in the November 9, 1827, issue of *Freedom's Journal*, see appendix B. Andrews acknowledges that Russwurm sent issues of the newspaper to the trustees of New York African Free Schools and they were part of the school library on Mulberry Street. A proposal for Andrews's *History of the New-York African Free-Schools* appeared in the August 7, 1829, issue of *Freedom's Journal*.
110. For instance, Nazera Sadiq Wright, in *Black Girlhood in the Nineteenth Century*, maintains that "Equiano's tale was decidedly not fodder for the colonization movement" (43), and Martha J. Cutter, in "The Child's Antislavery Talking Book," claims that scholars cannot locate "any evidence that [Abigail Field Mott] supported abolitionist attempts to move freed slaves back to Africa in plans promoted by the American Colonization Society" (130).
111. See Margaret Hope Bacon, "Quakers and Colonization," *Quaker History* 95, no. 1 (2006): 26–43.
112. Mott, *Biographical Sketches*, 141, ii.
113. For other notable differences between *Life and Adventures* and authorized editions of Equiano's *Interesting Narrative*, see Tikoff, "A Role Model for African American Children," 98–102. Tikoff observes, for instance, that Mott does not include Equiano's commentary on slavery in his Eboe nation, the qualities of the Eboes' religion that do not align with Christianity, interactions with numerous individuals of African descent in the Atlantic world, including his participation in the slave trade, along with his overseeing and purchasing of slaves when he was involved with Dr. Charles Irving's Mosquito Coast plantation. For other notable differences, consult Cutter, "The Child's Illustrated Antislavery Talking Book," 137–38.
114. According to Carretta, in *Equiano, the African*, "The black loyalists arriving from America at the end of the American Revolution joined the thousands of blacks already resident in England. Estimates of the total number of blacks in England in the last quarter of the eighteenth century range between five and twenty thousand" (216). Consult Carretta's biography on Equiano for a discussion of the economic and social conditions that led to the creation of the resettlement project (202–35). In *Short History of Sierra Leone* (London: Longman, 1979), Christopher Fyfe succinctly describes these conditions: "During the war the British offered slaves freedom if they left their American masters. Many ran away and joined the British army and navy. After the war some of them came to London, where they were free. But, though free, they were unemployed and had to beg in the streets" (22).
115. Bryant, *The Fluid Text*, 4.
116. G. Thomas Couser, *Vulnerable Subjects: Ethics and Life Writing* (Ithaca: Cornell University Press, 2004), 36.
117. Equiano, *The Interesting Narrative and Other Writings*, 226.
118. Equiano, 227, 228–29; emphases added. For more on Equiano and the Sierra Leone resettlement project, consult "The Will and Codicil of Gustavus Vassa [Olaudah Equiano]," in Equiano, *The Interesting Narrative and Other Writings*, 373–75. Equiano decided that if both of his children, Ann Marie and Johanna Vassa, predeceased him, he chose to "give[,] devise[,] and bequeath" the "whole of my Estate and Effects ... to the Treasurer and Directors of the Sierra Leona Company for the Use and Benefit of the School established by the said Company at Sierra Leona" (373). The resettlement project Equiano names here is not the same one he was involved with in 1787. For additional information on this will, consult Paul Edwards, "A Descriptive List of Manuscripts in the Cambridgeshire Record Office Relating to the Will of Gustavus Vassa (Olaudah Equiano)," *Research in African Literatures* 20, no. 3 (1989): 473–80.
119. Equiano, *Life and Adventures*, 24; emphases added.
120. For the Sierra Leone resettlement scene in the first edition of Mott's *Biographical Sketches*, see 64; for this scene in the second edition, consult 82–83.

121. Olaudah Equiano, *The Interesting Narrative of the Life of Olaudah Equiano, or Gustavus Vassa, the African. Written by Himself*, vol. 2 (New York: W. Durell, 1791), 180; emphases added.
122. In *Address*, published in 1818 by the Woods, Leggett's name appears in the list of trustees (24).
123. Andrews, *History of the New-York African Free-Schools*, 132. For the complete speech, see appendix B.
124. Anna Mae Duane, *Suffering Childhood in Early America: Violence, Race, and the Making of the Child Victim* (Athens: University of Georgia Press, 2010), 171.
125. For more on Fields's speech, see Duane, "'Can You Be Surprised at My Discouragement?,'" 331–38.
126. Andrews, *History of the New-York African Free-Schools*, 119, 118, emphases in original.
127. Andrews, 119.
128. Duane, *Suffering Childhood*, 172. For two narratives explaining why Andrews was fired, see Duane, *Educated for Freedom: The Incredible Story of Two Fugitive Schoolboys Who Grew Up to Change a Nation* (New York: New York University Press, 2020), 214–15n19.
129. Power-Greene, *Against Wind and Tide*, 29.
130. Equiano, *Life and Adventures*, 25.
131. Perhaps Mott's endorsement of the colonization of Liberia, including her rewriting of the Sierra Leone resettlement scene, contributed to the quarrel that permanently divided the white Quaker and Douglass between 1848 and 1850. According to John R. McKivigan, editor of *The Frederick Douglass Papers, Series 3: Correspondence*, vol. 1, the source of this divide "remains unknown" (114n1).
132. Equiano, *Life and Adventures*, 12.

Appendix B

Pedagogy, Politics, and Regulations at the New York African Free Schools

An Address to the Parents and Guardians of the Children Belonging to the New-York African Free-School, By the Trustees of the Institution (New York: Samuel Wood and Sons, 1818)

Respected Friends,

WE, the trustees of the School, feeling a desire that your Children should become useful and respectable in society, are impressed with the propriety of addressing you in this way, in order to call your attention to a few subjects connected with their and your present good, and consequent future happiness.

It will, we presume, be admitted by you, that great pains are taken at the school to teach your children, not only how to read, write, &c. &c. but also, that considerable care is bestowed in order to implant virtuous and correct principles in their minds. Nor can too much solicitude be felt on this subject, by those who take an interest in their real welfare. And who, we would ask, can or ought to feel more concern, that a child should be "trained up in the way he should go," [1] than the parents of such child. Nothing, perhaps, is calculated to be so useful in successfully prosecuting that object, as the well directed efforts of a prudent parent. We, therefore, recommend your frequent perusal of our ideas on the following subjects.

Example.

Children, as well as ourselves, are creatures of habit, and at all times observing the words and actions of their superiors; not an idle word that passes the lips of the parent, (if it be within the comprehension of the child) but the child will endeavour to imitate. Few are the parents, though they are ready to acknowledge the truth of the remark, make it of that importance as to put a proper restraint upon these feelings or expressions. Your words, your manner, your actions are all observed and practised by your children. Therefore[,] strive to think twice before you speak to, or in the presence of a child.

Of [A]ttending Places of Public Worship.

Children should be taught and encouraged to attend places of public worship at the stated times of service, and especially in company with their parents or other friends, and to behave in a becoming and reverent manner while there, as well as in going and returning.

This is an important duty to be performed by all parents and others having children under their care, as it is calculated to produce an inclination to good things, even from habit.

On Reading the Scriptures.

Such of your children as can read the Scriptures, should be encouraged and required to do so, at all suitable opportunities, when at home. If parents were to fix on stated times, (in the evening for instance) for this exercise, it would, perhaps, be productive of much good, especially if all present, during the time of reading, were to desist from every thing else, and spend half an hour, or more in solemn attention to the exercise. Let it be observed, that the [S]criptures should never be read in a careless irreverent manner, but with serious attention, seeing that they are given by the inspiration of God, and that with his blessing, they are able to make us wise unto salvation.

Of Speaking the Truth.

Parents should endeavour to impress upon the minds of their children the importance and excellence of always speaking the Truth, and also, to inform them, how *wicked* it is to utter a falsehood; as it is clearly pointed out in the Scriptures to be a very great offence against God; and he has sometimes punished liars in a very awful and exemplary manner: witness the case of Ananias and Saphira, recorded in the 5th chapter of the Acts.[2] A liar is always looked upon, by our fellow-men, as a mean and dishonourable person, unworthy of respect or esteem.

The following few lines, we consider appropriate, and would recommend them, not only to be read, but committed to memory by all the children capable of learning them.

> O! 'tis a lovely thing for youth
> To walk betimes in wisdom's way,
> To fear a lie, to speak the truth,
> That we may trust to all they say.
>
> But liars we can never trust,
> Though they should speak the thing that's true;
> And he who does one fault at first,
> And lies to hide it, makes it two.
>
> The Lord delights in them who speak
> The words of truth; but every liar,
> Must have his portion in the lake,
> Which burns with brimstone and with fire.[3]

On [G]iving Commands to Children.

While the Scriptures strongly enjoin it on children to be obedient to their parents, they likewise point out the duty of parents to their children; hence, in the proverbs of Solomon, and in some of the Epistles, much instruction may be gathered on this important subject; and we earnestly recommend such passages as treat on it, to the careful perusal of parents.[4]

We are persuaded that considerable trouble and unhappiness are experienced in families, in consequence of the improper manner in which many parents give their commands to their children. Parents and others who have the care of children, are obeyed and respected in proportion to their own good or bad management of them. Those who expect obedience, should first observe that their commands are given with prudence and moderation, and then enforce them with a becoming resolution. It is, however, to be regretted, that many persons give their orders in a boisterous and tyrannical manner, or else in a careless and indifferent way, so that they are hardly ever obeyed or respected by their children or domestics: for, in the first case, they only produce in the mind of the child, a slavish fear, dread, and hatred; and in the second, little else is produced but inattention and carelessness, and both of course, tend to disobedience.

Never make a promise to a child unless you intend fulfilling it; and when made, be careful you do not forget it. Many parents by the neglect of these simple rules, in effect, tell their children that they are not to believe what they say. The child hears your commands, but hopes, and often finds that you have either forgot what you have said, or you did not mean as you said.

Never correct in anger, but if a degree of it is felt, always wait till the mind becomes calm, the only state wherein a person can be qualified to correct in reason, without which, it will tend only to do harm, having a tendency of hardening or souring the mind, instead of convincing the judgment.

Of Industry.

As idleness leads to wickedness, so industry will be found happily to conduce to virtue and sobriety; and it is incumbent on parents to find employment for their children, at a suitable age, as it is to furnish them with food and clothing, for a want of employment, or rather of suitable inducement to it, will soon deprive them of both food and raiment.[5] Much more might be said on this subject, but we will only add one short sentence, viz.[6] To suffer children to run the streets freely, with promiscuous herds of idle[,] wicked companions, is only fitting them for *close Confinement at maturer age in a state prison or house of correction.*

Of Cleanliness.

Parents can, perhaps, scarcely show a greater proof of their care for their children, than by keeping them clean and decent, which contributes much to their health and comfort, and when they are sent to school, it is indispensable. It is also a very pleasing sight to see a large collection of children with their hands, faces, and heads perfectly clean, and their clothing clean and in good order. The appearance of the children exhibits to every observing mind, the character of the mother.

Of Dishonesty.

It is observable, though greatly to be lamented, that frequently children very early show a propensity to possess what does not belong to them, which if not checked in proper time, grows to a fixed and settled vice. It is, therefore, highly essential, that those who have the care of them should keep a watchful eye on the first buddings of this dangerous propensity. It generally shows itself first by cheating in the various games of play, well known among children, such as marbles, buttons, &c. &c. The stealing of a needle, pin, or a bit of thread, when known to the parent, should be treated with *great seriousness*, and if repeated, followed with timely correction, which, although it might not accord with the tender feelings of the indulgent parent, yet it is believed, that a steady perseverance would gradually lessen the painful task, and may be the means of saving the child from future disgrace and ruin, and the whole family from sharing in the same.

Of [U]sing Profane and Indecent Language.

There are few crimes more degrading to human nature than that of making use of profane and indecent language; and yet, how often is the ear of modesty and piety assailed by the horrid imprecations, and the disgusting vulgarity of the passing multitudes. Parents should be careful, whenever they hear any improper expressions of the child, and by timely and moderate reproof, endeavour to show the evil tendency thereof. Too great, alas! is the number of youth, who, indulged or neglected, are suffered to become a nuisance to society. It is believed that much of this great and growing evil might be prevented by the timely admonition and care of those who have a daily opportunity of hearing, and authority to correct their children.

Of Cruelty to Brutes, &c.

Parents should discountenance[7] every act of cruelty which they may discover in their children. The minds of youth are very susceptible of strong impressions: these may be turned either to their advantage or disadvantage; and it is greatly in the power of those who are entrusted with their moral instruction, to influence their tender minds to acts of kindness and humanity, even to the brute creation.

It is very probable, that many men of noted savage cruelty, began their first career in youth, by torturing and killing poor harmless flies, &c. &c. even in the presence of their own parents; who, not reflecting on the evil consequences, have suffered their children to indulge in such *wicked sports*, until they have grown up, hardened and unfeeling, and at length think, perhaps, as little of the lives of their fellow-men, and even of their own, as in their youth they did of the lives of insects, birds, or beasts.

We extract a few lines on this subject from the well[-]known Cowper,[8] and would recommend every child to learn and observe them.

> The spring-time of our years
> Is soon dishonour'd and defil'd in most
> By budding ills, that ask a prudent hand

To check them. But, alas! none sooner shoots,
If unrestrain'd, into luxuriant growth,
Than cruelty, most devilish of them all.
Mercy to him that shows it, is the rule
And righteous limitation of its act,
By which Heaven moves in pardoning guilty man;
And he that shows none, being ripe in years
And conscious of the outrage he commits,
Shall seek it, and not find it, in his turn.[9]

Ye therefore, who love mercy, teach your sons to love it too.

Education of Children.

All well[-]organized schools are governed by regular system, and this is strictly to be observed by the scholars: but a close conformity to such regulations as the system embraces, depends greatly upon the parents who must feel a sufficient interest in them, or the pupil will be prevented from fulfilling their requirements.

But, as it would be unreasonable to expect the parents of the children composing the school under our care, to feel an interest in the rules adopted for its government, unless they become acquainted with them, we have considered it proper herewith to furnish some of the most prominent of them, which are as follows:

1st. The school commences at nine o'clock in the morning, and at two in the afternoon, when every scholar is required to be present. Every monitor[10] is required to be present ten minutes before the above-mentioned hours. At half past nine, and at half past two o'clock, a monitor is placed at the door, to take down the names of the scholars who then enter, and these are, at the conclusion of the school, dealt with according to the lateness of the hour at which they may have come in.

2nd. Every scholar who comes to school after the regular hours of nine and two, is required to bring a note, signifying the reason of his or her detention, and every one that is once or twice absent at school hours, is required in like manner to bring a written excuse, or one of the family to call and give a verbal reason.

3rd. Every scholar is expected to come to school with his or her hands and face clean, hair combed, and their clothes clean and in good order; those who come dirty, will be washed and combed in school, before all the scholars.

4th. No scholar is allowed to talk, or make any unnecessary noise, during school time, and if any one wants to ask a question, he will be attended to by his holding up his hand.

5th. The school being conducted on the Lancasterian system,[11] every scholar is required to be obedient to the orders of the monitors, who have their appointments from the master.

6th. Such scholars as are appointed as monitors are required to perform their respective duties with promptness and fidelity.

7th. The master will hear any complaints which any child has against a monitor, by the scholar's holding up his hand.

8th. Every scholar, at the dismission of school, is required to go immediately, and quietly home, and parents are requested to correct every violation of this rule themselves.

9th. Any parent or other person sending a child to the school, is at liberty to call on the teacher at the school room, for explanations on any subject relative to the treatment of such child: but the teacher may use his discretion, whether to enter upon such explanation before, or after school closes.

10th. It is required that, previous to a child's leaving school, the parent or guardian of such scholar, will inform the teacher of his intention, together with the reason thereof, so that due notice of it might be taken, and a certificate prepared of the good behaviour of the scholar, if deserving it, and that the dismission may be conducted in due form, in the presence of the trustees.

11th. Any person wishing to send a child to the school will, by calling at the school room, during school hours, be informed by the teacher how they may effect the same, observing that no child under six years of age, nor girls above the age of fourteen and boys of fifteen will be admitted.

Sewing School.

The trustees viewing it very essential for the girls to learn the use of the needle, have provided a separate apartment near, where about 60 or 70 girls are taught with great success, by a well[-]qualified teacher, in divers[12] branches of needle work. The business of this school is conducted according to the late new method of female instruction.[13] Such girls as are in, or above the fourth reading class[,] have the privilege of learning to sew.

All scholars attending the sewing school are required to be clean, orderly, obedient, and to behave in the most respectful manner to their instructress.

There are several other regulations adopted for the internal government of the school, and which are to be strictly observed by the scholars; the above, however, are all that are deemed requisite, for our present purpose.

Order and system is the characteristic of a Lancasterian school, and it is the object of the trustees of this Institution, that it continue to be distinguished in those respects: much, however, depends upon the [co]operation of the parents and guardians of the pupils, for it is greatly in their power to aid or impede its salutary regulations.

Emulation and reward are observed throughout the whole; to aid which, a considerable sum is annually appropriated by the [t]rustees, for the express purpose of furnishing daily rewards to the scholars who merit them. The sum appropriated is subdivided into tickets, the nominal value of which is, one eighth of a cent each: every scholar who gains the head of each reading draft, of seven or eight boys each, receives one of these tickets, and for excelling in the other branches, or for being promoted to higher classes, in any of them, liberal rewards are given in tickets, and it is not uncommon to find several scholars at the time of calling in the tickets, (which is once in two weeks) who have from forty to sixty of them: which, according to some instances of trial, they would be unwilling to part with for as many cents, before the regular day appointed for redeeming them: on that day they bring them up with evident pleasure, and receive their value in cakes, toys, &c. &c. This with suitable expressions of approbation from the teacher, or from the trustees, produces the object designed.

Another important use is made of those tickets, besides expending them as pay and rewards to the scholars who deserve them, viz. they are to be returned by way of *fine*, for various offences, which may be committed by idle and unruly boys who may read, spell, or cipher well enough to earn them, but, may in other respects, behave too bad to keep them; if however the offender has no tickets, then other modes of punishment, though with regret[,] are necessarily resorted to.

A list of offences, with their penalties annexed, is kept hung up in the school room, which has the tendency of preventing much trouble, the Law being always in full view of the whole, and is occasionally read aloud.

A copy of this list, we think, may also be useful to the parents, as it may serve to assist them, when they are advising their children as to their behaviour in school, &c.

List of Offences with [T]heir Fines [A]nnexed.

	Tickets
For talking, playing, being out of seats, &c.[,]	4
For being disobedient, or saucy to a monitor,	4
For disobedience of inferior to superior monitors,	6
For snatching slates,[14] books, &c. from each other,	4

For blotting or soiling books,	4
For moving when the signal is given for silence,	2
For stopping to play, or making a noise in the streets when going home from school,	4
For staring at persons who may come into the school,	2
For monitors reporting scholars without cause,	4
For monitors neglecting their duty,	5
For general monitors neglecting their duty,	6
For a monitor asking the master a question without having it written on a slate,	4
For making a noise in, or near the school house, before school hours,	4
For having dirty hands and face, to be washed and fined[,]	4
For coming to school late, for every ten minutes[,]	1
For eating, or exposing any fruit, &c. during school hours, to forfeit the same and be fined[,]	4
For throwing stones or snow balls,	10
For calling ill names,	10
For fighting,	20
For playing truant, first time,	20
For playing truant, second time,	40
For scratching or cutting the desks, &c. or defacing the walls,	40

Further Regulations.

1st. No scholar is permitted to lend his tickets, in order to pay his fines, without the special consent of the master, and in no case shall any boy be indebted to another at any time more than five tickets.

2nd. No scholar is allowed to sell, give, barter, or bargain away his tickets to another, under any pretence what[so]ever.

3rd. No scholars are permitted to join in partnership in tickets.

4th. Any scholar who may be found violating any of these regulations, shall be fined or punished at the discretion of the teacher.

The trustees would improve this opportunity of again calling your attention to the subject of indenturing your children. It has been deemed proper by the Manumission Society,[15] (that society which has laboured with so much zeal for a long course of years, to meliorate the condition of the coloured people in the United States) that the power of putting out to trades or service, those children who may have received their education at the school, shall be left with the trustees, and a committee appointed by the society: it being understood that the parents, shall, in every case, if they desire it, be previously consulted. It has been a subject of much regret to the Manumission Society, that many of the children who have been educated in their school, have, after leaving it, been suffered to waste their time in idleness, to mingle in bad company, and to contract those vicious habits, which are calculated to render the subjects of them pests to society. If the children of this school are given up to such courses, their previous education will have little or no other effect than to render them more ingenious in the devices of wickedness, thereby, bringing scandal upon the school itself, and frustrating its grand object, which is, to improve the condition of your children by making them good citizens, and intelligent members of society.

For the more complete accomplishment of this important object, the Manumission Society have considered it their duty to continue their parental care over your children, even after they have left the school. In the selection of places for those scholars whom the trustees may think it advisable to put out to trades, or service, they will have a single eye to their welfare, and be careful that they are put with persons of kindness and humanity. During their apprenticeship, or term of employment, the trustees will act as the guardians of their rights, and while on the one hand they shall insist that your children demean themselves with fidelity and industry in their several employments, on the other they will effectually resist and cause to be punished those acts of oppression that may be practised upon them. We dismiss this subject with a single remark, that there is no disgrace incurred by the pursuit of any honest calling, however humble. It is the duty of every one to do all the good in his power, in that sphere in which Providence has placed him.

> Honour and shame from no condition rise,
> Act well your part, there all the honour lies.[16]

Before closing this communication, we would advert[17] to one more topic, and that is the subject of those charitable institutions, called Sunday schools. To those of you who have not had the advantages of an early education, we would earnestly recommend your attendance on the first day of every week, Sunday, at some school; and to those who cannot otherwise provide for the education of their children, we would recommend the sending them to some [one] of these numerous schools in the city; in so doing, you will, in the minds of the trustees, be pursuing the path of one of your most sacred duties. By attending these schools both you and your children will be able to improve yourselves in the acquisition of useful knowledge, and will be kept from spending improperly that day which has been set apart for public worship, the improvements of the mind, and pious meditation. At those schools you will have the opportunity of hearing the scriptures read, and of learning to read them yourselves, whereby you will become more fully instructed in those moral and religious duties, the practice of which will not only afford you peace of mind here, but render you happy hereafter: the history of those called Sabbath, or Sunday schools affords many instances where they have been the means, under God, of bringing those who have attended them, from darkness to light, and from error to the knowledge of true religion. When you consider that this may be the happy result to all who have been brought to understand and practice their duty, and that those schools have been thus blessed, you ought to give them every encouragement in your power.

It only remains for us now to conclude, by advising both parents and children, often to peruse what we have here presented them, and renew our hopes, that they will cordially unite with us in rendering the regulations which are adopted for the welfare of the school, fully effectual, so that the advantages may be derived from them, which we think they are calculated to produce.

> John Murray, Jun. *Chairman*.[18]
> Isaac Collins, *Secretary*.[19]
> Robert C. Cornell,[20]
> Joseph Curtis,[21]
> Nathan Comstock,[22]
> Hiram Ketcham,[23]
> Reuben Leggett,[24]
> Charles Miller,[25]
> Willet Seaman,[26]
> Jeremiah Thompson,[27]
> Samuel Wood,[28]
> John R. Willis.[29]

Charles C. Andrews's Letter to John B. Russwurm from the November 9, 1827, Issue of *Freedom's Journal*

N[ew]-Y[ork] A[frican] F[ree] S[chool].

Mr. John B. Russwurm.[30]

Dear Sir—It becomes my pleasing duty, at the request of the Board of Trustees of the "*New-York African Free School,*" to acknowledge, in their behalf, your generosity in furnishing gratuitously, the regular weekly numbers of the *"Freedom's Journal,"*[31] for the benefit of the Library in the School in Mulberry-street.

I do this with great satisfaction, first, because the act which merits it bespeaks a liberal heart; and, secondly, because much good may be calculated to result from *such a journal* being perused by *such readers*, as will have access to its pages.

It cannot but be acceptable to you, Sir, to be informed, that our Library now consists of about three hundred well selected volumes. Allow me, in this place, to relate the following pleasing fact.

One of our little scholars, aged about ten years, was questioned on some astronomical and other scientific subjects a few months ago, by a celebrated and learned doctor of this city;[32] the boy answered so readily and so accurately to the queries, was at last asked, how it was that he was so well acquainted with such subjects? His reply was that he remembered to have read of them in the books of the School Library.

> Very respectfully,
> C[harles] C. A[ndrews],[33]
> *Teacher of African Free School, No. 2.*

"A[FRICAN] F[REE] S[CHOOL]" FROM THE JANUARY 25, 1828, ISSUE OF *Freedom's Journal*

NOTICE.—Parents and Guardians of Coloured Children are hereby informed, that a male and [f]emale school [have] long been established for coloured children, by the Manumission Society of this city—where the pupils receive such an education as is calculated to fit them for usefulness and respectability. The male school is situated in Mulberry-street, near Grand-street, and the female school in William street, near Duane street;[34] both [are] under the management of experienced teachers. The Boys are taught Reading, Writing, Arithmetic, Geography and English Grammar—and the Girls, in addition to those branches, are taught Sewing, Marking, and Knitting, &c.

T[erms] [of] A[dmission].

Pupils of 5 to fifteen years of age are admitted by the Teachers at the Schools, at the rate of twenty-five cents to one dollar per quarter, according to the circumstances of the parents, and the children of such as cannot afford to pay any thing are admitted free of expense, and enjoy the same advantages as those who pay.

Each school is visited weekly by a committee of the trustees, in addition to which a committee of Ladies pay regular visits to the [f]emale school. Care is taken to impart moral instruction, and such have been the happy effects of the system pursued in these schools, that although several thousand have been taught in them since their establishment (now more than thirty years) there has never been an instance known to the trustees where a pupil having received a regular education has been convicted of any crime in our Courts of Justice.

> By order of the Board of Trustees.
> PETER S. TITUS,[35]
> RICHARD FIELD.[36]
> New-York, Jan. 10, 1827.

A "[R]esolution" from the February 7, 1828, Issue of the *Commercial Advertiser*

A resolution was adopted some time since by the Manumission Society of this city, to procure from the African free schools, specimens of the progress made by the pupils in writing and composition, drawing maps, &c., to transmit them to the Secretary[37] of the African Colonization Society[38] at Washington, to be deposited in the archives of that institution. This was done with a view of exhibiting the capabilities of the African intellect, to those who have entertained doubts as to its susceptibility of cultivation. Several specimens of penmanship, maps, drawings, solutions of trigonometrical propositions, &c., were forwarded in pursuance of this resolution, with the age of the pupils and certificates of the teacher. The following letter has been received in reply from the Secretary of the Colonization Society.

> Office of the Colonization Society,
> Washington, Dec. 17th. 1827.
>
> *Gentlemen*—I have been directed by the Board of Managers of our Society, to express their gratitude for the beautiful specimens of African ingenuity and talent; the productions of children in the African Free School of New-York, with which you have so obligingly favored them. No one surely, who has seen these specimens can question the ability of African children (under circumstances adapted to the development of their powers) to accomplish all, which is expected, from those of a fairer complexion. The evidence which your Society has exhibited is conclusive, and will doubtless be a powerful means of exciting more extensively and

deeply the sympathy and charity of our countrymen, in behalf of an unfortunate, neglected, and suffering people.

Our African colony is prosp[e]rous beyond example, and already gives proof that men of colour, when removed from a land in which their privileges are few, and their condition degraded, to one where they have no superiors, can feel themselves men, and act worthy of the dignity of their nature. Many such, who five years ago left our country with nothing, have acquired small fortunes of from four to ten thousand dollars each, are sharing in the offices and emoluments of a well[-]ordered government, and exerting on each other and the neighboring barbarians the benign influences of their Christian faith. I have the honor to be, gentlemen, with perfect respect, your faithful servant,

R. R. GURLEY, Sec'y Am. Col. So'y.
To Messrs. W. L. Stone. Esq.[39]
Peter S. Titus, Esq.[40] and
Wm. F. Mott, Esq.[41]

SELECTIONS FROM CHARLES C. ANDREWS'S *The History of the New-York African Free-Schools, from Their Establishment in 1787, to the Present Time; Embracing a Period of More Than Forty Years: Also a Brief Account of the Successful Labors, of the New-York Manumission Society: With an Appendix* (NEW YORK: MAHLON DAY, 1830)

I[ntroductory] A[ddress],

Spoken by a pupil[42] at a public examination [in] 1819, embracing also his Valedictory[43] on that occasion.

Respected Patrons and Friends,

To me is allotted the honor of inviting the attention of this philanthropic assembly to the various specimens of improvement, which the constant efforts of the Trustees and Teachers of this school, have caused us to make, since the last public examination, and I am happy in having been one of the favored number who have enjoyed the blessed advantages of this Institution. We have been the objects of your care, and I still earnestly solicit your sympathy. Had I the mind of a Locke,[44] and the eloquence of a Chatham,[45] still, would there not be in the minds of some, an immeasurable distance that would divide me from one of a white skin? What signifies it! Why should I strive hard, and acquire all the constituents of a man, if the prevailing genius of the land admit me not as such, or but in an inferior degree! Pardon me if I feel insignificant and weak. Pardon me if I feel discouragement to oppress me to the very [E]arth. Am I arrived at the end of my education, just on the eve of setting out into the world, of commencing some honest pursuit, by which to earn a comfortable subsistence? What are my prospects? To what shall I turn my hand? Shall I be a mechanic? No one will employ me; white boys won't work with me. Shall I be a merchant? No one will have me in his office; white clerks won't associate with me. Drudgery and servitude, then, are my prospective portion. Can you be surprised at my discouragement? Child as I am, of the same Almighty Being, and equally accountable both here and hereafter, as much so as any of the great human family!

You will now have an opportunity of seeing that many of us have acquired a commendable knowledge of the various branches taught in this School. This, the exercises now to be introduced, will, I hope, more fully demonstrate.

A D[ialogue],

Spoken between J. M. S. and W. H. at a Public Examination, written for the occasion.[46]

William.

Good morning, James, where are you going so early?

James.

I am going to school, William.

William.

To school! Why, do you go so soon as this? I am not going yet this long while.

James.

That may be your pleasure, William; this is mine.

William.

Not altogether *my* pleasure either, James; for I have been teasing my mother for my breakfast for some time, and she says, ["]No hurry, child, no hurry["]; and sends me to play a little longer.

James.

Well, I love to be obedient to my parents, and know it to be my duty; but I really think, that if I could not get my breakfast in time for early school, I should run off without it; for, half an hour's study over my sum[47] or any other part of my exercises at school, is of more consequence to me than even my breakfast.

William.

I have tried that, James, but I find that if I adopt such a plan, I may go without, not only my *breakfast*, but my *dinner* also; for, although my parents are, perhaps, as kind and indulgent as any parents can be, in other respects; yet, in this, they seem to take but little concern: I have often thought it a great pity, that they have not to pay three or four dollars a quarter, for my schooling, as our neighbor George's parents have to pay for his; I think, then, they would reckon every half hour that I were absent from school, a loss of *money* at least. They don't think of what Doctor Franklin says, that "Time is money,"[48] nor do they consider that time spent at school is to me *more precious than money*.

James.

Why, William, you both please and distress me. I am pleased to find, that the late hours at which you are noted for going to school, is not your fault, and am, at the same time, greatly distressed to hear that your parents, being so much older, and who ought to—

William.

Stop, James! I can't hear a word against my dear parents[;] I can excuse them, because they have but little learning themselves, and don't know the value of it; nor do they know how much time it takes to make one a good scholar.

James.

But, pray William, does it not subject you to great trouble at school; when you attend late, what does the master say?

William.

Why he says a great deal, and I often wish my parents could hear what he says[;] I think they would be more particular about the passing hours of the day. He says, among other things, that he knows of several boys, that are now great truants who used to be good boys, but, owing to the want of care in their parents, have become very troublesome by absence from school.

James.

I can't see how that can be; surely, their parents don't wish them to do so; they must be very much grieved, I should think, to see their children do what is so much to their own disadvantage, and be so troublesome to their teacher.

William.

That may be too, James, and yet, their parents may be frequently, the real cause of their bad conduct, though insensible of it at the time.

James.

How so, William? Do be more particular.

William.

Well, I will. You must know, our school is governed by such regulations as must be strictly observed by all concerned, which not only ensures good order throughout the school, but which are calculated to bring us on, in our learning, with greater speed.

Whenever a scholar distinguishes himself by orderly conduct, or by excelling in the performance of his exercises, he is noticed by the master, by Tickets of Reward; but, when any of us misbehave, or come late to school, we are fined and have to pay back our tickets: if we have none to pay with, we are necessarily punished. Now it is required that when a scholar has been detained till a late hour at home, or for a day or two, that he bring a note, or some of the family call and explain to the teacher, so that no fault may be laid to the charge of the supposed delinquent[;] all this[,] however, is neglected by many of our parents, and we are sent off without any thing to excuse us, and we, being sometimes disbelieved by the master, are accordingly punished, and thereby discouraged.

James.

What you have said, William, I think of so much importance, that I shall endeavor to remember it, and profit by the information you have given me, and am glad to find you capable of entering so thoroughly into such an interesting subject.

"L[ines] [on] [the] S[chool] F[air]."

By Andrew R. Smith.

The work of children here you find,
The fruit of labor and of mind,
Three months are past, the day is come,
And he that gains shall have the sum.
      Although our minds are weak and feeble,
      Some can use a knife or needle:
      If fortune by my side will stand,
      I mean to join the happy band.
A girl can make a frock or coat,
A boy, a pretty little boat;
Another girl, a pretty quilt,
A handsome cap, or gown of silk.
      T' excel we all will work and strive,
      Till to perfection we arrive;
      Many will work and strive in vain,
      The fifty tickets to obtain.
Our little fair to us is great
As any other in the state;
It is a cheerful time to some,
Though idle scholars will not come.
      The child that comes to this good school
      Should never rest an idle fool;
      Though there are many, once were so,
      We [f]ind them daily wiser grow.
The beauties of our little fair
You will not know, if you're not there;
It will be taking too much time,
To enter all the things in rhyme.
      You'll find mistakes I do not doubt,
And if you do, please leave them out.[49]

Notes

1. The trustees quote part of Proverbs 22:6.
2. According to Acts 5, Ananias decides to keep some of the proceeds from selling his land and not donate the full sum to the community. In Acts 5:4, Peter poses the following questions to Ananias: "Whiles it [the property] remained, was it not thine own? and after it was sold, was it not in thine own power? why hast thou conceived this thing in thine heart? thou has not lied unto men, but unto God." The punishment for Ananias lying is severe, according to Acts 5:5: "And Ananias hearing these words fell down, and gave up the ghost: and great fear came on all them that heard these things." In the children's book Isaac Watts, *Watts' Divine and Moral Songs* (New York: Samuel Wood, 1811), Samuel Wood includes a stanza in song VII, "Against Lying," that drives home the moral lesson from this Biblical narrative: "Have we not known, nor heard, nor read, / How God abhors deceit and wrong? / How Ananias was struck dead, / Catch'd with a lie on his tongue?" (12).
3. An extended version of this poem, titled song VII, "Against Lying," may be found in Watts, *Watts' Divine and Moral Songs*, 11–12. Wood sold this book at his Juvenile Book-Store.
4. The trustees likely had some of the following passages in mind concerning parental duty to children: Proverbs 13:24, 19:18, 22:6, 22:15, 23:13–14, 29:15, 29:17; Ephesians 6:4; and Colossians 3:21.
5. According to the *Oxford English Dictionary*, this term may be understood as "[c]lothing, clothes, dress, apparel."
6. According to the *Oxford English Dictionary*, this Latin term, an abbreviation for *videlicet*, may be understood as "[t]hat is to say; namely; to wit: used to introduce an amplification, or more precise or explicit explanation, of a previous statement or word."
7. According to the *Oxford English Dictionary*, this verb may be understood as "[t]o put out of countenance, put to shame, disconcert, discourage, abash."
8. The trustees refer to British poet and abolitionist Thomas Cowper (1731–1800). For more information on Cowper, his poetry that appeared in Abigail Field Mott's children's book designed for students at the New York African Free Schools, and her interest in him, consult the notes on *Life and Adventures of Olaudah Equiano*.
9. The trustees quote part of book 6, "The Winter Walk at Noon," from Cowper's *The Task, a Poem, in Six Books. By William Cowper, of the Inner Temple, Esq.* (London: Printed for J. Johnson, 1785), 261.
10. A helpful definition of the term "monitor" appears in *Manual of the Lancasterian System, of Teaching Reading, Writing, Arithmetic, and Needle-Work, as Practised in the Schools of the Free-School Society, of New-York* (New York: Samuel Wood and Sons, 1820):

    > [t]he value of this system consists in facilitating in an eminent degree, the business of instruction in the elementary branches of knowledge. It is founded upon a principle of order and discipline, by which the pupils, under the direction of the master, pursue a course of mutual instruction; those who have made the greatest progress in reading, writing, and arithmetic [transmit] the knowledge which they possess to others less advanced than themselves. These pupils have the titles of Monitors. Thus[,] by employing the children as teachers, in carrying forward instruction in the different classes, a single master, or professor, may superintend a school of 500, or 600, children. (20)

    Wood and Sons also sold this book.
11. The trustees refer to British pedagogue Joseph Lancaster (1778–1838), who implemented an educational system in England as early as 1801 in which more advanced

students called monitors were responsible for teaching younger students. This system reduced costs since Lancaster did not have to hire multiple teachers and extended education to poor students who traditionally did not have access to education. Lancaster, in his *Epitome of Some of the Chief Events and Transactions in the Life of Joseph Lancaster, Containing an Account of the Rise and Progress of the Lancasterian System of Education, and the Author's Future Prospects of Usefulness to Mankind; Written by Himself, and Published to Promote the Education of His Family* (New Haven: Baldwin and Peck, 1833), addresses the implementation of his educational system in the United States:

> 1806 exhibited the publication of the third edition of Joseph Lancaster's work in New-York, and the establishment of the first school, out of Britain, upon J. Lancaster's system, and thence has gradually arisen that noble exemplification of public school education, which excels in magnitude and the simple grandeur of public usefulness, all other cities of the same amount of population in the world. This also began chiefly with the *Friends* of that city, and their fellow citizens have never failed to give them the credit of early encouraging and persevering in the establishment of a useful design of patriotic as well as moral good. (9; emphasis in original)

John Franklin Reigart establishes, in *The Lancasterian System of Instruction in the Schools of New York City* (New York: Teachers College, Columbia University, 1916), that this method of teaching "remained the official system of the schools of the [New York Free School] Society until 1853 when the Board of Education assumed control of all the public schools" (17).

12. According to the *Oxford English Dictionary*, the term "divers" may be understood as "[d]ifferent or not alike in character or quality; not of the same kind."
13. The trustees likely refer to *Manual of the System of Teaching Reading, Writing, Arithmetic, and Needle-Work, in the Elementary Schools of the British and Foreign School Society. First American Edition* (Philadelphia: Benjamin Warner, 1817), another text which contains explanations on the logistics of the Lancasterian method of education. For an explanation regarding a "British System of Education for Girls," consult *Manual of the System*, pages 36–43. In 1820 Samuel Wood and Sons printed and sold *Manual of the Lancasterian System*. For an explanation regarding "The System of Education for Girls," see pages 38–45. According to the preface, trustees of the Free-School Society of New York maintained that the "interests of elementary education would be much advanced by the introduction of the Lancasterian System, in whole, or in part, into all the common schools in the State" (4). Additionally, the trustees circulated the manual for the "gratuitous instruction of teachers, or persons intending to become so, in the peculiarities of that mode of tuition."
14. According to the *Oxford English Dictionary*, this term may be understood as "[a] tablet of slate, usually framed in wood, used for writing on." According to *Manual of the Lancasterian System*, pedagogues used slates (and pencils) as "substitute[s]" "for paper and pens, which are only used in the higher classes. This plan is economical, and accelerates the progress of the children in writing" (13). For an advertisement indicating that Wood and Sons sold "Slates and Pencils," see the back cover of *Arithmetical Tables, For the Use of Schools* (New York: Samuel Wood and Sons, 1824).
15. The full name of this organization is the New-York Society, for Promoting the Manumission of Slaves, and Protecting Such of Them as Have Been or May Be Liberated, established in 1785. Digitized records of the New York Manumission Society from the years 1785 to 1849 may be found on the New-York Historical Society's webpage: https://digitalcollections.nyhistory.org/islandora/object/islandora:132346.
16. The trustees quote lines 193–94 from epistle IV, "Of the Nature and State of Man with

[R]espect to Happiness," in Alexander Pope's *An Essay on Man*, first published in London in 1733–34. This part from Pope's poem first appeared in *An Essay on Man. In Epistles to a Friend. Epistle IV* (London: Printed for J. Wilford, 1734), 70.
17. According to the *Oxford English Dictionary*, the term "advert" may be understood as "[t]o turn one's attention in a discourse written or spoken; to refer to."
18. Charles C. Andrews, in *The History of the New-York African Free-Schools, from Their Establishment in 1787, to the Present Time; Embracing a Period of More Than Forty Years: Also a Brief Account of the Successful Labors, of the New-York Manumission Society: With an Appendix* (New York: Mahlon Day, 1830), includes a biographical sketch of John Murray Jr. (1758–1819). In addition to being the chairperson of the trustees of New York African Free Schools as early as 1818, Murray Jr. "was among the early and most efficient founders" (24) of the New York Manumission Society, serving as Treasurer as well as member of the Standing and Correspondence Committees. For Andrews, Murray Jr. was especially devoted to the "moral and intellectual improvement of the descendants of Africa" (25). For instance, Murray Jr. "bequeathed in his will a legacy of five hundred dollars towards the support of the African Schools" (26). The information Andrews provides on the New York philanthropist may be supplemented by the entry on Murray Jr. in *A Biographical Dictionary; Comprising A Summary Account of the Lives of the Most Distinguished Persons of All Ages, Nations, and Professions; Including More Than Two Thousand Articles of American Biography*, 13th ed. (Philadelphia: H. Cowperthwait, 1859):

> For thirty-seven years he was a governor of the New York Hospital, took an active part in . . . promoting the instruction of the aboriginal inhabitants in the State of New York, and in procuring the repeal of the criminal code of that State, together with the establishment of the penitentiary system of punishment. He was the principal originator of the New York Free School Society, of which he was for some time Vice-President, and co-operated in the establishment of most of the charitable institutions which exist in that city. (891)

Murray Jr. also subscribed to William Durell's unauthorized edition of Olaudah Equiano's *Interesting Narrative*, published in New York in 1791, likely the base text from which Mott constructed *Life and Adventures of Olaudah Equiano*. Thomas Longworth, in *Longworth's New-York Register, and City Directory; For the Forty-Third Year of American Independence. Containing List[s] of Duties, Banks, Insurance Companies, and Post Office Establishment[s]* (New York: Published for Thomas Longworth, 1818), specifies that Murray Jr. lived at 335 Pearl Street (242).
19. Longworth, in *Longworth's New-York Register*, identifies Isaac Collins as a bookseller at 189 Pearl Street (87).
20. Longworth, in *Longworth's New-York Register*, identifies Robert C. Cornell as a merchant at 30 Cliff Street (93).
21. Longworth, in *Longworth's New-York Register*, identifies Joseph Curtis as an owner of a hardware store at 90 Maiden Lane (100).
22. Longworth, in *Longworth's New-York Register*, identifies Nathan Comstock as a merchant at 53 Catherine Street and commercial merchant at 248 Front Street (88).
23. Longworth, in *Longworth's New-York Register*, identifies Hiram Ketcham as an attorney at 13 Beekman Street (191).
24. Longworth, in *Longworth's New-York Register*, identifies Reuben Leggett as a merchant at 271 Pearl Street (202). Andrews, in *History of the New-York African Free-Schools*, writes that Leggett was a member of the New York Manumission Society (29). Leggett was also involved with the Association for the Instruction of Coloured Male Adults (New York) and occasionally wrote speeches that New York African Free School students delivered at examination days. For an explanation of examination days at the

New York African Free Schools, consult the notes on *Life and Adventures of Olaudah Equiano*.

25. Longworth, in *Longworth's New-York Register*, identifies Charles Miller as a rigger at 46 Broome Street (231). According to the *Oxford English Dictionary*, the term "rigger" may be understood as one in charge of the "arrangement of the masts, sails, etc., on a vessel."
26. Andrews, in *History of the New-York African Free-Schools*, notes that Willet Seaman was member of the "first Board of Trustees of the New-York African Free School" (14). Longworth, in *Longworth's New-York Register*, identifies Seaman as a merchant at 296 Pearl Street (290). Seaman was also a member of the New York Manumission Society.
27. Longworth, in *Longworth's New-York Register*, identifies Jeremiah Thompson (1784–1835) as a merchant at 273 Pearl Street (321). Fred Carstensen, author of the entry on Thompson in *American National Biography*, vol. 21 (Oxford: Oxford University Press, 1999), claims that in 1827 the New York merchant was "the largest shipowner" and "largest cotton exporter" (559) in the United States. Thompson was also a member of the New York Manumission Society.
28. Longworth, in *Longworth's New-York Register*, identifies Samuel Wood (1760–1844) as a printer and bookseller at 261 Pearl Street (362). For more on Wood, consult the notes on *Life and Adventures of Olaudah Equiano*, which he and his sons printed and sold, as well as "Rethinking Textual Paradigms in Early Black Atlantic Studies," which appears in appendix A.
29. Longworth, in *Longworth's New-York Register*, identifies John R. Wills as an "ironmonger" at 268 Pearl Street (358). According to the *Oxford English Dictionary*, the term "ironmonger" may be understood as "[a] dealer in ironware; a hardware merchant."
30. Andrews addresses his epistle to John Brown Russwurm (1799–1851), co-editor of *Freedom's Journal*, the first African American newspaper in the United States, and eventual governor of Maryland in Liberia Colony, West Africa. According to Penelope Campbell, who wrote the entry on Russwurm in the *American National Biography*, vol. 19, this African American taught briefly in African Free Schools in Philadelphia, New York, and Boston. Russwurm worked on *Freedom's Journal* until 1829, when he sailed to Liberia and helped establish the *Liberia Herald* (117–18).
31. John B. Russwurm and Samuel E. Cornish (1795–1858) founded *Freedom's Journal* in March 1827. In the first issue of the newspaper, published on March 16, 1827, Russwurm and Cornish state that they planned to include in *Freedom's Journal* "many practical pieces, having for their bases, the improvement of our brethren," "interesting subjects" that provide "an intercourse between our brethren in different states," and "[u]seful knowledge of every kind, and every thing that relates to Africa." Russwurm and Cornish also note in this first issue: "Education being an object of the highest importance to the welfare of society, we shall endeavor to present just and adequate views of it, and to urge upon our brethren the necessity and expediency of training their children, while young, to habits of industry, and thus forming them for becoming useful members of society." Cornish left the newspaper six months after the publication of the first issue, likely because of Russwurm's support of the colonization of Liberia. That is, Russwurm believed that African Americans needed to abandon the United States to experience freedom. The last issue of *Freedom's Journal* appeared on March 28, 1829. If Russwurm sent Andrews the May 18, 1827, issue of *Freedom's Journal*, New York African Free School students would have read the following biographical sketch:

> *Gustavus Vasa*, whose African name was Olando [sic] Equiano, was born in the kingdom of Benin in 1746. At the age of twelve he was torn from his country and carried to Barbadoes. After passing into various hands and making several

voyages to Europe, he at length obtained his freedom, and in 1781 established himself in London. There he "published his Memoirs, which have been several times reprinted in both hemispheres" and read with read interest. "Vasa published a poem containing 112 verses;" and in 1789 he presented to the British [P]arliament a petition for the suppression of the slave trade. His life and works are familiarly known in England.

32. Andrews refers to a conversation between Dr. Samuel L. Mitchell and New York African Free School student G. R. Allen. According to Andrews, in *History of the New-York African Free-Schools*, Allen was "a pupil aged 10 years" (145) when this dialogue occurred. Andrews includes this dialogue in *History of the New-York African Free-Schools*, 145–46.

33. For more information on Andrews, consult the notes on the selections from Abigail Field Mott's *Biographical Sketches* (appendix C) and "Rethinking Textual Paradigms in Early Black Atlantic Studies" (appendix A).

34. Designers of early nineteenth-century maps of New York regularly identified the locations of the New York African Free Schools. For instance, in the key to *Hooker's New Pocket Plan of the City of New York* (New York: Drawn, Engraved, Printed, Published, and Sold by W. Hooker, 1835), William Hooker (1782–1856) identifies the locations of three schools. Hooker notes that African Free School no. 1 may be located at "W[illiam] near Duane," African Free School no. 2 may be found at "Mulberry, b[etween] Hester & Grand," and African Free School no. 3 sits at "Amity, n[ear] Macdougal." Hooker included this information in his pocket plan for 1836 as well. For another helpful map of New York, see "Black New York City, 1785–1835," New-York Historical Society, https://www.nyhistory.org/web/africanfreeschool/map/map-print.html. The creators of this map identify the address for African Free School no. 1 as 245 Williams Street and 135 Mulberry Street for African Free School no. 2, home to the Female Department until May 1832, when it became African Free School no. 4.

35. Thomas Longworth, in *Longworth's American Almanac, New-York Register, and City Directory, For the Fifty-Second Year of American Independence* (New York: Thomas Longworth, 1827), identifies Peter S. Titus as a crockery merchant at 457 Pearl Street (482). Andrews, in *History of the New-York African Free-Schools*, names Titus as an individual who collected "Minerals, Shells, or other Natural Curiosities" for the New York African Free School on Mulberry Street's "Cabinet of Minerals and Natural Curiosities" (59). According to *The New-York Annual Register for the Year of Our Lord 1830* (New York: J. Leavitt, 1830), which the Woods sold, Titus served as a representative of New York City in the 52nd New York State Assembly in 1829 (232). According to the January 19, 1844, *Assembly Report in Documents of the Assembly of the State of New-York, Sixty-Seventh Session, 1844*, vol. 1 (Albany: Carroll and Cook, 1844), Titus served as director of the New-York Institution for the Instruction of the Deaf and Dumb from 1831 to 1834 (34). Titus also helped establish on May 25, 1836, "The Columbian Fire Insurance Company of the City of New-York," according to *Laws of the State of New-York, Passed at the Fifty-Ninth Session, of the Legislature, Begun and Held at the City of Albany, the Fifth Day of January, 1836* (Albany: E. Croswell, 1836), 733.

36. Longworth, in *Longworth's American Almanac*, identifies Richard Field as a merchant at 223 Pearl Street (195). Andrews, in *History of the New-York African Free-Schools*, includes a July 15, 1828, letter written by Field which requests contributions of "Minerals, Shells, or other Natural Curiosities" for the New York African Free School on Mulberry Street's "Cabinet of Minerals and Natural Curiosities" (59). Andrews identifies Field as the secretary of the board of trustees for the New York African Free Schools (60, 128). Field also served as secretary of the New-York Manumission Society (229, 284), according to *The New-York Annual Register for the Year of Our Lord 1833* (New

York: Peter Hill, 1833) and *The New-York Annual Register for the Year of Our Lord 1836* (New York: Edwin Williams, 1836).

37. The contributor to the *Commercial Advertiser* refers to Rev. R. R. (Ralph Randolph) Gurley (1797–1872). An obituary from the January 1873 issue of *The African Repository and Colonial Journal*, the newspaper of the American Colonization Society, contains the following information on Gurley:

> In 1822 he received his appointment as Agent of the American Colonization Society, and from that time to the present, a period of fifty years, his life has known no other first and all-absorbing object.... [H]e maintained a constant and extensive correspondence with every part of our country and with Liberia. He had also the entire editorial responsibility of the monthly publication of the *African Repository*, as well as the preparation of the Annual Reports of the American Colonization Society.

> Gurley wrote several books, including *Life of Jehudi Ashmun, Late Colonial Agent in Liberia: With an Appendix, Containing Extracts from his Journal and Other Writings: With a Brief Sketch of the Life of the Rev. Lott Carey* (Washington, D.C.: James C. Dunn, 1835), *Mission to England, in Behalf of the American Colonization Society* (Washington, D.C.: Wm. W. Morrison, 1841), and *Life and Eloquence of the Rev. Sylvester Larned: First Pastor of the First Presbyterian Church in New-Orleans* (New York: Wiley and Putnam, 1844). For a more complete biographical sketch of Gurley, consult Rev. Mason Noble's *A Discourse Commemorative of the Life and Character of Rev. Ralph Randolph Gurley* (Washington, D.C.: M'Gill and Witherow, 1872).

38. The contributor to the *Commercial Advertiser* refers to the Washington, D.C. chapter of the American Colonization Society. Eric Burin, in *Slavery and the Peculiar Solution: A History of the American Colonization Society* (Gainesville: University Press of Florida, 2005), observes that, by the early 1800s, members of this organization pushed for "black removal" as well as "secured federal funding, rallied an interregional constituency, and established the colony of Liberia as a place for black settlement. As sectional tensions heightened during the antebellum era, colonizationists became more vocal, pleading that only emancipation and deracination could solve the country's troubles" (1).

39. Longworth, in *Longworth's American Almanac*, identifies William L[eete] Stone, Sr. (1793–1844) as editor of the New York periodical *Commercial Advertiser* at 48 Pine Street (463). Stone was also secretary of the New York Colonization Society. In the July 1834 issue of *The African Repository, and Colonial Journal*, the newspaper of the American Colonization Society, his name appears as one of the "Managers" for "The Female Society of the City of New-York for the Support of Schools in Africa." According to this article, the objective of the Female Society was "to extend to the children of Africa the benefits of civilization, and the blessings of the [C]hristian religion" as well as "prepare and support [C]hristian teachers for the missionary settlement of New-York in Liberia, and, as far as practicable, for other portions of Africa."

40. For information on Titus, consult the notes on "A[frican] F[ree] S[chool]," published in the January 25, 1828, issue of *Freedom's Journal* (appendix B).

41. An obituary in the May 4, 1867, issue of the *New York Times*, titled "Death of an Old Citizen," provides a succinct biographical sketch of Mott (1784–1867):

> William F. Mott, a well-known citizen, died in his eightieth-third year, yesterday. He was born in this City, and until the infirmities of age abated his powers, was identified with the inception of almost every philanthropic effort. To the past generation his career was familiar, and the sterling qualities of his nature fully appreciated. He commenced life with moderate means, and, in connection with his brother Samuel F. Mott, successfully pursued what is now

known as the domestic commission business, from which, many years ago, he retired with an ample fortune, believing that Christian moderation forbade large accumulations by individuals. His active energies and benevolent impulses [were] then turned vigorously in the direction of public and private enterprises for the relief of the neglected, the poverty-stricken, and the diseased.

I am indebted to Julie Miller for this obituary. According to *Wealth and Biography of the Wealthy Citizens of New York City, Comprising an Alphabetical Arrangement of Persons Estimated to be Worth $100,000, and Upwards. With the Sums Appended to Each Name; Being Useful to Banks, Merchants, and Others*, 6th ed. (New York: Sun Office, 1845), Mott was of "a Westchester Quaker family, and in the Cotton and domestic Commission business" with his brother, Samuel F. Mott (23). In 1845 Mott's purported worth was $300,000. Mott's name appears under the category of "Managers" in *An Address to the Inhabitants of the City of New-York by the Board of Managers of the New-York Temperance Society, Together with the Constitution and List of Officers of Said Society* (New York: J. Seymour, 1829), 14, as well as among the "Life Members" of the New York Institute for the Deaf and Dumb in *Documents of the Assembly of the State of New-York. Ninetieth Session—1867. Volume VI. Nos. 86 to 113 Inclusive* (Albany: C. Van Benthuysen and Sons, 1867), 108. Mott also contributed to the Association for the Benefit of Colored Orphans in the City of New York, according to William Seraile, *Angels of Mercy: White Women and the History of New York's Colored Orphan Asylum* (New York: Fordham University Press, 2011), 9.

42. Though Andrews does not name this Black student orator, vol. 3 of the New-York African Free School Records, 1817–1832, New-York Historical Society Digital Collections, contains the following information: "Introductory Address (written by Reuben Leggett) Spoken by James Fields at the Public Exhibition of the School at the New-York Free School Chatham St[reet]." Leggett's name appears as one of the trustees in *An Address to the Parents and Guardians of the Children Belonging to the New-York African Free-School, By the Trustees of the Institution* (New York: Samuel Wood and Sons, 1818), 24. For the *Address*, see appendix B.

43. According to the *Oxford English Dictionary*, the term "valedictory" may be understood as "[u]ttered or bestowed in bidding or on taking farewell; of the nature of a valediction."

44. Fields refers to British philosopher John Locke (1632–1704). In *An Essay Concerning Humane Understanding. In Four Books* (London: Printed for Tho. Basset, 1690), Locke dismissed, according to Simon Blackwell in *The Oxford Dictionary of Philosophy* (New York and Oxford: Oxford University Press, 1994), "any place for 'innate ideas' in the foundations of knowledge, and is in that sense anti-rationalistic. [He] puts experience, or ideas of sensation and reflection, firmly at the basis of human understanding" (278).

45. Fields references William Pitt (the Elder), First Earl of Chatham (1708–1778) and British prime minister from 1766–1768. In *The History of the Life of William Pitt, Earl of Chatham* (London: Printed for the Author, 1783), biographer William Godwin offers the following on Pitt's oratorical skills: "But the eloquence of [L]ord Chatham was one of his most striking characteristics. *He far outstripped his competitors, and stood alone, the rival of antiquity.* . . . His eloquence was of every kind. No man excelled him, in close argument, and methodical deduction" (297–98; emphases in original).

46. Important information on this dialogue may be read in New-York African Free-School Records, 1817–1832, vol. 3. Before this dialogue, the following language appears: "Spoken by Ja. M. Smith and William Hill at a public exam. 1822. Written for the occasion by C. C. A. Teacher." This information indicates that a young James McCune Smith (1813–1865), the first African American to earn a medical degree and an

abolitionist, participated in this conversation and that white teacher Charles C. Andrews wrote this dialogue.
47. According to the *Oxford English Dictionary*, the term "sum" may be understood as "[t]he number, quantity, or magnitude resulting from the addition of two or more numbers, quantities, or magnitudes."
48. William refers to Benjamin Franklin (1706–1790), printer, editor, publisher, scientist, and author of one of the most famous autobiographies in the United States literary canon. Franklin played a key role during the American Revolution and in the formation of the United States. He signed the Declaration of Independence, Constitution of the United States, and Treaty of Paris.

   William may be quoting from *A Father's Gift to His Son, on His Becoming an Apprentice. To Which Is Added Dr. Franklin's Way to Wealth* (New York: Samuel Wood and Sons, 1821). In an introduction to Franklin's *Way to Wealth; or, "Poor Richard Improved,"* the writer (likely Wood) holds that "it is to be doubted, whether any other work of the kind equal to it has ever appeared. It has been repeatedly published, in different sizes; and made its appearance on both sides of the Atlantic" (99). The first page from Franklin's *Advice to a Young Tradesman, from an Old One. By Benjamin Franklin*, included in *A Father's Gift to His Son, on His Becoming an Apprentice. To Which Is Added Dr. Franklin's Way to Wealth*, reads: "Remember that time is money" (133). Franklin concludes this piece by writing, "In short, the way to wealth, if you desire it, is as plain as the way to market. It depends chiefly on two words, *industry* and *frugality*; i.e. waste neither your time nor money, but make the best use of both" (140). Extant records indicate that New York African Free School students were familiar with Franklin. See, for example, a drawing of Franklin by a thirteen-year-old James McCune Smith, the same James showcased in "A D[ialogue]," in *"Hope Is the First Great Blessing": Leaves from the African Free School Presentation Book, 1812–1816*, annotated by Anna Mae Duane and Thomas Thurston (New York: New-York Historical Society, 2008), 53.
49. Andrews, in *History of the New-York African Free-Schools*, offers the following description of the School Fair:

   > In accordance with these views [to encourage "ingenuity and skill" in the New York African Free School students], it has long been the practice in this school, both in the male and female departments, to encourage the scholars in the productions of their little works of art; and, in order, the more effectually, to bring the subject into a regular, and an interesting form, and to excite some degree of competition, an exhibition called a Fair, of all articles that the pupils may have made at home, is held every three months, in the male and in the female schools alternately, and the best piece of work entitles the manufacturer thereof to fifty school tickets. (109)

Appendix C

ADDITIONAL WORKS BY AND ABOUT ABIGAIL FIELD MOTT

A Short Account of the Last Sickness and Death of Maria Mott, Daughter of Richard and Abigail Mott, of Mamaroneck, in the [S]tate of New-York (NEW YORK: SAMUEL WOOD AND SONS, 1817)

"Wisdom is the gray hair unto men, and an unspotted life is old age." [1]

It having pleased an all-wise Providence, whose "judgments are unsearchable, and his ways past finding out," [2] to take to himself in the spring time of life, Maria Mott, the subject of this little memoir, her parents feel it to be a duty which they owe to her memory, to commit to writing a brief account of her short, but memorable life; entertaining a hope that it may prove useful and instructive to some of her young acquaintances, and believing that a sketch of the prominent features of her character, exemplified by some of her observations and sentiments while in health, will be rendered additionally interesting by the account of her last illness, extreme bodily sufferings, and death.

Traces of a vigorous mind were observed at an early period of her life; and the pleasing anticipation was indulged, that, by the operation of the subjecting and sanctifying power of truth, those gifts of the understanding, which are also "the treasures of God," [3] would, in after time, be devoted to the service of the blessed Giver. It was nevertheless evident to those who watched with affectionate interest the years of her infancy and childhood, that though possessed of an excellent understanding, and a tender, affectionate disposition, yet she was no less remarkable for her vivacity, and the strength and prevalence of that disposition generally denominated *will*; a disposition which was observed with concern to be taking root in her mind; and proofs were early given, that it would not be easy properly to regulate it. But as it was fully believed, that her will must be brought into subjection, before either the parents or the child could be happy, endeavours were used to convince her judgment of the impropriety and effect of wrong things, and the satisfaction and blessings attendant on a proper line of conduct. Her feelings were frequently much affected when thus reasoned with; but such was her propensity to self-indulgence, that she soon forgot her own tenderness, and again gave way to that kind of inattention, so peculiar to her disposition. The parents viewed their child with mingled emotions of hope and fear; and their tears were often strewed in secret on her account. But "hope travels through,"[4] and they indulged the cheering reflection, that on their efforts to discharge their parental duties, feeble as they felt themselves, the blessing of the Lord might at some time rest.

Such continued to be the state of trying suspense from the third to the ninth or tenth year of her age, when her parents saw, with great satisfaction, that the important point would probably be gained; and in this view were enjoyed those pleasurable feelings that compensated for all their anxiety and persevering care to give her mind a right direction.

Young as she was, her susceptible mind had often been sensible of the goodness of the Lord, but about the time mentioned, the Divine visitations made more perceptible and lasting impressions; and such were the happy effects produced thereby, that she became more and more affectionate, atten[t]ive, mild, and docile in her manners, which encouraged the pleasing idea, that she was becoming one of the Lord's children, "taught of him;"[5] and the observation of each succeeding year tended to strengthen and confirm the opinion. Indeed, so great was the influence of the heavenly principle in bringing her to a conformity to its teaching, that, from the time adverted to, her parents have no recollection of her committing any act which she knew would grieve, or be disagreeable to them. Her attachment to them, though always strong, by increasing submission, became an attachment of a superior kind, an attachment resulting from that love which is more than merely human. She possessed in the company of her parents and brother the society most dear to her, and often expressed the satisfaction and happiness she enjoyed in this little family circle. And this happiness was mutual: for as she made them her confidants, her stability, quickness of thought, and modest cheerfulness contributed, in no small degree, to comfort and enliven the domestic scene. Though her retiring disposition peculiarly fitted her for domestic enjoyment, yet she knew well how to appreciate the society, both of the friends of her parents, on whom she delighted in waiting, and of a select number of her contemporaries: but she had no inclination to cultivate an extensive and promiscuous acquaintance.

In the spring of 1815, her parents being about to leave home for a few weeks, while with her usual industry and affection, she was assisting in making the necessary preparation for the journey, she expressed herself to her mother as follows: "Though it is much against our inclination to part with you, as we feel the loss of your company very much, yet I hope you will not be anxious about home in your absence; for I think we endeavour to be as careful of our conduct as when you are with us, and to manage the affairs of the family as near as we can in a manner which we suppose would be agreeable to you: it is our practice to have the family collected, and to read the scriptures, as you do when at home."

From her mother she received a considerable portion of her literary instruction, and being early taught to read, and furnished with books suited to her age, she soon acquired a taste for reading, delighted much in it, and was careful, as long as she lived, to devote suitable portions of time to this agreeable and useful employment. The selection of her books was made with care, that what she read might be interesting and instructive, and such as her parents would approve; indeed, her tenderness for their feelings in this respect was so great, that it is believed she rarely if ever devoted much time to any book, without reading more or less of it to them. Though fond of history, and works on moral and literary subjects, she delighted most in religious books, which she read with great interest. She was well acquainted with the history of the society of Friends, and often made pertinent remarks upon their faithfulness, sufferings, &c. The last winter of her life, she read with attention and care, the Journal of George Fox,[6] and expressed much satisfaction in the perusal: and a short time previous to her last illness, [she] commenced a second reading of Gough's History of the society.[7]

The improvement of the human mind was not only a delightful theme to her, but was viewed as a subject of primary importance: hence, she highly estimated[8] that kind of conversation, and those opportunities which tend to inform, to improve, and to expand the intellect. A few months previous to her dissolution,[9] in conversation with her mother and a particular friend, on the benefit and design of social life, she said, "I have often regretted that so much precious time should be spent to so little purpose as it appears to be. I fear that in some places the practice is increasing, of young people collected in companies amusing themselves with various kinds of play, which appear to me not calculated to promote real happiness and enjoyment; nor is such an employment of time suited to that dignity of character after which we all ought to aspire.["]

In the summer of 1816, while employed in the tuition[10] of several little girls from New-York (an employment which was agreeable to her, because it was useful)[,] at a time too when the hope was cherished that her health, which had been delicate, was improving; and her connexions observed with much pleasure the consistency of her conduct, the sweetness of her disposition, and the purity of her mind, she was suddenly taken ill. The disease operated very severely, and being attended with distressing sickness of stomach for several days, soon reduced her strength so much that she was almost as helpless as an infant for a considerable time. Through the course of this long sickness, she showed a strength and firmness of mind not often met with, and during her confinement to her bed and chamber (nearly two months) manifested much patient resignation. From this illness she gradually recovered, and again took charge of the little flock; [she was] much pleased to be able to relieve her mother, whose care had necessarily been great during her indisposition.[11] Having been trained to habits of industry, she was fond of useful employment, and willing to put her hand to such business as was necessary; and being prompted by her great feeling and commiseration for the poor, she found opportunities to do much for those of that class in the neighbourhood, her needle being often used to make them comfortable in the inclement season of the year. As she was stimulated to such employment by the feelings of tenderness and benevolence, she derived peculiar satisfaction from it, and would often say, that time passed pleasantly on when she was thus occupied.

In the early part of the 11th month, in company with her parents, and their friend[s] John Cox and Nathaniel Coleman, she took a little journey to the north, as far as Stanford, in Dutchess County.[12] The ride and change of air appeared to be useful to her; she enjoyed much satisfaction in the tour, and frequently expressed her gratitude for the privilege of attending the meetings[13] held by the before mentioned friends. She was fond of attending religious meetings from her childhood, frequently spoke of the nature and importance of the duty, was herself an example of sobriety in them, and often expressed her admiration that any who made a profession of religion, and took pains to assemble on such occasions, could behave with lightness and irreverence. In passing from place to place during this journey, she made many interesting remarks on the beauties of creation, and being particularly fond of rural scenes, often drew instructive *morals* from them. Returning home after an absence of three weeks, with her health apparently improved, she was, as was usual on such occasions, much pleased, having a strong attachment for the scenes where her childhood had been past, and where she often discovered new beauties.

From subsequent remarks, it is evident that her mind had been seriously impressed in her late visit; and her opportunities for observation had occasioned her to reflect much on the importance of a proper cultivation of the minds of the rising youth. Having at one time made some pertinent remarks on the subject generally, she subjoined[14] with peculiar emphasis and feeling, "Oh, mother, how thankful I ought to be for the care and attention which I have received! From the peculiar texture of my mind, I think there is little doubt, that if I had been managed as many poor children are, I should have gone far astray: if instead of endeavouring to convince my judgement, and gain my affections, severity had been used with a view to coerce a compliance, the cord would probably have snapped, and no calculation can be made on the consequences that would have followed. On the other hand, if improper indulgences had been allowed me, as I had a desire for liberty, and a life in things improper for me, it is likely I should have taken wing, and wandered far from the path of simplicity." Soon after making these remarks, while still setting[15] beside her mother at work, she thus proceeded: "In time past, I had a strong inclination to have some articles of clothing different from those I had been accustomed to; and observing that many of the girls of my acquaintance were in the practice of curling the hair on the forehead, and thinking it pretty, I was inclined to take the same liberty: but as I reflected that father and thou would be uneasy with it; that it would grieve you, I became sensible that I could have no substantial enjoyment in it, for I never could feel happy, or enjoy true satisfaction in the practice of any thing, how much soever I have desired it, which I knew would be unpleasant to you; and although it has sometimes been rather difficult to submit cheerfully to your wishes, peace and satisfaction have always been the result of a ready compliance, and that to a much greater degree than I could possibly have experienced in a contrary procedure. My views[,] however, are much changed; I have not any wish for such things now." After a short pause, she proceeded: "It is a great favour to have religious and concerned parents and caretakers; and I have sometimes wondered how it can be that young people who have such, can have enjoyment or even be satisfied in the use of things disagreeable to them: their views of happiness must be very different from mine."

On fifth day, the 28th of [the] 11th month, she went to [a] meeting with her parents, being in usual health. It had been contemplated to make an evening visit to the family of a friend a few miles distant, but though the weather was unusually fine, and it seemed desirable to prosecute[16] the plan, yet as the time for leaving home approached, an uneasiness was felt, which, as it was not easily got over, was yielded to, and the proposed visit was deferred. To this disappointment Maria was perfectly reconciled, saying with her usual cheerfulness, "[W]ell, mother, we will sit quietly down to work by our own fireside; I don['t] know where we shall go to find more comfort than we can enjoy here."

About six o'clock in the evening, she began to experience pain, which indicated disease: in a short time it became severe, attended with great sickness at the stomach, and before the next morning, the complaint assumed a very serious aspect. And although, from its nature and uncommon severity, little composure of mind could be expected, yet from the early stage of the disorder, and indeed through the whole course of a painful illness, her remarks upon herself, and the connexion of remote ideas, evinced a range of thought really admirable: nor were her patience and resignation less remarkable. It was indeed wonderful to those who witnessed the affecting scene to observe, through the course of her sickness, such an entire command of herself, that an expression bordering on impatience was not known to escape her, nor did even the severity of the pain and suffering which she endured, in the least diminish that courtesy of manners and softness of expression which were peculiar to her: to her latest moments mildly acknowledging the kindness and attention of those who waited upon her.

On [the] second day, the physician[,] apprehending that the drink which she had taken tended to promote the puking without any prospect of relief, thought it necessary to withhold it principally from her. The thirst occasioned by an internal fever, so far from producing a murmur, seemed only to awaken her commiseration for those whose sufferings she supposed most to resemble her own; saying, "I have frequently thought of those people who traverse the deserts of Arabia, parching with thirst, but without water; but I have never until now been in a situation fully to sympathize with them: I apprehend that my tongue and throat are now in such a situation as to give me a pretty correct idea of the distress and suffering under which they must languish whose water fails in that burning clime."

In the afternoon, she adverted in a very feeling manner to the departure of her brother, whose engagements were such as to require his going to the city for a short time; saying, "[M]y poor dear brother, how I felt for him this morning when he left the room, his heart was so full."

Shortly after she mentioned the religious communication of a dear friend in a parting opportunity a short time previous to her illness, which had made a deep impression on her mind, and turning to her mother, who was sitting at the bedside, thus addressed her: "Oh, my dear mother, how often I have thought of what our friend ——, said to me on the morning he left us: 'Maria, dear Maria, whatever trials or afflictions may be thy lot, keep hold of the covenant which thou hast made.' I have endeavoured to do so previous to my sickness, and I will still strive to do it: but ah! how little did I think that I should so soon be brought to a situation like this. It is very desirable to have the mind composed, but it is not easily attained when the body is tortured with pain."

On the third and fourth days the animating hope was entertained that the symptoms were rather more favourable. She was not elated with the prospect, nor did she make dependence upon it; but [she] frequently spoke of her situation as being very critical, and said, that her feelings were very different from those which attended her sickness in the summer, although she was not yet reduced so low as she then was. She was remarkably composed and sweet, often craving that she might be endued with strength to bear with patience and resignation the severity of the pain which she had to endure.

On [the] seventh day morning, having passed the last twenty-four hours in extreme pain, and the most distressing sickness, her parents sitting by her bedside, one of them remarked the necessity there was of resignation to the divine will, both on her part and on theirs: after a pause, she replied with sweet serenity, "I have earnestly wished for it: I know the Lord is good; I felt his goodness this morning, and it was precious to me; and I then thought I was resigned whether to live or die, as it should please him."

About ten o'clock, her parents again sitting by her, she said, with a look replete with tenderness and affection, "[M]y dear parents, I weaken very fast, and think I shall not last long." Her father[,] observing that he hoped she was resigned, was answered, "[Y]es, I think I am, and I hope that you, my dear parents, will endeavour to be so too. I have very often been sensible of the kindness of the Lord to me. I do not see any thing in the way of my happiness; and though I have not always been as faithful as I ought to have been, and fear that I have sometimes been rather too much inclined to levity,[17] yet I have been favoured with many precious seasons, and divine visitations." A young woman with whom she was intimately acquainted, and to whom she was much attached, attending upon her, she said to her[:] "[D]ear ——, I shall not stay long, but I think I am quite willing to go. I have always loved you, (meaning the family)[,] but I never felt it so strongly as I have done many times during my present sickness."

A physician who had been called in for consultation by the attending physician, proposing that she should take an anodyne,[18] with a view of acquiring a temporary relief from the extremity of her pain, she asked, "Doctor, dost thou not consider my situation to be very critical?" [A]fter pausing a little, he replied, "[I]ndeed[,] I do;" Maria immediately added, "[A]nd so do I, but I hope my peace is made. I had a severe fit of illness last summer, and I think it weaned me very much from the world, though I little thought two weeks ago of being so soon reduced to such a situation as this. I fear the anodyne will lay me asleep, and I shall wake no more; and as my time will probably be short, I wish to improve it, and it is very desirable to have the exercise of my reason." She then concluded with saying, "Doctor, if thou thinks best, I will take a little of it." She then took a part of what was prepared, but brought it up again very soon.

About one o'clock, having gratefully acknowledged the partial relief which she experienced from the extremity of pain, and her precious mind being raised above all transitory things, and as if insensible to her weakness and debility, she broke forth in an audible voice and very animated manner to her parents, brother, and a young woman of the family as follows: "I have been desiring that we might have a solemn opportunity together before I die, but really I have been so distressed with pain for some hours past, that it has been difficult to have my mind composed, or my thoughts properly directed. This morning I had a sweet assurance that my peace was made, but during the extremity of my suffering, I have sometimes been almost ready to doubt. I am now thankful to feel it renewed; yes, to feel an assurance that there is a resting place for me in heaven; and to be admitted into bliss is all I wish, all I ought to desire. I do not ask for a high mansion; I have done but little, and am not entitled to one. My hope is in the Lord's mercy: I have always loved you, my precious parents and dear brother, and thee too Helen,[19] but I never felt the force nor understood the nature of love, as during this illness. Oh, when we are separated, you will often remember me with love; and if there is any such thing as departed spirits mingling with friends left behind, mine will often meet and mingle with yours, with whom it has been so closely united. I can't say much; I am but a child, and have done but little for the truth, yet I hope I have not done it harm. I have endeavoured to be a good example, and I know not that I have committed any flagrant sins."

She then added, "Some persons have said—Brother, I think Dr. Johnson said, that he did not believe that people felt what they said when they spoke of their willingness to die;[20] but I feel it to be true when I say that I am willing to die, and many others have known it to be true."

After a short pause she said, "[T]here are a few of my things which will be of little use to you, and it would be agreeable to me that they should be given to some of my particular friends, as tokens of my regard; and I have no doubt but my dear brother will preserve some trifles which he has in his possession as mementos of my love. But though these are things which ought to be attended to in a suitable manner, as long as they are necessary for the use of these poor bodies, higher and more noble considerations ought to claim our attention when we are about to leave this world; things that are durable, the others being no longer necessary."

A fear being expressed that she would exhaust herself, she replied, "[Y]es, my dear father, I am almost exhausted but I feel such a flow of love, love to all, that I cannot refrain from expressing it; and as the doctors consider my case a hopeless one, I may as well spend a little of my remaining strength in this way, as in any other. If it were the Lord's will, it is probable I might have a choice in continuing a little longer in this world; I have many strong attachments, such precious parents and a dear brother! Oh how dear they are to me! [B]ut if it is his will now to take me away, I am willing to go, yes, this very night." Perceiving that some of the family with others were at dinner below stairs, she said, "and when do *you* dine?" [B]eing answered, ["]we have no inclination to eat; this is an enjoyment far superior to dinner[."] [S]he rejoined in a very animated tone of voice, "yes, it is indeed a feast, [']a feast of fat things.[']"²¹

Soon after expressing the foregoing, the puking returned, attended with violent spasms, and her sufferings were so exquisite as deeply to affect those about her; but she bore them with a patience almost unexampled, nor did a murmur escape her.

About this time[,] she again adverted in a feeling manner to the religious communication of the friend before mentioned, saying, "I think I have been favoured to keep hold of the covenant." And soon after, looking on those who were sitting by, with a countenance beaming with sweetness and resignation, she mildly said, "I am going to the Lord, and hope you will follow me." About nine in the evening, her bodily distress being very great, she said, "[M]y dear father, I cannot last long; I think I shall not live through this night. May the Lord be with us all; with me who am going, and with you who stay." Notwithstanding such was the nature of the disorder, and the severity of its operation, that she seemed to be driven from dwelling upon particular subjects, yet the expression of the love which pervaded her mind, and dwelt richly there, could not be restrained; [she] frequently saying, "Oh, my dear mother, how I love thee!" [A]nd again, "Love I leave with you, love I give unto you."

About half past nine, for the first time during her illness, her thoughts wandered for a few minutes: but during the continuance of the delirium, so slight as scarcely to be observed, except by those immediately about the bed, not an incorrect expression escaped her: when again recollecting herself, as if sensible of the mental alienation which had taken place, she asked with much earnestness, "[H]ave I said any thing improper? [H]ave I hurt any body?" [B]eing told that she had not, she rejoined in a tone of voice denoting great pleasure, "[H]ow glad I am! I thought I had hurt some person. Have I not been very impatient?" [B]eing answered no, she continued, "I know I lost my reason, and I was afraid I had lost my patience."

The violence of the pain abating about this time, as did also the extreme restlessness which had been occasioned by the state of the nervous system, she became quite calm and composed, being evidently in the full enjoyment of her mental powers. A solemn, expressive silence prevailed in the room, and some drink being offered to her, she took it, and requested the person to feel the cold sweat on her forehead, adding, "I shall soon go:" and a short time after, "[M]y dear father, one more kiss; I long to be gone." Then remarking that her voice, which had been strong and clear, began to fail, and grow tremulous,²² and that her sight grew dim, she calmly said to her mother, "[N]ow I will lay me down to die. The fear of the Lord is round about to preserve us, yes, to preserve all:" and reclining her head upon the bosom of her mother, who at her request was lying beside her, she said distinctly, though in faltering accents, "[M]other, my precious mother, perform the last sad office." She spoke no more, but lying perfectly still, as if in a sweet sleep, breathed shorter and shorter for about ten minutes, until she quietly and peacefully expired, about half past ten o'clock, in the evening of the 7th of 12th month, 1816, aged 18 years.

"Mark the perfect man, and behold the upright, for the end of that man is peace." [23]

"G[ENERAL] R[EMARKS]" FROM ABIGAIL FIELD MOTT'S *Observations on the Importance of Female Education, and Maternal Instruction, with Their Beneficial Influence on Society. By A Mother* (NEW YORK: MAHLON DAY, 1825)

If we carefully examine the pages of ancient and modern history, we shall find, that where darkness and superstition have most prevailed, the female character has been most neglected and debased; and that where mankind have become enlightened by the influence of the Gospel, and have been sensible of the advantages resulting from early and virtuous impressions, they have seen the propriety of cultivating the female mind. And have we not reason to believe, that there is no part of the habitable globe, where females have a better opportunity, or where, if they were but attentive to their own best interest, there would be greater encouragement given for their improvement, than among the enlightened and reflecting sons of America? Why then should we neglect so great a blessing, and suffer our minds to be engrossed with trifles and vanity, which end in disappointment; or to fall into that apathy which induces us to suppose, that what women can do is of little avail. Have we not all talents, for the improvement of which we must be accountable? Have we not all duties to perform, for the neglect of which no excuse will be accepted? How often do we find the historian, the biographer, and even the ready writer in our periodical publications, when relating the lives of men eminent for their talents, piety or usefulness, recurring to early impressions, and to pious maternal care.

It is therefore, very necessary in our first setting out, seriously to reflect, and to ascertain what is the object we wish to obtain, by the cultivation of our own minds, and the education of our children. If it is, as it most certainly ought to be, that we may increase our own usefulness, and prepare our children for the enjoyment of those rational blessings pertaining to this life, and for the reception of that principle of light and grace, which, as it is attended to, will qualify them for permanent and everlasting happiness in the life to come, let us not neglect any opportunity that will promote the object of our wishes. Delays are always attended with danger, and often with irretrievable mischief.

It cannot be supposed, that other persons will feel the same affectionate interest in children as their parents ought to do, particularly the mother, who has them under her immediate care. Those passions which are so manifest in early life, and require so much attention to counteract or bring into proper subjection, leave no time for a mother's indolence, or delay to a future period. And the time present only being at her disposal, it is of the utmost importance that it be employed to the best advantage: that if her days should be few, she may leave as good and lasting impressions as possible on the tender minds of her children; or, if her days should be many, that she may with them enjoy the precious fruits of her labour. The husbandman scattereth the seed, and hath long patience for its increase.[24]

The improvement and happiness of the human family, so materially depend on the right formation of the infant mind, that it certainly is of great importance that those to whom children are intrusted, should be prepared by the cultivation of their own hearts to discharge that trust with fidelity.

Experience and a knowledge of mankind fully prove, that what parents wish their children to understand and practice, they are most careful to instil[l] into their minds in early life, because the most lasting impressions are then made. And is it not by suffering improper ideas to be infused, that superstition and bigotry, together with a numerous train of evil dispositions, take possession of the heart, from which it is very difficult to eradicate them, even when the judgment is convinced of their impropriety?

To make proper impressions on the minds of children, to guard and strengthen them as they advance in life, and to show them by example and precept, the comfort and enjoyment derived from virtuous and circumspect conduct, careful attention must be given to that precept of Christ, "What I say unto you, I say unto all, watch."[25] Watchfulness, and obedience to what is manifested in the heart by the light of truth, are the alone source of preservation to parents, and the qualification for the performance of all their relative duties.

The rising youth have greatly the advantage of those who are now in the meridian[26] of life. On the subject of female education, and virtuous accomplishments particularly, much has been said, calculated to assist in forming the mind for usefulness; in qualifying it for domestic enjoyments; enlarging and ennobling the heart with virtuous sensibility, and thereby preparing the young to become interesting and agreeable companions, and to act their part with dignity and propriety in that sphere wherein they may be placed. To be fully sensible of, and carefully to improve this blessing, would be of incalculable benefit to them, and to posterity.

It was the design of an All-wise and benevolent Creator in the formation of woman, that she should be a help-meet[27] and companion to man. If, in a state of innocency, her company and assistance were necessary to his comfort and happiness, how much more so, when his cares, his toils, and his anxieties, are multiplied. This sentiment is finely illustrated by one of the ancients, when speaking of the excellent qualities that adorn a virtuous woman. "Favour is deceitful, and beauty is vain: but a woman that feareth the Lord, she shall be praised. Give her of the fruit of her hands, and let her own works praise her in the gates. She looketh well to the ways of her household, and eateth not the bread of idleness. The heart of her husband doth safely trust in her, so that he hath no need of spoil. She will do him good and not evil all the days of her life. She openeth her mouth with wisdom, and on her tongue is the law of kindness." [28]

Although there are many very useful persons of interesting character, who prefer a single life, yet I think the celebrated Montesquieu, when speaking of the influence of females on public manners, &c. must have considered them in the capacity of wives and of mothers. He says, "The safety of the State depends on the virtue of the women." He also observes, that "Greece owed much of its wise policy to their chastity and economical virtues." [29] But we need not go to Greece or Rome for examples to prove the effects of female influence.

It is said, that soon after the conquest of England, and while it was divided into many small kingdoms, and when Ethelbert, king of Kent, was soliciting the hand of Bertha, a princess of Paris, "one of the stipulations insisted on, was, that she should have the free enjoyment of her religion, which was that of Christianity." "When she was introduced to the Court of her husband, the steadfastness of her principles, the sweetness and suavity of her disposition, and the conciliatory influence of her deportment, were so attractive, that not only the king, but his courtiers were brought to the acknowledgment of [C]hristianity, and through them it was spread over the whole English nation." [30]

If we carefully examine the sacred writings, the history of some of the kings of Israel and Judah, will furnish abundant proof of the effects of female influence. It is stated as one of Ahab's first and great transgressions, that "he took to wife Jezebel, the daughter of Ethbaal, king of the Zidonians, and became a worshipper of Baal: and that there was none like unto Ahab, which did sell himself to work wickedness in the sight of the Lord, whom Jezebel his wife stirred up." [31] When his son came to the throne, "he did evil (also) in the sight of the Lord, and walked in the way of his father, and in the way of his mother, and made Israel to sin."[32] It is likewise said of Jehoram, king of Judah, "he walked in the way of the kings of Israel, as did the house of Ahab: for he had the daughter of Ahab to wife;" and of Ahaziah, because his mother who was the daughter of Omri, and sister of Ahab, "was his counsellor to do wickedly."[33]

Another essential circumstance is observable in this history. When those kings governed, who endeavoured to serve the Lord, and to teach the people to do so, (though they were not exempt from human frailties) they generally prospered in their undertakings, enjoyed the good things of the land, and their enemies were not suffered to tyrannise over them. But during the reign of those kings who worshipped other gods; thereby setting their subjects a bad example, there were wars and famine almost continually. And from the great suffering of man and beast, the Prophets might well say—"When the wicked bear rule, the land mourneth."[34]

In this view of the subject, we may clearly discover the propriety, and more fully estimate the advantages, arising from a proper cultivation of the female mind. It is often asserted, and with great propriety, that on a proper education, the safety and happiness of a nation very materially depend. If so, is not the foundation of that education to be laid in the virtuous culture of females; that they may be prepared to watch carefully the opening buds of infantile intellect, and to distinguish between those propensities which should be fostered with care, those that want regulating, and those which ought to be entirely eradicated? Is it not on the lap, or by the side of a pious and judicious mother, that the foundation of what is good and great is generally laid?

For a woman to be a true help-meet to her husband, and a faithful mother to her children, she must be virtuous, industrious, and economical: studiously careful to live within the limits of their income, and by her neatness and cheerful deportment, always to make their home agreeable. And nothing but want of health should prevent her, (in whatever station she is placed,) from a general oversight of her domestic concerns. Every mother who is under the necessity of committing her offspring to the care of a nurse, should have a watchful care over that nurse, and spend as much of her time with her children as she can. What employment can a mother be engaged in, that affords equal pleasure, and is of equal importance with the proper instruction of her children and family?

By indulging a desire to appear more wealthy, and to make a greater show, than their circumstances would admit, many have improperly extended their business, and in the end, lost what they had, and been reduced to poverty. How much more desirable to a virtuous and feeling mind is a cottage, (even a solitary one) with a competency, through the means of industry and frugality, than the show of that wealth and grandeur, which must end in sorrow and disappointment. But this is not all. There are circumstances attending, that are of much greater importance than loss of property. A man who in his business, is straining every nerve to accomplish this desire of obtaining wealth, to gratify the wishes, and to indulge the solicitations of his wife and children, cannot have that leisure for the proper improvement of his own mind, and for the cultivation of his own talents, that he ought to have, and which his station as an accountable being, placed at the head of a family, certainly requires.

Were children taught by the example of their parents properly to estimate the advantages of wealth; and were the virtues of frugality, temperance, and economy, brought into proper estimation, and were that estimation, which is now bestowed on grandeur, made the reward of merit, have we not reason to believe that it would not only produce domestic, but national prosperity[,] "built, not on the quicksands of extended commerce; not on the bloodstained treasures of the east or west; but on the solid rock of public and of private virtue[?]" [35]

Let every mother, then, who has a sufficient degree of [C]hristian philanthropy, and parental tenderness, to feel a glow of heart in the contemplation of such a picture, consider herself as an instrument in the hand of a kind Providence to promote its realization. Let her reflect how much the proper education of one single family may eventually contribute towards it. And that while the fruits of her labour are a rich compensation of peace, virtue[,] and contentment, which may descend through generations yet unborn, she will herself enjoy a suitable and permanent reward. But should she see her beloved children, in the bloom of youth, languishing under the pressure of disease, and about to enter into a state of fixedness, how sweet would be the consolation, that she had endeavoured, according to the best of her understanding, to prepare them for such a state! And that He who had blessed her pious care, would take the precious treasure He had loaned, into the mansions of eternal bliss.

Happy would it be for mankind if this care were more generally extended: we should not then see so many of our young people trifling away in idleness, vanity, and dissipation, that time which is lent them for great and important purposes. There would not be so much anxiety and expense in decorating those poor bodies of clay, which are seen today, and tomorrow are consigned to the silent tomb, there to mingle with their parent earth. We should then see more of our sons pursuing those objects which tend to ennoble the mind, and to promote the welfare and happiness of the human race, and our daughters uniting with them in the practice of those virtues which are best calculated to answer the end of our existence: glorifying God while here, and thereby becoming prepared to enjoy and adore [H]im in the life to come.

What must be the feelings of that mother, who has unhappily been the instrument of sowing and cultivating in the bosoms of her children, the seeds of pride and ostentation, even in the nursery! [F]or to the nursery may be traced many of the evils which abound. For instance: how common it is, when children are dressed in something new or clean, instead of informing them that it is to make them sweet and comfortable, they are sent to the other side of the room that we may see how pretty they look! [A]nd for performing this with an air of ostentation, they are rewarded with a kiss! Can this be the object of a fond mother's ambition for the darling children of her bosom? Is it to this, she would devote the offspring, a benevolent Creator has committed to her care?

Many are the females, who might have shone with brightness, been ornaments to their sex, and useful members of the community, but for the influence of those destructive mental associations which have been early and deeply rooted, and which are seldom, if ever, entirely subdued. But where these unhappy associations have already taken place, it is our duty, as well as our interest, properly to ascertain how they may be most effectually counteracted. It cannot be done by grave lessons, and serious arguments alone, or by formal declamations against the vanity of dress. One remedy, and one only remains, in which there can be any probability of success. The mother who would have her children superior to pride and vanity, must be superior to them herself. Every lesson to be taught with effect, must be enforced by example.

The following testimony to the watchful and affectionate care of a mother, is given after her decease, by her son, a late and well known writer:—"A few hours after my birth, she lost the use of one arm, and almost [all] of her left side. Being also afflicted with the stone,[36] she lived in a state of continual pain. Yet under all these afflictions, she was cheerful, and had the full use of her excellent understanding. She told me that when young, she frequently excused herself from going to public places, and private parties, that she might obtain an opportunity for reading. And the best authors were her favourites. The fruits of this early application amply repaid her for the pains which she had taken to cultivate her mind. Besides fortitude under real sufferings, exemplary piety, and an excellent understanding, she was possessed of a remarkably generous disposition. Her own wishes and opinions were never pursued merely because they were her own; the ease and comfort of every one about her, were necessary for her well being. In her own family, domestic order, decent economy, and plenty were combined; and to the education of her children, her mind was particularly bent from every ordinary occupation. She inspired me with the love of truth, and admiration of what was generous, and a dislike to low company. She took various means early to give me honourable feelings, and good principles; and to the influence of her authority and instructions, I owe the happiness of my life."[37]

He also relates a circumstance which occurred when he was very young, and in which his mother's prudence and care were strikingly exemplified. When he had, by giving way to a violent fit of anger, thrown an iron which endangered the life of his elder brother, he was brought into the presence of his mother. Though she was struck with horror at his conduct, she said nothing to him in anger. He thus relates the interview. "She ordered every body out of the room except myself, and then drawing me near to her, she spoke to me in a mild voice, but in a most serious manner. First, she explained to me the nature of the crime which I had run the hazard of committing. She told me she was sure I had no intention seriously to hurt my brother, and did not know, that if the iron had hit him, it must have killed him. While I felt this first shock, and while the horror of murder was upon me, my mother seized the moment to conjure me in future to command my passions. 'You,' said she to me, 'have naturally a violent temper; if you grow up to a man without learning to govern it, it will be impossible for you to command yourself; and there is no knowing what a crime you may, in a fit of passion, commit, and how miserable you may in consequence of it become. You are but a very young child, yet I think you understand me. Instead of speaking to you as I do this moment, I might punish you severely; but I think it better to treat you like a reasonable creature. My wish is, to teach you to command your temper; no body can do that for you so well as you can do it for yourself.' The impression made by the earnest solemnity with which she spoke, never has been effaced from my mind; and I am conscious that my mother's warning frequently recurred to me when I felt the passion of anger arising within me, and that these words of early advice had a most powerful and salutary influence in restraining my temper." [38]

Here we have a striking instance, worthy the imitation of every female, of the advantages arising from early self-cultivation, and proper maternal instruction. It not only prepared the mother to sustain with cheerfulness, fortitude, and resignation the privations many years, attendant on close confinement, accompanied with great bodily pain and infirmity, but qualified her for governing her family with dignity, and educating her children with success. If we pause for a moment, we are almost involuntarily led to contemplate the excellency of true

P[arental] [and] F[ilial] L[ove].

The language addressed to the mother of Moses, when her darling infant was committed to her care by the Egyptian princess, is very appropriate to the subject. "Take him away and nurse him for me, and I will give thee thy wages." [39] What mother of common understanding and sensibility, does not feel the assurance that if she nurses her offspring with maternal care, under the guidance of that principle of love, which is to be her light, and her leader, she will receive her wages from Him, who has committed them to her care: and that she will be laying a good foundation in their minds, for the enjoyment of every rational blessing.

How long Moses remained under the paternal roof, we are not told. But we may reasonably suppose that the mother (the father being oppressed with rigorous servitude) spared no pains to impress on the mind of her little son, the promises of future and innumerable blessings that were to be conferred on the Israelites. For although he was instructed in all the knowledge and accomplishments of the Egyptian Court, as being the adopted son of the Princess, his mind did not become so contaminated by its allurements as to indispose him to acknowledge his brethren. And although they were then in a very degraded situation, he preferred associating with them, that he might partake of the blessings in store for the nation to which he belonged.

It remains to be a fixed principle, that if we desire to have companions in our children when they arrive to years of maturity, we must prepare their minds by furnishing them with proper ideas, and inculcating proper sentiments. Mutual love, and mutual interest, form a much stronger, and more durable tie between parents and children, than any other that can be devised. Coercion may, in childhood, produce prompt obedience, but if it destroys affection, what hope can we reasonably entertain, that when such children get from under parental authority, they will retain a respect for what they have been compelled to adopt, without a conviction of its propriety, or necessity? If the rod is ever used, it ought only to be done after there has been sufficient time to reflect upon the nature of the fault, and to ascertain that correction would be for the child's real benefit. But there should be no anger manifested in the presence of the child, and certainly there should be none felt at the time of correcting it. Special care must therefore be taken, to correct and govern our own passions, as children observe their effects much sooner than we are aware.

As love is the foundation of all our happiness, so it ought to be the predominant motive of all our actions. We must convince children that our requisitions to do, or to leave undone, are the effects of love, and that obedience to our commands will contribute to their own comfort and enjoyment. For similar reasons, it is of the utmost importance, that children be early, and properly informed, respecting the attributes of the Supreme Being. He must not be represented to them as a partial, tyrannical Sovereign; but as a kind, merciful, and affectionate parent, providing for all our necessities, and acting for the benefit and everlasting happiness of his children; and that his love and his care are universal, as is shown by the general tenor of the Holy Scriptures. Numerous passages might be selected thence, for the support of this doctrine. When Cain was wroth[40] and his countenance was changed, because his brother's offering was more acceptable than his own; was it not said to him, "If thou doest well, shalt thou not be accepted? And if thou doest not well, sin lieth at the door."[41] The royal Psalmist, when speaking of the goodness of the Lord, of which he appears to have been very sensible, says, "As a father pitieth his children, so the Lord pitieth them that fear him."[42] At another time[,] "Bless the Lord, O my soul! and forget not his benefits."[43] In the Revelations, it is recorded by John in the name of the Most High, "I will give to him that is athirst, of the fountain of life freely. He that overcometh shall inherit all things, and I will be his God, and he shall be my son."[44]

The advantages arising from early mental associations of this kind, are incalculable. An instance of their happy effect, is very feelingly set forth by Elizabeth Hamilton, in her letters on education,[45] in the following narrative. "One young man, it has been my happiness to know, who entered upon life at the age of sixteen, without any guide but his own principles, without monitor, but the precepts of education, and the dictates of his own heart. Unsullied by the temptations of a capital, he was plunged into the temptations of a camp. Fond of society, where his cheerful temper and easy manners formed him to shine; but still fond of improvement, neither the inducements of camp, or city, interrupted his unwearied pursuits of literature and science. Surrounded by companions, who had caught the contagion of skepticism, he, at this early period of life, listened to their arguments, weighed, examined, detected their futility, and rejected them! In prosperity and adversity, in public and in private life, the sentiments of religion retained their influence on his heart. Through life they were his guide; and in death his consolation. When sinking, by painful steps, into an early grave, 'With what gratitude,' he exclaimed, 'With what delightful gratitude do I look back to my infancy, and to the judicious conduct of my mother, who made religion appear to me in colours so engaging, and so congenial! Had I been taught as other boys are taught, my passions would have made me an easy prey to vice; my love for enquiry, would have led me to infidelity. She prepared me for the trial of faith and virtue, and, thanks to God, I have come off victorious. Had religion been made to me a gloomy task in infancy, where would now have been my consolation!'"[46]

If the principle of love were more generally fixed in the human mind, and children were induced to obey, because they love, what a good foundation would be laid for the operation of that Holy Spirit, which is love itself. And how many more of the votaries of religion should we then see holding forth to the world this animating language—The ways of virtue are ways of pleasure, and in pursuing her paths there is great delight. Thus[, it] would be fulfilled the command of Him, who said, "Suffer little children to come unto me, and forbid (or hinder) them not."[47]

Selections from Abigail Field Mott's *Biographical Sketches and Interesting Anecdotes of Persons of Colour. To Which Is Added, A Selection of Pieces in Poetry. Compiled By A. Mott* (New York: Mahlon Day, 1826)

A[frican] S[chools] [in] N[ew]-Y[ork].

1. The "Clarkson Association," for instructing adult females of colour, commenced in the spring of 1811, and was conducted [for] ten or twelve years by a number of young females of the Society of Friends.[48] This was the first institution that came under the appellation of Sabbath School in that city, where there are now so many. It was taught on that day, because those people had generally more leisure to attend, than on other days of the week: but these benevolent females soon appropriated also one afternoon in the middle of the week, for such as were at liberty to attend. There were a considerable number of aged women, as well as those in the prime of life, who learned to read, and rejoiced greatly in the acquisition. There were also schools kept by young men, for adults of colour.[49]

2. The African Free Schools, under the care of the Manumission Society in New-York, have engaged the attention of many distinguished persons, who have visited the city: and many encouraging observations on these schools, have appeared in the public prints.

3. The following remarks are taken from one of the daily papers of 1824:[50]— "We had the pleasure of attending the annual examination of the scholars of the 'New-York African Free School[']; and we are free to confess, that we never derived more satisfaction, or felt a deeper interest in any school exhibition. The male and female schools were united on this occasion, and the whole number present was about six hundred. The exercises of the scholars were commenced by an address spoken by one of the lads; in which were included thirteen lines from Cowper, in favour of liberty, beginning with

'For there is yet a liberty unsung.'[51]

4. "The examinations were in reading, writing, arithmetic, a critical examination in American geography, and a grammar class; with a recitation of several appropriate pieces; and an exhibition of work done by the females in their

department (this branch of their education is under the care of a committee of females, annually appointed by the Trustees of those schools, whose business it is to visit the school, once or more every week)[.] A list of the articles exhibited, made within the past year, are as follows:— Shirts, 93; pillowcases, 61; sheets, 7; cravats, 49; towels, 23; handkerchiefs, 15; wristbands and collars, 25 pair; dresses for scholars, 13; fine samplers, 9; bench covers, 1 pair; pocket-books, 2;—knitting, 27 pair of children[']s socks; 26 pair suspenders; 7 pair of stockings, and 6 pincushions. These specimens of knitting and needlework, all appeared to much advantage.

5. "The number in this department is 154; of which there are 56 acquainted with making garments and marking, and 42 with knitting socks, stockings, suspenders, &c.; the remainder are progressing in those branches. Of this school Eliza J. Cox[52] is teacher,—and Charles C. Andrews[53] that for boys.

6. "The whole scene was highly interesting, and we never beheld a white school, of the same age (of and under fifteen), in which, without exception, there was more order, neatness of dress, and cleanliness of person. And the exercises were performed with a degree of promptness and accuracy, that was surprising. We could plainly perceive (notwithstanding what is asserted to the contrary) that the effects of education were as visible upon the countenances of these children, as they are upon those that are white. Their countenances beaming with intelligence, and the liveliness of their spirits, with their apparent happiness, was a subject of universal remark. There were two or three southern gentlemen present, and we should have been pleased had there been many more.

7. "There is one remarkable fact connected with the effects of this excellent school upon the moral condition of the blacks. At every term of the court of sessions in this city, there are many blacks convicted of crimes, and sent to the state prison or penitentiary. This school has now been in operation a number of years, and several thousand scholars have received the benefits of a good thorough English education, *and but three persons, who have been educated here, have been convicted in our criminal courts.* This *single fact* speaks volumes in favour of education, and endeavouring to improve the condition of this unfortunate class of people. It is the cultivation of the mind and the heart, which teaches them to be honest, makes them quiet and orderly citizens, and leads them to a knowledge of the means whereby they may obtain comfort in this life, and happiness in the life to come."

8. Several girls, who have received their education at this school, have gone with their parents to Hayti, where they will be capable of teaching schools, and may be of singular benefit.—Two interesting letters from one of these girls has been received by E. J. Cox; extracts from which are here subjoined.

Republic of Hayti, City of St. Domingo, Sept. 29, 1824.

"Dear Teacher,

9. "With pleasure I hasten to inform you of our safe arrival in St. Domingo, after a passage of twenty-one days: mother and myself were very much afflicted with sea-sickness, for about nine or ten days, but after that, we enjoyed a little of the pleasures of our voyage.[54]

10. "On our arrival, we were conducted by the captain[55] of the port to the Governor's house,[56] where we were received by him with all the friendship that he could have received us with, had we been intimately acquainted for years. After informing him of our intention of residing on the Island, we were conducted to the residence of the second General in command,[57] where we had our names registered. From thence we went to see the principal chapel[58] in the city; to give a description of which, it requires a far abler pen than mine; (she[59] however mentions many particulars) but you cannot form an idea of it, unless you could see for yourself. After we had viewed the church throughout, we were conducted to our lodgings, at which place we are at present.

11. "Since we have been here, my sampler and bench cover have been seen by a number of ladies and gentlemen, and have been very much admired by all who have seen them.—Dear Teacher, notwithstanding we are hundreds of miles from each other, I hope you will not think that I shall forget you, nor those kind friends (I mean the Trustees)[,] who have been so kind to me: for had it not been for them and yourself, perhaps I never should have known one half what I do, as respects my education; for which, for them and you, to God I shall offer up my humble prayers for your welfare, both in this life, and that which is to come. Please to give my kind respects to Mr. Andrews, and my love to all my school-mates.—Father, mother, and brothers join in love with me to you and Mr. Andrews.

"P. S.—Please to get 3 yards of fine white canvass, 3 yards fine yellow, 3 sets of knitting needles, and 2 skeins[60] of blue worsted—which I forgot.—Mother has enclosed four dollars for the same."

"I am with respect, yours,
S[erena] M. B[aldwin]."

"Republic of Hayti, City of St. Domingo, June 30, 1825

"Dear Teacher,

12. "I received your letter, dated November 11, 1824, and was truly happy to hear from you:—the canvass, worsted, and books, I received also—for which I thank you kindly. The advice that you have given me, I shall cherish in my bosom, and hope the impression it will make there, shall be such as time can never destroy. Although we are separated from each other [by] hundreds of mile[s], I shall ever consider it my duty to adhere to your advice; especially when it is such as concerns my eternal welfare.

13. "Among your good wishes, you wish I may live to enjoy freedom. Dear Teacher, if ever there was a country where Liberty dwells, it is here. It is a blessing enjoyed alike by all men, without respect to fortune or colour—it cannot be otherwise, as our motto is 'Liberty and Equality.' As respects our situation, it is a pleasant one. Picture to yourself a farm a quarter of a mile from the city, containing about twelve acres of even land, in the centre of which stands a little white cottage, surrounded by every kind of fruit trees that the Island produces, besides vegetables of every kind, which we have raised since we have been here. Add to these, two cows, one calf, geese, ducks, and upwards of one hundred chickens, and I am certain you will agree with me, in saying our situation is truly pleasant.[61]

14. "On New-Years day, which is the anniversary of our Independence,[62] we went to the parade, where the troops were assembled in the public square at an early hour—(after mentioning divers particulars, she concludes with saying,) at ten o'clock, the inhabitants with one accord, retired to their respective homes, without the least noise or tumult. Thus passed the day of Haytian Independence.—My parents join with me in love to you and Mr. Andrews, &c.

S[erena] M. B[aldwin]."

[These letters were written in a very fair intelligible hand, by a girl about fourteen years old.]

N[ew]-Y[ork] A[frican] S[chool] [for] B[oys].

[Communicated to the Compiler.]

1. In the African School for boys, in Mulberry [S]treet,[63] a class has long been established, which is perhaps the only one of the kind in the city of New-York: it is composed of such boys as are the best behaved, and most advanced in their learning, say in arithmetic, as far as the Rule of Three.[64] They are distinguished in school, by a medal suspended to the neck, on which are engraved the words, "*Class of Merit.*"

2. This class has a regular meeting once a month, to transact business, and to hear the reports of standing and other committees. It is allowed one hour each session to conduct its business. Its officers are a Chairman, Secretary, Register, and Treasurer. The class by a vote determine in what branch of learning a member shall excel to entitle him to the chair at the next succeeding meeting—the teacher always deciding. I have seen some specimens of penmanship, map drawing, composition, both in prose and verse, the performance of those lads, the result of this laudable emulation.

3. The Chairman preserves order and decorum at the meetings of the class: the Secretary records, in a neat manner, their proceedings: the Register enters in his book the names, qualifications, character, and other particulars, of every member when admitted: and the Treasurer collects voluntary contributions[65] of the members at every stated meeting. On the admission of a new member, he is addressed by the Chairman, and received in due form, in presence of the whole school.

4. The class appoints a committee at each stated meeting, whose duty it is to take notice of the general deportment of the members when out of school, and to report to the class, if they discover any thing in the conduct of a member immoral, or unbecoming, and the member so reported, is dealt with in such manner as the circumstances of the case may require: such as suspension, expulsion, or otherwise; even reproof by the Chairman has been known to have a very striking effect. Another committee observe the appearance of the members, as it respects cleanliness, and report if occasion require; and a third is called the Health Committee, who, on hearing of the sickness of any member, visit him, and render services of kindness, and report on such subjects every regular meeting.

5. I now subjoin an instance of the good effect of this juvenile tribunal. Some time ago, at a meeting of the class, held then in the back part of the school

room, one of the members was observed by the teacher to be in considerable trouble. The rest of the class seated, and the Chairman standing in the attitude of addressing this poor fellow, who it appeared had been doing wrong: the scene being one which interested the teacher, he walked towards the class, and the following dialogue took place:—

6. *Teacher.* May I be permitted by the Chairman, to ask, what is the cause of the grief which seems to afflict this member of the class? (pointing to the boy in tears.)

Chairman. Yes, Sir—he has been reported by the Standing Committee, as having made use of bad language out of school;[66] it has been proved against him here, and he has been sentenced by the class, to be by the Chairman reproved in this manner.

7. *Teacher.* It is a serious sentence, and a still more serious crime which has occasioned it; but I perceive that the offender is in great distress.—Have you gone through with what you intended to say to him?

Chairman. No[,] Sir—I have considerable yet to say to him.

8. *Teacher.* Shall I request one more indulgence, and that in behalf of poor William [(the name of the offender)]?—I wish to speak a few words to him.

Chairman. By all means, Sir.

9. *Teacher.* How is this, William; did you not know that it was very wicked, as well as offensive to your classmates, thus to transgress?

William. O, yes, Sir [(the tears all the while streaming down his cheeks)]! I know it was very wrong—but do pray, Sir, please to ask the class to forgive me; I will never be guilty of the crime again—I know I have disgraced myself, and am very sorry—I have done very wrong.—Can't I be forgiven?

10. It appears that this was spoken with so much earnestness, as to affect the whole class, and a readiness to forgive seemed evident in every countenance. The Teacher then turning to the Chairman, asked him if he could[,] with propriety, dispense with saying any thing further to William than to express his forgiveness, on condition of a promise that he will be more careful in [the] future?

11. The Chairman (a boy of fourteen years of age) bowed assent; and handing back to the little penitent his medal, of which he had been deprived on conviction of guilt, expressed the forgiveness of the class in a becoming manner. Poor William thanked his teacher for interceding for him (still in tears)[,] resumed his seat, and soon appeared greatly relieved.

One of the Trustees.

A V[aledictory] A[ddress].

The following is a Valedictory Address, composed and spoken at an Annual Examination,[67] by *Andrew R. Smith*, aged 14 years, on his and others leaving the New-York African Free-School, April, 1822.

Respected Patrons and Friends,—

1. With much diffidence, I rise to address you on a subject which is of great importance, both to myself and to those of my fellow-schoolmates, who are about to leave this school. I feel it my duty, on this occasion, to return my humble thanks to those gentlemen who have so long been, and still are, the supporters of this valuable institution. I consider myself under many and great obligations to you; and my ardent desire and wishes are that you may flourish and prosper in this benevolent undertaking.

2. To you, my much[-]respected Teacher, I am greatly indebted. For your kind attention to me, while under your care, I most sincerely and humbly thank you. When I first became your pupil, I was ignorant of letters, and learnt my A, B, C, by means of writing in the sand: since that time, I have passed regularly through every class in the school, and have had the honour of filling almost every office in the same; and more than this, down to the present day, I have had the pleasure of enjoying the expressions of approbation[68] of my teacher.

3. My books and exercises, exhibited before you this day, will, I doubt not, be regarded by you, gentlemen, who are Trustees of this school, as testimonials in my favour, that your labour, and that of my preceptor,[69] have not been bestowed upon me in vain.

4. As the various exercises of the day have detained you some time, it requires me to be short. In conclusion, let me remind you, my fellow-schoolmates, who are about to leave with me, that we are now entering into a wide field, and that we must be industrious and upright to make respectable members of society; and to be an honour to our parents, we must make such use of our learning, as will prove a blessing to ourselves, and to the community with which Providence now calls us to mix.

Appendix C

Selections from Abigail Field Mott's *The Mother and Her Children, or Twilight Conversation* (New York: Mahlon Day, 1828)

"First Evening"

William. It is now near dusk, and before the lamps are lighted, why may we not have a little pleasant conversation?

Mother. It is a very suitable time: now all is quiet, and before we begin our evening work.

Eliza. What shall we talk about?

Mother. It makes but little difference, my dear children, what we begin with: if the object be for improvement, we may make as long a story as we please from a small beginning. A small seed will produce a large plant, and a little nut a great tree, if the soil is good.

William. Let us begin then, with Gustavus Vassa's three pence.[70]

Maria. What can we make of that? I never have heard any thing about it; who is Gustavus Vassa?

William. He was an African, and stolen from his parents when he was about seven years old, carried to the West Indies, and sold several times, like a great many of his country folks; but he at last had a kind master, who told Gustavus when he could get as much money as had been given for him, and would let him have it, he should be free.[71] The three pence, I suppose, was given to him for something he had done.[72] By trading with that little, he got more, and so on, until by great industry and prudence, he got money enough, paid it to his master, and became free.

Mother. Here we have one striking instance already, of what a small beginning will do.

Eliza. And what did he do, when he was free?

William. He went to sea for many years, and suffered a great deal, in many ways. When he was about forty years old, he gave that up, and wrote a history of his life, which was printed; and by reading that, I learned what I have just told you.

Eliza. Going to sea is very dangerous business I believe, is it not?

Richard. There are a great many vessels lost at sea, and sometimes all the people on board are drowned. But I remember reading in the book William has just mentioned, that when Gustavus was in the ship [*Nancy*], she got on the Bahama banks, and the sailors all got into the little boats, and landed on an island; but when they came near the shore, they saw some creatures walking on the beach, and they were afraid they were Cannibals; but being birds they soon spread their wings and flew away, for they were only flamingos.[73]

Maria. What are Cannibals?

Mother. They are a fierce barbarous kind of people, who, when they kill those they dislike, sometimes eat them. It was not far from where the [*Nancy*] was lost, that a vessel, many years ago, in coming from the West Indies, with a number of passengers on board, was cast away.[74] The people got on shore in East Florida, which now belongs to the United States, though then it was inhabited by Cannibals, who treated them very cruelly. One of the passengers speaking the Spanish language, and the Cannibals being afraid of the Spaniards, they did not kill them.[75] In the company, there was an old man named Robert Barrow, and also Jonathan Dickinson, his wife, and a baby only a few months old, and several black people, besides the sailors.[76] The Cannibals having taken nearly all their clothes, and the weather becoming cold, they suffered very much for want of food and clothing in traveling a great distance on foot, and the negroes mostly died with cold and hunger on the journey.[77]

Maria. Did the old man or the baby die?

Mother. Not then. Several of the company, after travelling and suffering greatly for many weeks, reached St. Augustine, where they met with kind treatment from the Spaniards; were provided with clothes, and sent in a vessel to Philadelphia, where Robert Barrow soon after died;[78] Jonathan Dickinson went with his wife and child to Long-Island, where Thomas Chalkley, from Pennsylvania, mentions attending his funeral in 1727, just a century ago.[79] The baby lived to be a man, but I don't know how old a one.

Eliza. What birds were those that Gustavus Vassa and his companions saw, that they were so much afraid of[?]

William. They were Flamingos. A tall bird, with long legs and necks, and their plumage being red, they thought they were men with red coats on.[80]

Maria. What is plumage?

William. It is feathers. What a bird is covered with, is called its plumage.

Eliza. Where those people travelled, and suffered so much with cold, were there any Bears?

Mother. Not that I know of. Bears generally live further north. In Greenland there are a great many Bears; some of them are black, and some are white. They sometimes get on cakes of ice which float away with them. If the ice goes into the ocean they must be drowned or starve to death. When it goes to some other shore, they get off. There [have] been many instances of their going quite to Iceland on cakes of ice.

Maria. How large are the cakes of ice?

William. They are of different sizes. I think Guthrie, in his [*Geography*], says that some of them are more than a mile in length, and upwards of a hundred feet in thickness: and that the Dutch had thirteen ships crushed to pieces with them in one season, off the coast of Greenland:[81] I suppose they were there after whales or some other fish.

Eliza. That is wonderful! [T]hey must be a great while making, or the weather a great deal colder there than it is here.

Mother. In those northern regions it is so cold that the ice never all melts. When some of it melts, and the water runs on that which is not melted, and freezes again, it makes the cakes thicker. And when there comes a heavy storm, or milder weather, some of them break loose and float away.

Richard. Such great cakes of ice must be very dangerous, if vessels come near them, even when they are out on the ocean.

William. Yes, a great many ships are injured by them, and some quite lost. There was a very fine new ship called the [*Liverpool*], which sailed from New-York in the summer of 1822, with a number of passengers on board. When they had been out about ten days, the weather being foggy, a cake of ice came very hard against the ship, and broke her side, so that the people were all obliged to get into the small boats as quickly as they could, without taking any thing with them but a little provision; and the ship sunk almost immediately. They being in all thirty-six persons, steering their course for Nova-Scotia, and it being then fine weather, they arrived safely in seven days.[82]

Maria. Did they stay in Nova-Scotia?

William. No. Captain Lee, with his sailors, and some of the passengers, came back to New-York. The others went to England in another vessel.[83]

Richard. Iceland, I suppose is called so, because it is such cold weather there. How far is it from Greenland, that the Bears could go to it on the ice?

Mother. Iceland is an island north of Ireland, but not so far north as Greenland; they are a considerable distance from each other, but those large mountains of ice float a great way sometimes. The most particular account we have of Iceland was published by E. Henderson, an Englishman, who visited it in 1814, and stayed about fifteen months; in which time he travelled almost over the whole island.[84]

Richard. [What] did he do to travel, if it is so cold there?

Mother. He arrived the fore part of one summer, and stayed until the latter part of the next: so that he was two summers and one winter on the island. When it is winter[,] they have so much snow, and the weather is so very cold, that they are obliged to stay at home. The houses for their cows and sheep are very near to those the people live in.

Eliza. Their cows give them milk, I suppose; and the wool of their sheep makes their clothes: do they weave their cloth?

Mother. Not much of it. They knit most of their clothing. In long winter evenings the men knit as well as the women.

Richard. Do they raise [I]ndian corn or wheat there?

Mother. No, their summers are too short for such grain.[85] They have a wild grain that looks a little like our oats, which they gather, as they also do the moss that grows on the rocks and on the ground. For their winter food, they catch some fish, and wild ducks, and dry them. The ducks are very fat, and have fine feathers like down, which is called e[i]der[-]down.[86] The women and children all help in summer, to gather what they can for winter.

Richard. Is it a smooth country?

Mother. No, it is very mountainous, and the travelling difficult even in summer. There are several volcanoes on the island; the most noted one, called Hecla, is on the south side of it.

"Second Evening"

Eliza. I think when we were talking last evening about Iceland, Mother said the people there gathered moss to eat.

Maria. Eat moss! [T]hat I think must be very poor eating.

Mother. The Iceland moss is very nourishing.[87] Some of it is brought to America and sold by the apothecaries. It is used for persons who have been very much reduced by sickness. By boiling it in water several hours it becomes like jelly; when the liquor is strained through a cloth, and milk and sugar put with it, as we do in coffee or chocolate, it makes a very wholesome drink.

William. I suppose it is the same kind of moss that the reindeer in Lapland[88] live upon, which they get by digging through the snow. [It] having so much nourishment in it, a little keeps them alive in winter.

Richard. It must be very difficult, in Iceland, for children to get to school in winter[.] [H]ow do they do then?

Mother. They have not many public schools. Henderson said there was but one on the island, and that one was for teaching such young men as were to be employed in state affairs, and public offices. Mothers teach their children, and those they have under their care to read, as soon as they are capable of it. And the father instructs them in such other branches of learning as he wishes them to acquire. In this way, not only their own children, but even their little servant girls get very good learning.[89]

Eliza. How clever that is, to learn[90] those poor children. When they get to be women, then they can teach their own children.

William. Yes, if every body would do so, we should not have so many ignorant folks as we now have. It sometimes happens that two persons marry who do not either of them know how to read; and then if they get a letter from a friend, they are obliged to wait until they can get somebody to read it for them. They are very much to be pitied, for there is great satisfaction in reading good books, and exchanging letters with our absent friends. Of this pleasure such are almost deprived.

Mother. They are so. I recollect to have heard a woman say, that when she received a letter from her daughter who resided at a distance from her, she was obliged to wait sometimes all day for her husband to return home before she could know what it contained; and added, "I am now very sorry I did not learn when I was a big girl and lived with you, and you so kindly offered to instruct me. But I was so naughty, I have often wondered how you could have so much patience with me as you had."

Richard. What a pity it is, that when people have an opportunity, they are not willing to learn. If they are large, they might learn the better for that.

Mother. There is too much of what may be called false shame in the world. Many of those who are ignorant, are not so much ashamed of being so, as they are that it should be known; and by this means they remain ignorant all their days: whereas if they were only desirous of learning, they could generally find some one willing to instruct them. There is one thing that sometimes occasions very unpleasant feelings to persons of limited education; that is, when they are requested to sign their name as a witness, and are obliged to acknowledge they can only make a mark for it. I wish every one so circumstanced, would be convinced by the experiment, how soon this difficulty may be remedied by having their name written on a piece of paper, or a slate, and copying it. In this way many persons have learned to write their names intelligibly in a few hours. There was a school taught several years by young women, in New-York, on purpose for women of colour; and a number who were quite aged learned to read, and were very much pleased when they could read the Bible for themselves.[91]

Maria. How clever that was: did they go every day?

Mother. No, they only went once or twice in a week: they could not be spared from their business to go oftener. It is probable they studied when they had leisure at home, and that the children or mistress of the family where they lived, heard them say their lessons. Don[']t you remember my telling you of a good little boy named William, who was so fond of a book that he learned all the large letters before he was two years old? When he was a little older, he would stand by his mother and say his lesson, while she was at her work, or nursing her baby.

Richard. I think he must have been a very nice little boy.

Mother. He was indeed. When he was about four years old, there came a black man to live in the family, who seeing how easy it was for William to learn, asked the child to learn him: he replied, "I don[']t know much myself, but I am willing to learn thee, as fast as my dear mother learns me." When evening came, the man would take William on his knee and say his lesson to him, and they both appeared to enjoy these opportunities very much; but it was not long before the dear little boy was taken sick and died.

Eliza. How sorry it makes me feel that such a good little boy must die; when he was so kind too in learning the poor black man his lesson.

Maria. Mother, what is dying? I know they put folks in the ground when they are dead.

Mother. It is ceasing to breathe, and becoming insensible to every thing around us, so that we cannot see, nor feel any more than those dolls you play with.

William. But there is a part of us that cannot die; that is spirit.

Mother. Yes, my dear, that's right, and when the body dies, the spirit goes to God who gave it, and if we have been good, and minded what [H]e has made known to us to be right, He will let us live with Him for ever: for as William said, the spirit never dies.

Richard. We read in the Testament what Christ said about those who did right, and those who did wrong. I often think of that about the rich man, who had so many nice things, and lived so high every day, and poor Lazarus, who was so full of sores that he could not work, and was obliged to beg even for something to eat. But though he suffered so much in this world, when he died he was a great deal better off than the rich man. I suppose he was very patient, and bore his many trials without murmuring, while the rich man was feasting, and perhaps keeping bad company.[92]

William. How necessary it is we should be kind to the poor too; especially those who are sick, or lame, or old, and can't take care of themselves. I think that passage about feeding the hungry, clothing the naked, and visiting the sick[93] is also one that we ought to keep in mind, if we wish for happiness in the discharge of our duty.

Mother. Those ideas are very correct, and it ought to be done seasonably too. I well recollect a circumstance that occurred in New-York a few years since. A poor man was very sick, and had been so for a long time, and his wife could not work to earn any thing. She sat down by his bed-side and wept, for they were strangers in the city, and it seemed to her as if they must suffer and die together. A person hearing of their situation sent a little girl with some provision, who got to the house just at the time the poor woman was bemoaning their sad and destitute condition.

Eliza. How comfortable that must have been to them. I think I should be willing to spare part of my own dinner in such a case.

Maria. And did the little girl go again to see them?

Mother. Yes, she went a great many times; and sometimes when she went to the house, the sick man would call her a little angel for bringing him food, and being so kind to him, though he could eat but very little at a time. And it is not only comfortable to the sick, but to the person who sends it also; for by attending to what we believe to be right, our own happiness is increased, while it relieves those in distress. So that those who give, and those who receive, are made to rejoice together.

William. I think it is very proper for children to do such errands; it gives us an opportunity of seeing how poor folks live, and we shall be likely to have more thought about them, and feel more tenderly for them. And when we are at home where we have plenty, we shall not be disposed to waste, or throw away any thing that would be useful to the poor.

"Report of [the] Ladies' Anti-Slavery Society of Albany" from the July 2, 1845, Issue of *The Albany Patriot*

Treasurer's Report.—The close of our last year's operations, ending April 18, left us a balance in the treasury of $33[.]57. During the present year there has been paid into the Society's funds, from the sale of articles and donations, $7[.]30. Our expenditures, including $10 sent to Mrs. Torrey,[94] have been $24[.]71—leaving a balance in the treasury of $16[.]35.

Two years have now elapsed since the formation of our Society.[95] Being still in its infancy, and compelled to contest with a host of opposing influences, its operations have necessarily been narrowed down to a very small compass. The unaccountable apathy of the community at large, and the total disregard which most of the professed church of God manifest to the claims of the crushed, bleeding, groaning victim of Southern oppression, are obstacles in our progress of no small magnitude. While one portion of the religionists of the country are selling Christ "in the shambles"[96] with a degree of guilt that calls loudly for the speedy vengeance of Heaven, most of the remaining portion are not only winking at the crime, but actually sustaining the system, by their unlawful deeds and unholy connections. Instead of remembering those in bonds as bound with them, and those that suffer adversity as being themselves also in the body, the people have perverted the right way of the Lord.

Though our numbers are exceedingly small, and a tremendous tide of influence sweeping against us, we are in no w[ays] daunted. We expect to be borne aloft on the mighty wings of Truth, though the [E]arth pass away, and the mountains are removed into the midst of the sea.[97] Our motto is—Awake to the contest! [A]nd having done all, *stand*. Let "neither life nor death, principalities nor powers, things present nor things to come, height, depth, or any other creature,"[98] lead us to aim a blow at the foundation[al] principles of Christ's religion, by refusing to defend the God-given, blood-bought rights of our fellow-men.

Our Society has sustained some severe losses in its membership during the past year. Three have been called to exchange the armor for the harp and the crown.[99] One of this number was our Corresponding Secretary.[100] We most cordially acquiesce in the Divine will, which has removed them from our ranks, and given them an inheritance among the saints in light, far away from the clanking of chains, and the "sighing of the needy."[101] Some choice spirits have left us for distant fields of labor, where their influence will no doubt be felt for the good of the cause.

We have sustained a monthly meeting for prayer, and the execution of plans for the assistance of fugitives on their way to Canada. A number have been furnished with clothing, and strengthened with "a cup of cold water"[102] to go on their way rejoicing. Some have come under our observation that hardly knew their right hand from their left. We have been led to conclude that American *church-manufactured heathen* would range very well with Hottentots.[103]

The Society has at present a box of clothing on hand of some considerable value, solicited by a committee, designed for the benefit of the Mission at Canada, under the care of Mr. Rice.[104]

Mothers! sisters! daughters! come and help us! Religion and humanity demand it. Come! [A]nd we will try to secure to ourselves the blessing of those that are ready to perish.

"[*Narrative*] of Douglass" by A. M. [Abigail Field Mott] from the July 6, 1845, Issue of *The Liberator*

Dear Garrison:[105]

I received, yesterday, through the kindness of some friend in Boston, the [*Narrative of Frederick Douglass*]—his *multum in parvo*.[106] His account is brief, though admirable for its comprehensiveness. Whole volumes are therein contained, it being replete with the strong features of that most odious monster Slavery. The scenes through which he passed are exhibited with a clearness, and stamped upon the mind with a strength, which ever accompanies a strong, commanding evidence of truth.

My language is inadequate; therefore[,] I shall not attempt to describe my feelings, as I went with the Narrator through his twenty years' experience in slavery.

I have wept over the pages of Dickens' [Oliver Twist][107]—I have moistened with my tears whole chapters of Eugene Sue's [Mysteries of Paris][108]—but Douglass's history of the wrongs of the American Slave, brought, not tears—no, tears refused me their comfort—its home truths crowded in such quick succession, and entered so deep into the chambers of my soul, as to entirely close the relief valve. For I am an American woman, and for American women I bleed. I groaned in the agony of my spirit, and said, ["]Oh, Lord! [H]ow long shall these things be? How long shall the spoiler mark his prey?["] I have many times heard the author vividly portray the evils of slavery. I have often heard him recount with deep feeling the endless wrongs they are made to endure—but, oh! never before have I been brought so completely in sympathy with the slave—never before have I felt myself so completely bound with them—never before have I so fully realized the doctrine of our blessed Saviour, ["]whatsoever ye do unto the least one of these, ye do it unto me.["][109]

May his [Narrative] incite us to renewed diligence in our labors for the slave! May the author become a mighty instrument to the pulling down of the strong holds of iniquity, and to the establishing of righteousness in our land!

Affectionately thine for the slave,
A. M.

P. S.—I know of no way in which I can better serve the cause of the oppressed, than to enclose $5 to the author of the book, for extension of its publicity.

Albany, May 24, 1845.

Our correspondent chooses to affix to her letter only the initials of her name; but we know her to be a most faithful friend of the oppressed. Copies of the [Narrative], to the extent of her donation, shall be distributed with judgment and care.

Memoir of Purchase Monthly Meeting, Concerning Abigail Mott
(NEW YORK: JAMES EGBERT, 1852)

Our beloved friend Abigail [Field] Mott having recently been removed from us by death,[110] we feel engaged to preserve a brief [Memoir] concerning her, both from the regard we had for her as a distinguished member of our Religious Society, and as a bright example of the efficacy of Divine Grace, when admitted as a governing principle into the heart, to regulate and elevate the character, to qualify for the performance of the varied duties of life, and to sustain under the trials and afflictions incident to it.

She was the daughter of Uriah and Mary Field, and was born in the year 1766.[111] Her parents were worthy members of the Religious Society of Friends, belonging to Purchase Monthly Meeting,[112] in West Chester County, New York; and of this Monthly Meeting Abigail Mott continued to be a member to the close of her life.

In her childhood she was remarkable for the sweetness of her disposition and her orderly deportment, and at this early age was disposed to counsel and encourage her brothers and sisters in a dutiful course of conduct.

Her parents were concerned to train up their children in a manner consistent with the principles of the Religious Society of which they were members, and through their pious care, joined to a tender susceptibility of mind on her part, she was preserved from those deviations from Christian simplicity in appearance and deportment, which too frequently mark the youthful period of life.

She labored under peculiar disadvantages in obtaining a competent portion of school learning, in consequence of the low state of schools at that time, yet such was her fondness for intellectual improvement, that through untiring application, this difficulty was overcome, and she made a progress in literature that prepared her for usefulness in Religious Society, and in the community.

At an early age she was united in marriage with our beloved friend Richard Mott,[113] and being happily united with each other in a religious concern to "[s]eek first the kingdom of God and his righteousness,"[114] the union proved a mutual blessing through the varied stages of their future life; and in their experience was verified the promise of our blessed Redeemer to those who make the performance of their religious duties their first and chief concern, "[a]ll things necessary shall be added unto you."[115]

Impressed with the weight of responsibility connected with the sphere in life which she had now assumed, she entered upon it with a desire faithfully and discreetly to perform the duties connected with her new position. Sensible of the advantage to be gained by the observance of method and order in the business and arrangements of the family, she was enabled to introduce a system of management by which the benefit in view was secured, and which procured for her household the enjoyment of quiet and comfort.

Through the force of the "[l]aw of kindness[,]"[116] she obtained an influence over those within the province of her control so fully, as to render unnecessary the harsher features of authority. While by this means she gained the heart-felt respect of those around her, and also a faithful attention from them to their respective duties—reciprocal attachment contributed largely to the prevalence of domestic peace. This "[l]aw of kindness[,]" united with her humble piety, endeared her to all who were acquainted with her.

So fully was she satisfied with the benefit resulting from the system of management she had adopted, that in later life she was induced to labor as an author to draw attention to the advantages to be derived from such a course.

By an early submission to the discipline of the Spirit of Christ, she became a very valuable member of our Society, "[a]dorning the doctrine"[117] by her circumspect life.

About the twenty-eighth year of her age she was appointed to the station of an Elder,[118] and through the remainder of her life was enabled to discharge the duties of this office to the satisfaction of her friends—an Elder worthy of double honor, because she filled the station and performed its duties in the fear of the Lord.

The public labors of her husband in the ministry commenced about the same time; and he frequently feeling constrained to leave his home and its many attractions, to travel in the service of the Gospel—while she sympathised with him in the exercise, she uniformly resigned him willingly to the service, encouraging him in a faithful attention to his duty, and cheerfully taking upon herself the charge that devolved on her during his absence.

She entertained a lively sympathy for those who were called to the work of the ministry, and willingly received and entertained them when travelling in this service. To such her home proved a quiet resting place. While attentively administering to their temporal wants, she was qualified to enter into feeling with them in their spiritual trials and exercises, and to hand forth the counsel or encouragement that they needed—thus performing the duties of a mother in the Church.

Firmly attached to the doctrines of the Gospel as held by the Religious Society of which she was a member, she felt deeply interested in the preservation of a sound and pure ministry. Hence every appearance of a departure from soundness of doctrine was regarded by her with much solicitude.[119] Her concern on account of the Ministry, and her views respecting it, are expressed in the following extract from a paper written by her, dated [the fifth] month [of] 1831:[120]

> I think there is cause to apprehend that the Ministry in our Society, notwithstanding the sifting we have experienced, is yet too superficial—that in some instances there is a want of that deep indwelling that mortal man should witness, to bring him into a suitable state to visit the immortal seed and word of life, in the hearts of his hearers. And this being too often the case when attempts are made to instruct the people, the matter communicated, coming only from the superficial part in the speaker, cannot penetrate the heart and produce conviction in the mind of the hearer.
>
> The ministry of the Word[,] in the power and demonstration of the Spirit, is a very solemn office, and the rightly qualified are often induced to adopt the query, "who is sufficient for these things?"[121] But when they feel the "wo[e]" alluded to by the Apostle,[122] and are attentive to the word given, an evidence attends, and the word preached generally meets the witness for truth in the hearts of the audience, and while the sincere are comforted, the weak strengthened, the lukewarm aroused, even the gain-sayer[123] is brought to a secret acknowledgment of the excellency of the Christian's hope. It ought therefore to be the prayer of all the truly exercised amongst us, that the ministry may be purged, not only from its *dross*,[124] and its *tin*, but from its reprobate silver also.[125]
>
> Until this is experienced, and the people are made willing, instead of depending on the minister, to *dig* and to *beg* for the arising of that life in themselves which will enable them to worship in reverential fear before Him who is the true Head of the Church, and to cast away all depend[e]nce upon man, whose breath is in his nostrils,[126] we cannot reasonably look for much increase of vital religion within our limits or for much enlargement of our borders. The foundation of Christianity must be sought for, and built upon in its own simplicity, or the superstructure raised, will not stand.

As a wife she was very affectionate and discreet: calm and deliberate in her disposition, she was prepared to meet the various contingencies of life with composure, and, possessing a sound judgment, she was qualified to aid her husband in seasons of trial, by her prudent counsel, and to comfort him by her sympathy.

As a Mother, she was much impressed with the importance of her charge, and was concerned to seek for ability rightly to train the infant minds committed to her care. Sensible how much the opening faculties of the child require the mother's care to give them the right direction, and to furnish the expanding mind with ideas suited to its age and strength, she carefully sought for opportunities thus to guide and nurse the growing intellect.

The twilight of the evening was a favorite season with her, for collecting her little ones around her, to enter into free and cheerful conversation with them, on subjects suited to their capacity, and calculated while enlivening their feelings to enlarge their sphere of useful knowledge—watching on these occasions, [she wished] to draw from the subject some moral that might aid in forming the character, or to catch a thought that might lead to the contemplation of the power, and wisdom, and goodness of their Creator, and of the obligation resting upon us all, to be grateful to Him for his multiplied favors, and to love and serve Him according to His will.[127]

Instruction thus given, scarcely could fail to produce salutary effects. So fully was she satisfied with the benefit resulting from care thus extended, that she believed it right to invite the attention of parents (mothers especially) to the subject, in several essays prepared and published by her.

By an unusual dispensation of Divine Providence, she was called to endure severe trials of a domestic nature, being bereaved of all their children (four in number) by sickness and death, at different periods—two of them when only a few years old—a third, an only daughter, at an interesting age, just entering upon the stage of womanhood.[128] Their remaining son attained to mature age, leaving at his decease a wife and infant son.[129]

Being affectionately attached to her children, she felt these bereavements keenly; yet regarding them as a dispensation of her Heavenly Father, she submitted with exemplary resignation. It had been her concern to "bring them up in the nurture and admonition of the Lord;"[130] and in their early removal from this probationary state of being, she was comforted in the belief, that through Divine Mercy, they were admitted into those eternal joys which are prepared for the righteous. In resigning these *plants* which she had nursed with the tenderest maternal care, she was enabled to adopt the language, "The Lord gave, and the Lord hath taken away, blessed be the name of the Lord."[131]

She entertained a lively sympathy with the suffering class of her fellow creatures, from whatever cause those sufferings might arise. Hence[,] she was very attentive in endeavoring to administer to the relief of the sick, who were within her reach. Those who were struggling with scanty means of subsistence, as well as the more abject poor, found in her a steady friend; and her hands were often employed in preparing articles of clothing for the destitute. Many mementos of her generous regard for this class of persons, like "the coats and garments which Dorcas had made,"[132] bear testimony to the kindness of her heart.

She felt tenderly for that oppressed portion of the human family, whose rights as men are torn from them, and they [are] doomed to a state of bondage that is to be transmitted from parents to their children, with the disheartening prospect ever present, that "on the side of their oppressors there is power—but they have no comforters."[133] To her it was a pleasing anticipation, to look forward in hope to the time when, through the humanizing influence of the Christian religion, those having the power should be induced to restore to this injured people, the full enjoyment of that liberty which is the inalienable gift of our common Creator.

The depressed condition of the people of color in the "Free States" likewise attracted her attention and her commiseration. From a desire to promote their improvement, she wrote and published [Sketches][134] of the characters of those of their own people who had most distinguished themselves, with the hope of exciting a spirit of emulation by such examples, that might tend to the elevation of their character. This work was favorably received, and has been extensively circulated.[135]

Sensible of the duty of maintaining a watch over our words as well as conduct, her circumspection[136] on these accounts was such, that rarely, if ever, was an expression, or an act indulged, that could cause uneasiness to another. She was fond of the company of her friends, and her social intercourse with them was free and interesting, often edifying. By her affability and sweetness of disposition, a numerous circle of young persons [was] warmly attached to her. She took pleasure in mingling with them, and was careful to embrace these opportunities to impart instruction and counsel to them.

She was through life diligent in the attendance of religious meetings, when the state of her health would admit of it, and her appearance and deportment on these occasions were such as to bespeak a mind intent on heavenly things. In meetings for discipline, she was particularly serviceable. Sensible of the importance of faithfully maintaining our [C]hristian discipline, she was concerned not only to encourage others in the exercise of this care, but willingly united with her friends in the labor.

For many years she filled the office of Overseer.[137] Her mild and conciliating manner qualified her for this service, and obtained for her a ready ear, from those who were the objects of her concern, to receive the counsel she felt engaged to impart.

She highly prized the Scriptures of Truth, as proceeding from "holy men of God,"[138] who "spake as they were moved by the Holy Ghost,"[139] and as being "written for our learning, that we through patience and comfort of the Scriptures might have hope."[140] Entertaining this view, she was concerned to promote the daily reading of them in her family, and to encourage others in this practice. In the later years of her life, when her hearing had become impaired, it was very interesting to see her at the stated time, seated by the side of her husband, or [an] other person who read, seriously and intently tracing the page with her eye as the reader proceeded.

In the summer of 1847, with her husband she made a visit to her daughter-in-law and [grandson],[141] then residing in Burlington, New Jersey; [they] design[ed] to spend a few months with them, and return. Bodily infirmities had been gaining upon her for several years, and at this period experiencing an increase of debility, and feeling the need of the sympathy, and the kind and watchful attention of her children, she was induced to prolong her stay, and eventually closed her days with them.

To this time[,] we have spoken of the subject of this Memoir, as residing within our own limits, and coming under our own observation. During the few remaining years of her life, her daughter above referred to has furnished the following testimony concerning her.

While residing here, the same mild and Christian virtues exerted their influence over the domestic circle; and very striking and instructive was it, to observe the constant cheerfulness of spirit with which she submitted to the privations which her increasing bodily weakness subjected her to. Early rising was with her a principle as well as a practice, and when she came from her chamber, into the family band, she brought with her a sunshine of peace and serenity, which seemed to diffuse itself on all around her. Separated as she was from her early friends, and from her own particular meeting, her loving spirit attached itself to those objects that were within her reach; and she felt bound to attend meetings both for worship and discipline, as long as she was able to do so. Her example and influence attracted those around her, and attached them to her in a remarkable manner[.] Not only those of the same standing in age and experience, but many young persons sought her society, deriving both pleasure and profit from it. For the poor and needy around her, wherever her lot was cast, her sympathies were called into action; and her hands were often employed in preparing such articles of clothing for their comfort, as lay within her power. These labors of love evidently brought a sweet reward of peace to her mind.

In [the] [n]inth month [of] 1849, she was seized with paralysis[142] from which her recovery appeared doubtful. The power of articulation was for a short time suspended, but her mind under this shock appeared composed and unimpaired. On regaining the use of speech[,] she said, "The will of the Lord be done;"[143] and this state of confiding submission to the will of her Heavenly Father was manifested throughout this afflicting dispensation. Observing her husband to be affected, with much tenderness she said to him, "A happy union such as ours has been, cannot be severed without a pang." Many other instructive and comforting expressions were uttered by her, evincing the strength and clearness of her faith and hope—illustrative of the truth of the declaration, "Thou wilt keep him in perfect peace whose mind is stayed on thee, because he trusteth in thee." [144]

Recovering from this illness, she nearly regained her previous state of health, manifesting the same clearness and strength of mind that had marked her course through life; and was able frequently to attend religious meetings, in which she took great delight. On the [ninth] [day] of [the] [s]eventh month [in] 1851, while seated beside her daughter—to whom she was tenderly attached—with her sewing work in her hand, and apparently as well as usual, a second severe shock of paralysis occurred, by which her whole left side, including that eye, was entirely disabled, and so continued while she lived. The use of speech was lost for some time—her consciousness, not entirely.

The following particulars respecting this illness, and the close of her life, are taken from notes preserved at the time.

Her husband was from home at the time of this attack, attending the Monthly Meeting of which he was a member. His return was hastened by a message informing him of her illness. On his entering her room, she was able to receive and greet him with her usual affection, saying with a sweetness that seemed almost heavenly, "Welcome, always welcome, even from our youth."

Hopes were for a time entertained, that the disease might so far yield, as to admit of her being again about, still a little longer to cheer the family circle by her delightful society. But it soon became evident that the disease was progressing with a steady pace. With true Christian fortitude, and entire resignation to the Divine Will, she submitted without a murmur to the afflictive dispensation; nor did she during its continuance, at any time[,] express a desire that it should be otherwise. Her trust for support was in her Saviour, whom she had long loved, and she loved him to the end. Her faith was unwavering in the salvation that cometh by Jesus Christ.

Such was the pressure of the disease, while her physical powers were becoming a wreck, that it was feared the mind would also give way; but it was wonderful (and we record it with gratitude to our Heavenly Father) that throughout this sore disease of five weeks' continuance, her recollection remained clear; and such an extensive range of thought, such an interest in passing events, such warm affection for her friends, such solicitude for the progress of vital religion and the support of the testimonies of our religious society, were manifested as was truly admirable. Whatever she said of herself, all was in reference to her Heavenly Father, her darling[145] theme being, "[']The will of the Lord be done,['] that is what I desire." [146]

During the progress of the disease, though often so distressed with restlessness that it was impossible for her to be still, she uttered many expressions indicating her abiding trust in the everlasting Arm of Divine support. Pretty early in her sickness she remarked that she was very sick; that she did not know how the disease would terminate, but that a few days would show, and that she was content.

For several days in the fore part of her illness she appeared inclined to quiet and deep thoughtfulness. During this season of comparative seclusion, though under much physical suffering from nervous irritability, she was wonderfully preserved, not only in patience and resignation to the Divine will, but in thankfulness also, which she often expressed, frequently repeating the language, "'The will of the Lord be done.'"

She uniformly spoke of herself with great humility and abasedness; and when alluding to her hope of happiness, it was always with subdued language.— There was nothing e[cs]tatic in her views, very little allusion to *feelings*, and the *brightness* of her prospects; but a living faith in that grace which had been her guide through life, and which she felt to be sufficient for her on the bed of sickness and suffering.

On one occasion, when some beloved friends were sitting by her, without anything being said to lead to the subject, she repeated distinctly those lines of Cowper, "'I would not have a slave to till my ground, / To carry me, to fan me while I sleep, / And tremble when I wake, for all the wealth / That sinews[147] bought and sold have ever earned;'" [148] adding, "'what is done for me is done freely:'" and then [she] spoke encouragingly to those friends, to bear their testimony against slavery, by declining the use of articles produced by the unrequited labor of the poor slaves, who are as much the objects of Redeeming love as ourselves.[149] This is a subject respecting which she had long felt concern.

[On the] morning [of the] 28th of [the] [s]eventh month[,] [t]he dear invalid was favored to be rather more free from nervous distress, than was generally the case. She said, "It is a great favor to be thus relieved," adding, "I trust the Lord will have mercy upon me," and repeating the following lines: "'There is mercy in every place, / And mercy, encouraging thought, / Gives even affliction a grace, / And reconciles man to his lot.'" [150]

Shortly after she said, "There may be a struggle at last, I don't know[.] I can't see much, but I have peace and happiness. [']The will of the Lord be done['] for ever." Then speaking to a person who was waiting upon her, and for whom she had a great regard, she said, "I hope thou wilt be rewarded for all thy kindness to me." Soon after she said, "I have prayed, for your sakes, as well as my own, that I may have an easy passage when I go hence. But [']the will of the Lord be done[']—that is what I desire."

[On the] morning [of the third day during this illness,] [a]s her husband was sitting by her side, her countenance radiant with heavenly love, she said to him with much sweetness, "Don't be sad, endeavor to be cheerful. Thou wilt be cared for.—We have many kind, good friends."

On one occasion she was told, that the doctor said, he thought her situation even on the bed of sickness, was so happy, that he would be glad to exchange with her, if he could. "Tell him then, to do as I have endeavored to do—[']strive to enter in at the straight gate[']¹⁵¹—there is no other way to the kingdom," was the emphatic reply.

At another time she spoke of the parable of the vine and the branches, as being beautiful and instructive, repeating much of it, and saying, "Oh, the blessedness of abiding in the vine, that we may bring forth fruit, and thus become the disciples of Christ." ¹⁵² Soon after she repeated the passage, "'The foxes have holes, and the birds of the air have nests, but the Son of man hath not where to lay his head.'" ¹⁵³ "The Lord of all had no house in which to dwell." ¹⁵⁴

[On the] morning [of the third day of the eighth month], while a beloved relative was sitting by her side, with a sweet and impressive countenance[,] she said, "There is rest, and peace, and joy, in Heaven: I know nothing of myself; but I feel that it is so: I had hoped to be in the enjoyment of it before this time. But we must have patience—we shall have to wait a little longer." She then spoke of the great goodness and mercy of a kind Providence in bestowing upon *man* so many good things—and every thing so exactly suited to his capacity for enjoyment. "Yes," said she, "there have been many favors extended, even to poor me." Shortly after she said very sweetly, "'Our Father which art in Heaven.'" ¹⁵⁵ "Oh, what a favor to be able to call Him our Father, and to feel him truly to be so." At another time, as her husband approached her bed-side, she said, "It is a great comfort to believe that we have four dear children in heaven."

The same evening she had a low sinking turn—such [problem] had several times occurred during her illness. She appeared to think at this time, as did others also, that the last struggle was near; and she distinctly uttered the heart-touching words, "Ready—all ready." Reviving again, she submissively said, "We must have patience a little longer. [']The will of the Lord be done.[']"

At this advanced stage of her disease, her numerous inquiries concerning absent friends, and events that were taking place in the world, showed plainly that an extensive range of thought was passing in her mind. She spoke very affectionately of a Friend[156] then engaged in an arduous and important mission in Africa, desiring that a blessing might attend her labors. With deep concern she inquired whether there was a probability that the war[157] that was then going on in a part of that continent, would soon be ended—saying, "Oh, it is so cruel!" And then expressed in strong terms, her great desire that universal peace might prevail in the world.

[On the] morning [of the seventh day of the eighth month,] [she,] [h]aving passed a wearisome night, [became] more easy, and as she was lying comfortably upon the pillow, with a look beautifully serene, she said, "If I could have my wish, how I should love to pass quietly away, as I now lay. But the Lord's will be done."

[The] [s]ixth day [of this period of illness] to her was one of much suffering. Great nervous irritability rendered it exceedingly difficult to be still, which she regretted. She had declined taking nourishment through the day, until about four o'clock in the afternoon, when she took a little from a glass in her own hands. After this she answered several questions, showing that her recollection was yet clear. About this time she was taken from her bed to have it made comfortable for the night, which she bore, apparently, as well as usual. On being again replaced in bed, she appeared exceedingly feeble, and after lying a short time entirely still, she was observed to gasp once or twice, and life was extinct.

Thus was answered her petition, that if consistent with the Divine will, she might have an easy passage out of time. So easy was her release, as to be like falling asleep without the least distortion of her features, on the [eighth] [day] of [the] [e]ighth month [in] 1851.

Thus passed the venerable and beloved Abigail Mott, from a state of trial and probation on [E]arth, to a state, as we reverently believe, of rest, and peace, and joy, in Heaven—the hope of which had been her solace through life, and her support in the solemn hour of death.

"Here is the patience of the saints; here are they that keep the commandments of God, and the faith of Jesus." [158]

Notes

1. The Motts quote The Wisdom of Solomon 4:9.
2. The Motts quote part of Romans 11:33.
3. The Motts likely reference Isaiah 33:6.
4. The Motts quote part of line 274 from epistle II, "Of the Nature and State of Man with [R]espect to Himself, as an Individual," from Alexander Pope's *An Essay on Man*, published in London in 1733–34. This part from Pope's poem first appeared in *An Essay on Man. In Epistles to a Friend. Epistle II* (London: Printed for J. Wilford, 1733). The stanza in which this language appears reads as follows: "See! some strange *Comfort* ev'ry *State* attend, / And *Pride* bestow'd on all, a common Friend; / See! some fit

Passion ev'ry *Age* supply, / Hope travels thro', nor quits us when we die" (17; emphases in original).

5. The Motts likely quote part of Ephesians 4:21.
6. The Motts refer to *A Journal or Historical Account of the Life, Travels, Sufferings, Christian Experiences and Labour of Love in the Work of the Ministry, of that Ancient, Eminent and Faithful Servant of Jesus Christ, George Fox; Who Departed this Life in Great Peace with the Lord, the 13th of the 11th Month, 1690* (London: Printed for Thomas Northcott, 1694). The title of Fox's *Journal* mutates through its publishing history. Isaac Collins printed the corrected, fourth edition of Fox's *Journal*, composed of two volumes, in New York in 1800. According to Larry Ingle, a contributor to the *Historical Dictionary of the Friends (Quakers)*, ed. Margery Post Abbott, Mary Ellen Chijioke, Pink Dandelion, and John William Oliver Jr., 2nd ed. (Plymouth, UK: Scarecrow, 2012), Fox may be considered the "principal founder and organizer of the Religious Society of Friends" (133). According to Elizabeth Cazden, in "Quakers, Slavery, Anti-[S]lavery, and Race," in *The Oxford Handbook of Quaker Studies*, ed. Stephen W. Angell and Pink Dandelion (New York: Oxford University Press, 2013), Fox "preached to enslaved Africans in the West Indies" (348).
7. The Motts refer to *A History of the People Called Quakers. From their [F]irst Rise to the [P]resent Time. Compiled from Authentic Records, and from the Writings of that People. By John Gough*, 4 vols. (Dublin: Printed for Robert Jackson, 1789-1790). In the preface from the first volume, Gough pinpoints why he chose to offer a fresh history of Quakers:

> Yet some modern authors of reputation in the learned world have thought it worth their while to revive long refuted calumnies, and debase the page of history with a delineation of this people, copied from the distorted caricatures of their bitterest antagonists; the consideration whereof pointed out the propriety of a new review of their real history, drawn from authentic memoirs, and genuine records, preserved in their own archives; that by comparing their own accounts of themselves, with those of their adversaries, a more impartial judgment may be formed of their real character. (iii-iv)

8. According to the *Oxford English Dictionary*, this term may be understood as "[t]o value (subjectively); to attribute value to; to appreciate the worth of; to esteem, hold in (higher or lower) estimation."
9. According to the *Oxford English Dictionary*, this term may be understood as "[h]urtful relaxation, softening, or weakening; enfeeblement."
10. According to the *Oxford English Dictionary*, this term may be understood as "[t]he position of a guardian or tutor in relation to a ward; guardianship."
11. According to the *Oxford English Dictionary*, this term may be understood as "[d]isordered bodily condition; ill health, illness, ailment."
12. In *The Cox Family in America: A History and Genealogy of the Older Branches of the Family from the Appearance of Its First Representative in This Country in 1610* (New York: Printed for the Author, 1912), Henry Miller Cox identifies Quaker John Cox (1754-1847), occasionally referred to as John Cox Jr., as "a prominent member and well known preacher of the Society of Friends . . . [who] became the head of the Friend's Meeting" in Burlington, New Jersey (219). Additionally, in her March 15, 1822, letter to James Mott Sr., included in *Selected Letters of Lucretia Coffin Mott*, ed. Beverly Wilson Palmer (Urbana: University of Illinois Press, 2002), Lucretia Mott references having spent "several days" (10) with John Cox and his wife, Ann Dillwyn Cox (1746-1838). According to this letter, the Coxes wished to inform Richard and Abigail Mott via Lucretia Mott's missive to James Mott Sr. that they "generally look for a visit

from them next mo[nth]." In *First City: Philadelphia and the Forging of Historical Memory* (Philadelphia: University of Pennsylvania Press, 2002), Gary B. Nash identifies the Quaker Nathaniel Coleman as a Burlington, New Jersey silversmith (248). Coleman's home located at 320 High Street is part of the Burlington Historic District Tour. The Motts refer to Stanford, a town in the northern and central region of Duchess County, a part of the state of New York near the northwestern part of Connecticut.

13. According to Pink Dandelion, a contributor to Abbott et al., *Historical Dictionary of the Friends (Quakers)*, the term "meeting" is "the shorthand name for meeting for worship" (216).
14. According to the *Oxford English Dictionary*, the verb "subjoin" may be understood as "[t]o add at the end of a spoken or written statement, argument, or discourse."
15. According to the *Oxford English Dictionary*, the verb "set" may be understood as "[t]o cause to sit, seat; to be seated, sit."
16. According to the *Oxford English Dictionary*, the verb "prosecute" may be understood as "[t]o follow up, pursue; to persevere or persist in, follow out, go on with (some action, undertaking, or purpose) with a view to completing or attaining it."
17. According to the *Oxford English Dictionary*, this term may be understood as "[w]ant of serious thought or refle[ction]; frivolity."
18. According to the *Oxford English Dictionary*, this term may be understood as "[a] medicine or drug which alleviates pain."
19. Helen is likely the individual the Motts describe as a "young woman with whom she [Maria] was intimately acquainted." The Motts offer this description two paragraphs above the one in which Maria names her friend.
20. For this point on Dr. Samuel Johnson (1709–1784), author, editor, and lexicographer, Maria Mott likely draws from the following passage in volume 2 of *The Life of Samuel Johnson, LL.D. Comprehending An Account of His Studies and Numerous Works, in Chronological Order; A Series of His Epistolary Correspondence and Conversations with Many Eminent Persons; And Various Original Pieces of His Composition, Never Before Published. The Whole Exhibiting a View of Literature and Literary Men in Great-Britain, For Near Half A Century, During Which He Flourished. In Two Volumes. By James Boswell, Esq.* (London: Henry Baldwin, 1791):

    > The horrour of death which I had always observed in Dr. Johnson, appeared strong to-night. I ventured to tell him, that I had been, for moments in my life, not afraid of death; therefore I could suppose another man in that state of mind for a considerable space of time. He said, "he never had a moment in which death was not terrible to him." He added, that it had been observed, that scarce any man dies in publick, but with apparent resolution; from that desire of praise which never quits us. I said, Dr. Dodd seemed to be willing to die, and full of hopes of happiness. "Sir, (said he,) Dr. Dodd would have given both his hands and both his legs to have lived. The better a man is, the more afraid he is of death, having a clearer view of infinite purity." (143–44)

21. Maria Mott quotes part of Isaiah 25:6.
22. According to the *Oxford English Dictionary*, this term may be understood as "[c]haracterized or affected by trembling or quivering from nervous agitation or weakness, of mental or physical origin."
23. The Motts quote Psalm 37:37.
24. Mott references James 5:7.
25. Mott quotes Mark 13:37.
26. According to the *Oxford English Dictionary*, the term "meridian" may be understood

as "[p]ertaining to or characteristic of the period of greatest elevation or splendour (of a person, state, institution, etc.)."

27. According to the *Oxford English Dictionary*, this term may be understood as "[a] fitting or suitable helper; a helpmate: usually applied to a wife or husband."
28. Mott quotes Proverbs 31:30–31, 27, 11–12, and 26.
29. For these points from Charles-Louis de Secondat, Baron of Montesquieu (1698–1755), a French writer and political philosopher, Mott quotes John Burton's *Lectures on Female Education and Manners*, vol. 1, 2nd ed. (London: Printed for J. Johnson and J. Murray, 1793). In lecture 5, Burton makes the following points:

> The celebrated Montesquieu, speaking of the influence of the female Sex on public manners, says, that the safety of a state depends upon the virtues of the Women. Hence it is, that the sage Legislators of Republics have required of them a sedateness of behaviour; and have endeavoured to correct that false taste, which inspires them with a value of trifles, and which debases things of consequence. The same Author observes, that Greece owed much of its wise Polity to the chastity and [economical] virtues of [its] Women. (73–74)

For his commentary on Montesquieu, Burton draws on *The Spirit of Laws. Translated from the French of M. De Secondat, Baron de Montesquieu. With Corrections and Additions [C]ommunicated by the Author*, vol. 1 (London: Printed for J. Nourse and P. Vaillant, 1750), one of the first English translations. In book 8, "Consequences of the [D]ifferent [P]rinciples of the [T]hree Governments with [R]espect to [S]umptuary Laws, Luxury, and the Condition of Women," chapter 9, "Of the Condition or State of Women in [D]ifferent Governments," Montesquieu writes:

> In republics[,] women are free by the laws, and constrained by manners; luxury is banished from hence, and with it corruption and vice. In the cities of Greece, where they [women] were not under the restraint of a religion which declares that even amongst men a purity of morals is a part of virtue; cities where a blind passion triumphed with a boundless insolence, and love appeared only in a shape which we dare not mention, while marriage was considered as nothing more than simple friendship; such were the virtue, simplicity, and chastity of women in those cities, that in this respect no people hardly were ever known to have had a better and wiser polity. (149)

30. For these points on Ethelbert and Bertha, Mott mostly draws from David Hume's *The History of England, from the Invasion of Julius Caesar to the Accession of Henry VII*, vol. 1 (London: Printed for A. Millar, 1762). In chapter 1, Hume writes:

> But these causes might long have failed of operating their effect, had not a favourable incident prepared the means of introducing Christianity into Kent. Ethelbert, in his father's lifetime, had married Bertha, the only daughter of Caribert, King of Paris, one of the descendants of Clovis, the conqueror of Gaul; but before he was admitted to this alliance, he was obliged to stipulate, that the princess should enjoy the free exercise of her religion; a concession not difficult to be obtained from the idolatrous Saxons. Bertha brought over a French bishop to the court of Canterbury; and being zealous for the propagation of her religion, she had been very assiduous in her devotional exercises, had supported the credit of her faith by an irreproachable conduct, and had employed every art of insinuation and address to reconcile her husband to her religious principles. Her popularity in the court, and her influence over Ethelbert, had so well paved the way for the reception of the Christian doctrine, that Gregory, surnamed the

Great, the present Roman pontiff, began to entertain hopes of effectuating a project, which he himself, before he mounted the papal throne, had once embraced for converting the British Saxons. (22)

31. Mott quotes 1 Kings 16:31 and 1 Kings 21:25.
32. Mott quotes 1 Kings 22:52.
33. Mott quotes 2 Kings 8:18 and 2 Chronicles 22:3.
34. Mott draws on Proverbs 29:2, which she may have misremembered. The KJV reads: "When the righteous are in authority, the people rejoice: but when the wicked beareth rule, the people mourn."
35. Mott quotes from letter 12, "Associations [I]nspiring the Love of Wealth," in *Letters on Education* (Bath: Printed for R. Cruttwell, 1801), vol. 1, 325, written by Elizabeth Hamilton (1756?–1816). Hamilton, a friend of Sir Walter Scott (1771–1832) and Maria Edgeworth (1768–1849), wrote the following texts in addition to *Letters on Education*: *Translations of the Letters of a Hindoo Rajah* (1796), *Memoirs of Modern Philosophers* (1800), *Letters on the Elementary Principles of Education* (1801), *Letters Addressed to the Daughter of a Nobleman* (1806), and *The Cottagers of Glenburnie* (1808). For more on Hamilton's life, consult *Memoirs of the Late Mrs. Elizabeth Hamilton. With A Selection from Her Correspondence and Other Unpublished Writings. By Miss Benger* (London: Printed for Longman, Hurst, Rees, Orme, and Brown, 1818), 2 vols.
36. According to the *Oxford English Dictionary*, this term may be understood as "[a] hard morbid concretion in the body, especially in the kidney or urinary bladder, or in the gallbladder."
37. Mott selectively quotes from *Memoirs of Richard Lovell Edgeworth, Esq. Begun by Himself and Concluded by His Daughter, Maria Edgeworth* (London: Printed for R. Hunter, 1820), vol. 1, 105, 106, 107–8, 32, 26, and 108. Wells and Lily published an edition of *Memoirs* in Boston in 1821. Mott was likely attracted to the life of Richard Edgeworth (1744–1817) because of his popular book on education, *Practical Education* (1788), on which his daughter, Maria (1768–1849), a novelist and educational theorist, collaborated. The Edgeworths structured some of *Practical Education* based on conversations between children and adults. Mott used this same organizational structure in *The Mother and Her Children, or Twilight Conversation* (New York: Mahlon Day, 1828). In 1807 Samuel Wood sold Maria Edgeworth's *The Contrast*.
38. Mott selectively quotes from *Edgeworth*, vol. 1, 28–30.
39. Mott quotes part of Exodus 2:9.
40. According to the *Oxford English Dictionary*, the verb "wroth" may be understood as "[t]o become wrathful or angry; to manifest anger."
41. Mott quotes part of Genesis 4:7.
42. Mott quotes Psalm 103:13.
43. Mott quotes Psalm 103:2.
44. Mott quotes part of Revelation 21:6 and all of 21:7.
45. Some of the topics Hamilton addressed in her two-volume *Letters on Education* include the following: "An Examination into the End and Object of Education," "Associations Producing the Passion of Fear," "Religion," "On the Cultivation of Benevolence," "Partiality: [I]ts Pernicious Effects. Associations [P]roducing Contempt for the Female Character: [T]heir Consequences," "Objects of Sense: Use to be [M]ade of [T]hese in [I]nfant Education," "Associations Inspiring the Love of Wealth," "Children's Books," "Hints Toward Developing [Perception] Cultivation in [E]arly Infancy," "Religious Instruction of the Poor, of the Rich," "Imagination [D]efined," and "Character of [T]hose who Object to the Cultivation of the Reasoning Faculty in the Female Sex," among others. According to the *National Union Catalog* (London: Mansell, 1972), vol. 228,

Hamilton's *Letters*, with variations on the title, continued to be published as late as 1837 (455).
46. Mott quotes from letter 5, "Religion," in Hamilton, *Letters on Education*, vol. 1, 119–21.
47. Mott quotes part of Matthew 19:14.
48. Graham Russell Hodges provides the following information in *Root and Branch: African Americans in New York and East Jersey, 1613–1863* (Chapel Hill: University of North Carolina Press, 1999): "In the 1820s, the Clarkson Benevolent Association sponsored a school for aged black women who wished to learn how to read and write. The testimonies of the elderly students, ranging in age from sixty-eight to over one hundred years, were living reminders of the days of general slavery in New York" (219). Hodges notes that Mott included in *Biographical Sketches and Interesting Anecdotes of Persons of Colour. To Which Is Added, A Selection of Pieces in Poetry. Compiled by A. Mott* (New York: Mahlon Day, 1826) the testimonies of some students who attended this school. See the biographical sketches of Zilpha Montjoy (49–52) and Belinda Lucas (52–55), both of which appear before the biographical sketch of Gustavus Vassa or Olaudah Equiano. The numbering of the paragraphs in *Biographical Sketches* may be understood by the following "Note By The Publisher":

> By consent of the Compiler, and at the recommendation of the Trustees of the African Free Schools in New-York (who have liberally patronized the work)[,] the pieces in the following compilation have been divided into reading sections, with a view to have the volume introduced into Schools, as a Class Book. It is hoped this arrangement will be equally agreeable to Subscribers, and to those Trustees who may use it in their Schools. (ii)

49. The author of "A[frican] S[chools] [in] N[ew]-Y[ork]" likely refers to the New York Association for the Instruction of Coloured Male Adults. Two record books of this association, dated 1816–1819, may be found at the American Antiquarian Society. According to the American Antiquarian Society library catalog,

> Members of the Society of Friends organized the New York Association for the Instruction of Coloured Male Adults in 1816, with schools established at Rose St. and Flatbush. The stated purpose of the Association was to enable black Americans to read the scriptures through free instruction. The school met weekly under the management of Rueben [sic] Leggett (1791–1826) and Isaac Hatch ([birth and death dates unknown]).

As early as 1818, Leggett was a trustee of the New York African Free School. For more on the involvement of another trustee of the New York African Free School in the Association, Samuel Wood, consult "Rethinking Textual Paradigms in Early Black Atlantic Studies" (appendix A).
50. Charles C. Andrews, historian of the New York African Free Schools and teacher at one of the Free Schools, indicates that this information appeared in the New York periodical, the *Commercial Advertiser*, on Wednesday, May 12, 1824. See Charles C. Andrews, *History of the New-York African Free-Schools, from Their Establishment in 1787, to the Present Time; Embracing a Period of More Than Forty Years: Also a Brief Account of the Successful Labors, of the New-York Manumission Society: With an Appendix* (New York: Mahlon Day, 1830), 38.
51. The contributor to the *Commercial Advertiser* quotes part of book 5, "The Winter Morning Walk," from *The Task, a Poem, in Six Books. By William Cowper, of the Inner Temple, Esq.* (London: Printed for J. Johnson, 1785), 208. The line in Cowper's book (along with the three that follow) reads as follows: "But there is yet a liberty unsung /

By poets, and by senators unpraised, / Which monarchs cannot grant, nor all the powers / Of earth and hell confed'rate take away" (208–9). For more information on Cowper, consult the notes on *Life and Adventures of Olaudah Equiano*.

52. Not much is known about Eliza J. Cox. Andrews, in *History of the New-York African Free-Schools*, references Cox as a teacher who taught Black girls and helped "the female department [continue] to sustain its high character for order and usefulness" (22).

53. Andrews wrote *History of the New-York African Free-Schools*. Andrews identifies himself as "*Teacher of African Free School, No. 2*," located at 135 Mulberry Street, in his November 9, 1827, letter to John B. Russwurm, an editor of *Freedom's Journal* (appendix B). Andrews was dismissed from the school in 1833 for his support of Liberian colonization. See Anna Mae Duane, *Suffering Childhood in Early America: Violence, Race, and the Making of the Child Victim* (Athens: University of Georgia Press, 2010), 172.

54. Baldwin's letter to her teacher, Miss Cox, was printed in the November 9, 1824, issue of the New York periodical *Spectator*. The following paragraph appeared before Baldwin's letter:

> The following letter has been received within a few days past, by Miss Cox, the amiable and intelligent instructress of the Female African Free School in this city. It was written by a little black girl, one of her late pupils, of only 12 years of age, whose parents were among the Emigrants to Hayti, who sailed in the brig [*De Witt Clinton*] from this city. The letter is neatly and correctly written, and may be examined in this office. We publish it for two reasons. First, to show that the emigrants are pleased and happy in their new residence; and, secondly, to show that black children can learn to read and write with as much facility as white ones.

Ousmane K. Power-Greene articulates in *Against Wind and Tide: The African American Struggle Against the Colonization Movement* (New York: New York University Press, 2014) that

> over 8,000 black Americans settled in Haiti during the 1820s alone. Even though this number is no more impressive than the number of blacks who left for Liberia, free African American spokespersons and leaders seemed much more eager to promote Haitian emigration than colonization in Liberia. Such interest in Haiti actually worked to undermine the American Colonization Society because both Haitian emigration advocates and ACS colonizationists competed for funds and potential recruits in free black communities throughout the nation. (xviii)

55. Baldwin refers to Jean Pierre Henry, identified as the Port Captain of Santo Domingo in *Almanach pour l'année 1825, An 22 de l'Indépendance d'Haïti, Contenant les noms de tous les Fonctionnaires publics, civils, et militaires de l'Arrondissement de Santo-Domingo* (Santo Domingo: Imprimé par J. M. Gonzalez et Cie, 1824), Library of Congress, Washington, D.C., Microform and Electronic Resources Division, Collection Mangonès, Reel 6, 23–24, p. 40. For this source, I am indebted to Andrew Walker.

56. Baldwin likely refers to the highest-ranking military officer, Jérôme Maximilien Borgella (1773–1844), the division general of the District of Santo Domingo. See *Almanach pour l'année 1825*, 33.

57. Baldwin likely refers to Bernard-Philippe Alexis Carrié, the brigadier general for Santo Domingo. See *Almanach pour l'année 1825*, 39.

58. Baldwin likely visited the Cathedral of Santa María la Menor, the first Catholic cathedral constructed in the Americas by the Spanish, completed in 1541.

59. "She" refers to Baldwin. Unfortunately, Mott trims this part of the New York African Free School alumna's letter.
60. According to the *Oxford English Dictionary*, this term may be understood as "[a] quantity of thread or yarn, wound to a certain length upon a reel, and usually put up in a kind of loose knot."
61. Baldwin's commentary on her family farming land outside of Santo Domingo mirrors one of the ways in which Jean Pierre Boyer, president of Haiti, marketed the Caribbean nation. In an April 30, 1824, letter, included in *Correspondence Relative to the Emigration to Hayti, of the Free People of Colour, in the United States. Together with the Instructions to the Agent Sent out by President Boyer* (New York: Mahlon Day, 1824), Boyer writes that he has "given land to those who wished to cultivate it" and maintains that the Haitian government "will give fertile lands to those who wish to cultivate them, will advance to them nourishment, tools, and other things of indispensable necessity until they shall be sufficiently established to do without this assistance" (8–9). Boyer further holds that "[t]he quantity of ground shall be as much as each family can cultivate" (9). Boyer also utilized the metaphor of African Americans as plants in a May 25, 1824, letter:

> What joy will it give hearts like yours [that of Mr. Collins of New York, the addressee of the missive], to see scions of Africa, so abased in the United States, where they vegetate with no more utility to themselves than to the soil which nourishes them, transplanted to Hayti, where they will become no less useful than estimable, because the enjoyment of civil and political rights, ennobling them in their own eyes, cannot fail to attach them to regular habits, and the acquisition of social virtues, and to render them worthy by their good conduct, to enjoy the benefits which their new country will bestow upon them! (16)

62. January 1 marks the day on which Haitians declared independence from France in 1804.
63. For information on the locations of New York African Free Schools, see the notes on "A[frican] F[ree] S[chool]" from the January 25, 1828, issue of *Freedom's Journal* (appendix B). Consult, as well, *Plan of the City of New-York* (New York: A. T. Goodrich, 1825), which offers the locations of several important New York City landmarks, many of which New York African Free Schools students would have passed on their way to and from the educational institution.
64. For an explanation of the rule of three, consult the notes on *Life and Adventures of Olaudah Equiano*.
65. Mott includes the following note on this page of *Biographical Sketches*: "These contributions chiefly consist of school tickets of reward, bearing a nominal value, which the teacher receives for cash, and places to the credit of the class. These funds, with the consent of the teacher, are disposed of by the class in purchasing books for the library, &c" (160n).
66. For information on how the trustees handled New York African Free School students' use of bad language, see the section titled "Of [U]sing Profane and Indecent Language," in *An Address to the Parents and Guardians of the Children Belonging to the New-York African Free-School, by the Trustees of the Institution* (New York: Samuel Wood and Sons, 1818), 11. For the *Address*, see appendix B.
67. For an explanation of examination days at the New York African Free Schools, consult the notes on *Life and Adventures of Olaudah Equiano*.
68. According to the *Oxford English Dictionary*, the term "approbation" may be understood as "[t]he action of expressing oneself pleased or satisfied with anything; or the mere feeling of such satisfaction; approval expressed or entertained."

69. According to the *Oxford English Dictionary*, this term may be understood as "[o]ne who instructs; a teacher, instructor, tutor."
70. For a definition of the word "pence," consult the notes on *Life and Adventures of Olaudah Equiano* (15).
71. Willliam refers to Equiano's final master, Philadelphia Quaker Robert King. For Equiano's and King's conversation on the slave acquiring his freedom, see *Life and Adventures of Olaudah Equiano* (17).
72. In *The Interesting Narrative of the Life of Olaudah Equiano, or Gustavus Vassa, the African. Written by Himself* (New York: W. Durell, 1791), vol. 1, Equiano offers the following commentary on three pence: "After I had been sailing for some time with [Captain Farmer], at length I endeavoured to try my luck and commence merchant. I had but a very small capital to begin with; for one single half bit, which is equal to threepence in England, made up my whole stock. However[,] I trusted to the Lord to be with me; and at one of our trips to *St. Eustatia*, a Dutch island[,] I bought a glass tumbler with my half bit, and when I came to Montserrat I sold it for a bit, or six pence" (166–67). See *Life and Adventures of Olaudah Equiano* for Equiano's commentary on the three pence (15).
73. For this shipwreck scene on one of the Bahama islands in William Durell's edition of the *Interesting Narrative*, consult vol. 2 (29–41). Equiano notes the following after approaching the flamingoes, who some crew members mistaken for cannibals: "Accordingly[,] we steered towards them; and when we approached them, to our very great joy and no less wonder, they walked off one after the other very deliberately; and at last they took flight and relieved us entirely from our fears" (37). For this shipwreck scene in Mott's abridged edition, consult *Life and Adventures of Olaudah Equiano* (18). In *Life and Adventures*, Mott excises Equiano's comment, one found in Durell's edition, that him and his colleagues were transporting "several slaves" (28) from St. Eustatia to Georgia when they shipwrecked in the Bahamas. Mott also eliminates the fact that a team composed of Equiano, "three black men[,] and a Dutch creole" (34) were largely responsible for saving their colleagues, many of whom turned to drink instead of orchestrating ways to survive.
74. For this point by Mother and ones that follow on the shipwreck of Commander Joseph Kirle's *Reformation*, Mott draws on *God[']s Protecting Providence Man's Surest Help and Defence in the Times of the [G]reatest [D]ifficulty and [M]ost Imminent [D]anger; Evidenced in the Remarkable Deliverance [o]f [D]ivers Persons, [f]rom the [D]evouring Waves of the Sea, amongst which [T]hey Suffered Shipwrack. And also [f]rom the [M]ore [C]ruelly [D]evouring [J]awes of the [I]nhumane Canibals of Florida. Faithfully [R]elated by [O]ne of the [P]ersons [C]oncerned [T]herein, Jonathan Dickenson* (Philadelphia: Reinier Jansen, 1699). Evangeline Walker Andrews and Charles McLean Andrews identify fourteen reprints in English of *God[']s Protecting Providence*, also known as Jonathan Dickinson's *Journal*, between 1700 and 1868 (177). For their work on the publishing history of this text, see "Reprints" in *Jonathan Dickinson's Journal or, God's Protecting Providence. Being the Narrative of a Journey from Port Royal in Jamaica to Philadelphia between August 23, 1696 and April 1, 1697*, eds. Evangeline Walker Andrews and Charles McLean Andrews (New Haven: Yale University Press, 1945), 177–96. Samuel Wood identified this narrative as "Jonathan Dickerson's [sic] Shipwreck" in his advertisement on books "For Sale By Samuel Wood" on the last page of Jupiter Hammon's *An Address to the Negroes in the State of New-York* (New York: Samuel Wood, 1806). Evangeline Walker Andrews writes, in the introduction to the Andrews' edition of Dickinson's *Journal*, that the *Reformation* was "laden with the usual trading cargo of sugar, molasses and rum, beef and pork, barreled and on the hoof, clothing, and varieties of stuffs, wine, chocolate, 'a great glass wherein was five or

six pounds of butter,' ginger, and Spanish money in the form of plate and pieces of eight, the eventual loss of which, as we learn later, came to £1500, a very large sum at that time" (8). She also speculates on why Dickinson, along with family members and slaves, boarded the *Reformation*:

> For exactly what reason Jonathan Dickinson was sailing at this particular moment, we do not know; but it seems reasonable to believe that he had chartered the *Reformation* as a strictly commercial venture, made necessary by the earthquake which had laid so much of Port Royal under water, though miraculously sparing his father's store. Also, it is possible that the general disorder which had befallen the island—both because of the earthquake and of the continuing French attacks that devastated scores of plantations along the eastern coast—may have decided him to transfer his business as a whole to Philadelphia. The fact that he took with him on this voyage not only his wife and child but also ten Negroes seems to confirm this opinion, though later, at Philadelphia, he sometimes queried the advisability of keeping a permanent residence there. (8)

75. In the entry for "7 Month, 23; the 4th day of the week" from *God[']s Protecting Providence*, Dickinson writes: "As we were under a deep exercise and concernment, a motion arose from one of us that if we should put ourselves under the denomination of the Spaniards (it being well known that that nation had some influence on them) and one of us named Solomon Cresson speaking the Spanish language well, it was hoped this might be a means for our delivery, to which the most of the company assented" (6–7). Dickinson identifies Cresson as one of the "Mariners" (1).

76. According to the 1699 edition of *God[']s Protecting Providence*, Dickinson names twenty-five individuals who were on the *Reformation* when it left Port Royal, Jamaica, for Philadelphia, Pennsylvania, on August 23, 1696. Dickinson identifies Barrow, his wife, Mary Dickinson, his young son, Jonathan Dickinson ("a sucking Child six months old") and Benjamin Allen as "Passengers" (1). Dickinson categorizes passengers Peter, London, Jack, Cesar, and Cajoe ("a Child") as "Negro Men," "[b]elonging to Jonathan Dickinson" (1). Dickinson classifies passengers Hagar, Sarah, Bella, Susanna, and Quensa as "Negro Women" "[b]elonging to Jonathan Dickinson." Venus, "an Indian Girl," last on the list of women "[b]elonging to Jonathan Dickinson," concludes the author's list of passengers on the *Reformation*. Dickinson includes Richard Limpeney ("Mate"), Solomon Cresson, Joseph Buckley, Thomas Fownes, Thomas Jemmet, Nathaniel Randall, John Hilliard ("the Master's Boy"), and Ben ("the Master's Negro") as "Mariners."

77. In the entry for "9 Month, 15; the [1st] of the week" from *God[']s Protecting Providence*, Dickinson observes: "Robert Limpeney and those that went with him had a hard travel for thirty-six hours without ceasing, in which travel three of our Negroes that went with them were lost (viz Jack, Cesar, and Quensa), by sitting down to rest themselves they were in a little time so numbed that they could not go, and there perished" (72). In the entry for "9 Month, 14; the 7th of the week" from *God[']s Protecting Providence*, Dickinson writes: "I understood that our Negro woman Hagar got hither late last night having her child [Cajoe] dead at her back, which the Spaniards buried" (70).

78. In the entry for "2 Month, 4; the [1st] of the week" from *God[']s Protecting Providence*, Dickinson comments on Barrow: "This day in the evening Robert Barrow departed this life and was buried the 6 instant having passed through great exercises in much patience; and in all the times of our greatest troubles was ready to counsel us to patience and to wait what the Lord our God would bring to pass" (96). In an earlier part of *God[']s Protecting Providence*, Dickinson writes:

Sometime before night Robert Barrow was exhorting us to be patient and in a godly manner did he expound the text of scripture: *Because thou hast kept the word of my patience &c.* Rev., 3 Chap., 10 ver., after which he ended with a most fervent prayer desiring of the Lord that whereas He had suffered us to be cast amongst a barbarous and heathenish people, if that it was His blessed will, he would preserve and deliver us from amongst them, that our names might not be buried in oblivion; and that he might lay his body amongst faithful friends: and at the close of his prayer, he seemed to have an assurance that his petition would be granted. In all which some of us were livingly refreshed and strengthened. (15–16)

79. For this point by Mother, Mott draws from *The Journal of Thomas Chalkley. To Which is Annexed, A Collection of His Works* (New York: Samuel Wood, 1808). In his *Journal*, Chalkley writes that "[i]n this year [1722] also, I was at the burial of our friend Jonathan Dickinson, at which we had a very large meeting[;] he was a man generally well beloved by his friends and neighbors" (95). Mott likely misquotes or misremembers the year in which Dickinson died. In the paragraph preceding his comment on the death of Dickinson, Chalkley identifies the "year 1722" (94).

80. In vol. 2 of Durell's edition of the *Interesting Narrative*, Equiano offers the following commentary on flamingoes:

> On that part of it [one of the Bahama islands] where we first attempted to land there stood some very large birds, called flamingoes: these, from the reflection of the sun, appeared to us at a little distance as large as men; and, when they walked backwards and forwards, we could not conceive what they were: our captain [William Phillips] swore they were cannibals. This created a great panic among us; and we held a consultation [on] how to act. (37)

81. For this point by William, Mott draws on William Guthrie's *A New Geographical, Historical, and Commercial Grammar; And Present State of the Several Kingdoms of the World* (London: Printed for J. Knox, 1770). Writing on Greenland, Guthrie observes:

> The taking of whales in the seas of Greenland, among the fields of ice that have been increasing for ages, is one of the greatest curiosities in nature. These fields, or pieces of ice, are more than a mile in length frequently, and upwards of a hundred feet in thickness; and when they are put in motion by a storm, nothing can be more terrible; the Dutch had thirteen ships crushed to pieces by them in one season. (2)

Confirming William's point about hunting whales and fishing in Greenland, Guthrie, in the next three paragraphs, outlines the logistics of the whale industry (2–3).

82. The entry for July 25, 1822, from the "American Chronological Table" in *Longworth's American Almanac, New-York Register, and City Directory, for the Fifty-Ninth Year of American Independence* (New York: Thomas Longworth, 1834), provides the following information on the *Liverpool*: "The ship, of the New-York and Liverpool Line of packets, Capt. W[illia]m Lee, [J]r. lost on the Banks of Newfoundland, on her first voyage, by running upon an island of ice; crew and passengers saved" (30).

83. An article from the September 10, 1822, issue of the *American Repertory and Advertiser* (Burlington, VT) confirms William's point:

> The ship [*Liverpool*], Capt. Lee, sailed from New-York July 16, with 19 passengers. On the 25th, lat. 43, 45, long. 48, in a thick fog, ran foul of an Island of Ice, which carried away her bowsprit, and started her timbers in such a manner, that in less than two hours she went down, notwithstanding both pumps were kept going. The crew and passengers (36 in number) took to their boats, and after

being in them seven days, reached Newfoundland, from [whence] all the passengers save one, took passage for England. Nothing was saved from the ship, except the clothes on the passengers and crew. The passengers speak in high terms of the good conduct of Capt[.] Lee, before, during, and since the disaster. He had been apprehensive of ice, and was under short sail, but when the accident happened the fog was so thick that no one could see the length of the ship.

In *An Universal Dictionary of the Marine: or, A Copious Explanation of the Technical Terms and Phrases Employed in the Construction, Equipment, Furniture, Machinery, Movements, and Military Operations of A Ship* (London: Printed for T. Cadell, 1769), William Falconer defines "bowsprit" as

a large boom or mast, which projects over the stem, to carry sail forward, in order to govern the fore part of the ship, and counter-act the force of the sails extended behind, or, in the *after* part. It is otherways of great use, as being the principal support of the fore-mast, by confining the *stays* whereby it is secured, and enabled to carry sail: these are great ropes stretching from the mast-head to the middle of the bowsprit, where they are drawn tight.

84. For this point by Mother, Mott refers to Ebenezer Henderson's book *Iceland; or, the Journal of a Residence in that Island, During the Years 1814 and 1815. Containing Observations on the Natural Phenomena, History, Literature, and Antiquities of the Island; and the Religion, Character, Manners, and Customs of Its Inhabitants. With an Introduction and Appendix* (Edinburgh: Oliphant, Waugh, and Innes, 1818), 2 vols. Perkins and Marvin published Henderson's *Journal* in Boston in 1831. Mott includes portions from Henderson's *Journal* in *Observations on the Importance of Female Education, and Maternal Instruction, with Their Beneficial Influence on Society. By A Mother* (New York: Mahlon Day, 1825), 72–79.
85. In vol. 1 of the *Journal*, Henderson occasionally references wild corn. He names, for instance, "*Myrdals-sand*, a desert tract, consisting for the most part of lava and ashes, which have been deposited on it by the neighbouring volcano of *Kötlugiá*," where he and others "observed a number of people cutting the wild corn, a vegetable which grows in different parts of the island, but nowhere more plentiful than among the sand and ashes which cover the grounds along the coast at this place" (306–7).
86. According to the *Oxford English Dictionary*, this term may be understood as "[t]he small soft feathers from the breast of the eider duck."
87. In vol. 1 of his *Journal*, Henderson offers the following commentary: "For supper they have either *skyr*, a little bread and cheese, or porridge made of the Icelandic moss. To a foreigner this is not only the most healthy, but the most palatable of all the articles of [the] Icelandic diet" (113).
88. Part of the dialogue, "On Lapland," from *A Short But Comprehensive System of the Geography of the World; By Way of Question and Answer. Principally Designed for Children and Common Schools* (Elizabeth-Town, New Jersey: J. Woods, 1801), provides helpful information on this geographic location:

    Q: What is the situation and location of Lapland?
    A: It extends from the north cape in Norway, in the latitude of 71 deg. 30 m. to the White Sea under the Arctic Circle.
    Q: To what states does Lapland belong?
    A: It belongs to three, [that is] to Denmark, to Russia, and Sweden . . .
    Q: What animals are there in Lapland?
    A: The only animal peculiar to Lapland, which we know, is the Zibelin. It is highly valued for its skin. By far the most useful animal in Lapland is the ReinDeer. The other animals are common to all those northern countries. It

>is observable that all the animals which run wild in those countries change their colour with the season, and in winter turn white. (16–17)

89. In vol. 1 of his *Journal*, Henderson offers the following commentary on education in Iceland: "There being no parish schools, nor indeed any private establishments for the instruction of youth in Iceland, their mental culture depends entirely on the disposition and abilities of the parents.... The children are taught their letters, either by the mother, or some other female; and when they have made some progress in reading, they are taught writing and arithmetic by the father" (369). He adds, "I have frequently been astonished at the familiarity with which many of these self-taught peasants have discoursed on subjects, which, in other countries, we should expect to hear started by those only who fill the professor's chair, or who have otherwise devoted their lives to the study of science" (370).
90. According to the *Oxford English Dictionary*, the verb "to learn" may in this context be understood as "[t]o teach (a person)."
91. Mother refers to the Clarkson Benevolent Association's school for aged Black women, established in the 1820s. For more on this school, consult the notes on the selections from Mott's *Biographical Sketches* (appendix C).
92. For this point by Richard, Mott draws upon Luke 16:19–31.
93. For this point by William, Mott draws upon Matthew 25:35–36.
94. Unfortunately, I have not been able to identify this individual.
95. William J. Switala, in *Underground Railroad in New Jersey and New York* (Mechanicsburg, PA: Stackpole, 2006), identifies Lydia and Abigail Field Mott as individuals who helped establish this antislavery society (100).
96. The author of the "Report" quotes part of 1 Corinthians 10:25.
97. The author of the "Report" draws upon Psalm 46:2.
98. The author of the "Report" quotes parts of Romans 8:38–39.
99. The author of the "Report" likely draws on Romans 13:12, Ephesians 6:11, Psalm 21:3, and Revelation 14:2.
100. Unfortunately, I have not been able to identify this individual.
101. The author of the "Report" quotes part of Psalm 12:5.
102. The author of the "Report" quotes part of Matthew 10:42.
103. According to the *Oxford English Dictionary*, this term refers to "[a] member of a native South African race of low stature and dark yellowish-brown complexion, who formerly occupied the region near the Cape of Good Hope." However, this word is "derogatory" and "considered both archaic and offensive."
104. This individual may be the "S. T. Rice" identified as one of the chairpersons for the Executive Committee of Young Men's Albany Anti-Slavery Society. Consult the articles "Circular" in the October 9, 1839, issue of the *Extra Globe* (Washington, D.C.) and "Antislavery in New-York" in the December 1, 1838, issue of *Niles' National Register* (Washington, D.C.).
105. Mott addresses her review of *Narrative of the Life of Frederick Douglass, an American Slave. Written by Himself* (Boston: Published at the Anti-Slavery Office, 1845) to William Lloyd Garrison (1805–1879), an abolitionist, editor of *The Liberator*, and principal founder of the American Anti-Slavery Society.
106. According to the *Oxford English Dictionary*, this Latin term may be understood as "[a] great deal in a small compass" and "applied to articles of small bulk but of great comprehensiveness."
107. Mott references the British novelist, Charles Dickens (1812–1870), who wrote *Oliver Twist; or, the Parish Boy's Progress*. According to Paul Schlicke, a contributor to and editor of *The Oxford Companion to Charles Dickens* (Oxford: Oxford University Press, 2011), *Oliver Twist* was first "serialized in *Bentley's Miscellany* from February 1837 to

April 1839" (438). Mott's emotional reading likely derived from Dickens's use of Oliver "less as a character than as a representative of oppressed childhood," as Schlicke puts it (440).

108. Mott references French writer Marie Joseph Eugène Sue (1804–1857). According to John Flower, who wrote the entry on Sue in *Historical Dictionary of French Literature*, ed. John Flower (Lanham, MD: Scarecrow, 2013), *The Mysteries of Paris* was serialized in the *Journal des débats* between June 19, 1842, and October 15, 1843 (423). Flower writes that in *The Mysteries of Paris* Sue is "critical of Parisian high society and offers a series of random portraits of workers and the underprivileged." Brian Rigby, who wrote the entry on the novelist in *The New Oxford Companion to Literature in French*, ed. Peter France (New York: Oxford University Press, 1995), claims that by completing *Mysteries of Paris*, "with its super-heroes, its obsession with criminality, and its irresistible blend of the fantastic and the mysterious," Sue "set the pattern for modern mass fiction" (782).
109. Mott quotes part of Matthew 25:40.
110. According to Thomas Clapp Cornell, in *Adam and Anne Mott: Their Ancestors and Descendants* (Poughkeepsie, NY: A. V. Haight, 1890), Abigail Field Mott died on August 8, 1851, in Burlington, New Jersey (212).
111. According to Cornell, in *Adam and Anne Mott*, Abigail Field Mott was born on October 20, 1766 (212).
112. According to Pink Dandelion, a contributor to Abbott et al., *Historical Dictionary of the Friends (Quakers)*, the term "meeting" is "found in the [seventeenth-century] records of Quaker faith and practice and used in a variety of distinctive and important ways" (216). For instance, Dandelion notes that the term is "used to refer to the corporate body of members at various levels, named by their frequency of occurrence: monthly, quarterly, or yearly meetings. Any decision which can be taken locally is thus the responsibility of that local group" (217). Dandelion also observes that "[t]he basic unit of organization, which records membership and makes basic local decisions, is the monthly meeting."
113. According to Cornell, in *Adam and Anne Mott*, Abigail Field and Richard Mott (1767–1856) married on January 17, 1787 (212). Abigail was twenty-one years old when she married Richard. Cornell describes Richard as "a handsome man, tall, erect, and of unusual grace and dignity of manner, and active in affairs of the Society of Friends." Moreover, Cornell states that Richard became "Clerk of New York Yearly Meeting as early as 1798" and "an esteemed minister in the Society, an easy and graceful speaker" (212–13).
114. The authors of *Memoir* quote part of Matthew 6:33.
115. The authors of *Memoir* quote Matthew 6:33 or Luke 12:31. Both passages address "seek[ing] . . . the kingdom of God."
116. The authors of *Memoir* quote part of Proverbs 31:26.
117. The authors of *Memoir* quote part of Titus 2:10.
118. According to Paul Lacey, a contributor to Abbott et al., *Historical Dictionary of the Friends (Quakers)*, an elder was "responsible for both the religious and moral health of the [Quaker] meetings and its members. . . . Today elders are the individuals responsible for nurturing the spiritual vitality of meeting for worship. Elders are charged with seeing to the good order of the meeting, with active discernment and encouragement of gifts of ministry among members, and with calling to order those who disrupt worship" (115–16).
119. The authors of *Memoir* reference the Great Separation, a conflict that impacted many nineteenth-century Quaker communities. A contributor to Abbott et al., *Historical Dictionary of the Friends (Quakers)*, offers important commentary: "In 1827, Philadelphia Yearly Meeting divided over issues of authority and theology into two entities,

both known by the same name and claiming to be 'the' Philadelphia Yearly Meeting. These two bodies were the first in what came to be known as the Hicksite and Orthodox branches of the Religious Society of Friends" (153). On one hand, Elias Hicks (1748–1830), leader of the Hicksites, "directed Friends to the Inward Light and to an understanding of Christ as one who had achieved divinity through perfect obedience to that Light," as Thomas D. Hamm, contributor to *Historical Dictionary*, makes clear (166). As Margery Post Abbott, contributor to *Historical Dictionary*, clarifies, Inner Light "is one of the many ways Friends speak of Christ's work in the human heart. . . . A central understanding is that Light will show sin and evil just as it will show the way to salvation" (202–3). On the other hand, as Hamm makes clear in another entry in *Historical Dictionary*, Orthodox Friends, critics of Hicksites,

> argued that the Bible, rather than appeals to other revelation or the Inward Light, should be the final arbiter of doctrinal questions. They bitterly attacked Elias Hicks's argument that Jesus Christ achieved divinity through perfect obedience, rather than being born as God incarnate. And they emphasized the redeeming power of the blood of Christ as shed on the cross, which Hicksites tended to spiritualize. (253)

H. Larry Ingle, in *Quakers in Conflict: The Hicksite Reformation* (Knoxville: University of Tennessee Press, 1986), identifies Richard Mott, Abigail Field Mott's husband, as an "Orthodox spokesman" who pinpointed "the want of religious education of the youth," including "home education" and "school education," as the "root of the defection" (69–70). Additionally, Ingle notes that "Hicksite reformers found it easy to attack" individuals like Mott "for they did appear self-serving. As defenders of established authority, they were trying to maintain their prerogatives and power and quite naturally assumed that the good order from which flowed their influence was worth saving" (149).

120. The authors of *Memoir* likely had access to an unpublished text written by Mott.
121. Mott quotes part of 2 Corinthians 2:16.
122. Mott likely references 1 Corinthians 9:16.
123. According to the *Oxford English Dictionary*, this term may be understood as "[o]ne who gainsays, speaks against or opposes."
124. According to the *Oxford English Dictionary*, this term may be understood as "[r]efuse; rubbish; worthless, impure matter."
125. Mott draws from Jeremiah 6:30.
126. Mott references Isaiah 2:22.
127. The authors of *Memoir* reference Mott's *The Mother and Her Children, or Twilight Conversation* (New York: Mahlon Day, 1828). For parts of *Mother and Her Children*, see appendix C.
128. According to Thomas Clapp Cornell in *Adam and Anne Mott*, Richard and Abigail Field Mott had "a daughter Maria, born 1799, died 1817, and two sons who died in infancy, each named William, one born 16th of 8th month, 1790, the other 3d of 2d month, 1796" (213).
129. According to Thomas Clapp Cornell in *Adam and Anne Mott*, Richard and Abigail Field Mott also had a "son[,] Robert F. Mott, born at Mamaroneck 22d of 5th month, 1794, died there 8th of 7th month, 1826, married Hannah B. Smith, born 21st of 3d month, 1793, died 17th [of] 12th month, 1866, [d]aughter of Richard S. and Hannah Smith, of Burlington" (213).
130. The authors of *Memoir* quote part of Ephesians 6:4.
131. The authors of *Memoir* quote part of Job 1:21.
132. The authors of *Memoir* quote part of Acts 9:39. Also, Andrews, in *History of the New-York African Free-Schools*, offers the following on the African Dorcas Association:

> As a large number of our coloured people are very poor, and unable to provide for their children suitable clothing to attend school, several benevolent *coloured females* have recently formed themselves into a society, under the name of "The African Dorcas Association," for the purpose of procuring and of making up garments for the destitute. The labors of this Society have already been productive of much good; and it is highly gratifying to find a feeling existing among these people, so honorable and praise-worthy. (57–58)

133. The authors of *Memoir* quote part of Ecclesiastes 4:1.
134. The authors of *Memoir* reference Mott's *Biographical Sketches*. For selections from *Biographical Sketches*, see appendix C.
135. *Biographical Sketches* was likely Mott's most well-known publication. In a letter to Frederick Douglass, dated January 1855, twenty-nine years after the publication of the first edition of *Biographical Sketches*, Samuel Ringgold Ward (1817–1866), a graduate of New York African Free Schools, abolitionist, newspaper editor, minister, and autobiographer, exclaims,

> Alas! the history of our unhappy people consists of a single term and its cognate—slavery—slave trade—there is negro history, and what is more, some of the darkest and most diabolical papers and chapters of *other* history as well; and while this has been our lot, and that of our fathers, how were we to raise up historians? That is done by people in far different circumstances. Who was to write about us? Alas! who cared enough about us to write *for* us or *of* us? ... We have nothing but Mott's *Sketches*, Mr. Armistead's *Tribute*, Mr. Nell's *Military Heroes*, and a few anecdotes. (413–14)

For the rest of Ward's letter, published in the February 23, 1855, issue of *Frederick Douglass' Paper*, consult *The Black Abolitionist Papers*, vol. 1, The British Isles, 1830–1865, ed. C. Peter Ripley (Chapel Hill: University of North Carolina Press, 2015), 412–16.
136. According to the *Oxford English Dictionary*, this term may be understood as "[t]he scanning of surrounding objects or circumstances, careful or wary looking about one; the faculty of doing this."
137. According to Paul Lacey, a contributor to Abbott et al., *Historical Dictionary of the Friends (Quakers)*, overseers are "[i]ndividuals charged with the pastoral care of the meeting" whose duties include "visit[ing] families; keep[ing] in touch with distant members; giv[ing] confidential attention to family crises, special needs, and conflicts between individuals needing mediation; and labor[ing] with members whose actions cause scandal or violate Friends' principles. In the past, overseers also had responsibility for physical property" (255).
138. The authors of *Memoir* quote part of 2 Peter 1:21.
139. The authors of *Memoir* quote another part of 2 Peter 1:21.
140. The authors of *Memoir* quote most of Romans 15:4.
141. According to Thomas Clapp Cornell in *Adam and Anne Mott*, Richard and Abigial Mott's son, Robert F. Mott (1794–1826) married Hannah B. Smith (1793–1866) (213). Robert and Hannah had a son, Robert F. Mott, born in 1825. Hannah B. Smith is identified in the next paragraph of *Memoir* as the "daughter above referred to [who] has furnished the following testimony concerning her [Abigail Field Mott]." Therefore, I categorize *Memoir* as collaborative life writing and use the phrase "authors of *Memoir*." Smith had access to "notes preserved at the time" (perhaps ones written by her), as the authors of *Memoir* later make clear.
142. According to the *Oxford English Dictionary*, this term may be understood as "[a] disease ... of the nervous system, characterized by impairment or loss of the motor or

sensory function of the nerves, esp[ecially] of those belonging to a particular part or organ, thus producing (partial or total) incapacity of motion, insensibility, or functional inactivity in such part." The term may also be understood as "[a] condition of utter powerlessness, incapacity of action, or suspension of activity; the state of being 'crippled,' helpless, or impotent."

143. Mott quotes part of Acts 21:14.
144. The authors of *Memoir* quote Isaiah 26:3.
145. According to the *Oxford English Dictionary*, this term may be understood as "[d]early loved, very dear; best-loved, favourite."
146. Mott again quotes part of Acts 21:14.
147. According to the *Oxford English Dictionary*, this term may be understood as "[s]trength, energy, force."
148. Mott recites part of Book II, "The Time-Piece," from William Cowper's *The Task, a Poem, in Six Books. By William Cowper, of the Inner Temple, Esq.* (London: Printed for J. Johnson, 1785), 46. Mott and the Woods included in *Life and Adventures of Olaudah Equiano* several lines from *The Task*. See page 30. For more on Cowper, consult the notes on *Life and Adventures of Olaudah Equiano*.
149. Mott reinforces arguments about "declining the use of articles produced by the unrequited labor of the poor slaves" articulated by the Quaker Elias Hicks in *Observations on the Slavery of the Africans and Their Descendants. Recommended to the Serious Perusal, and Impartial Consideration of the Citizens of the United States of America, and Others Concerned* (New York: Samuel Wood, 1811). In response to the thirteenth query, "Do the consumers of the produce of the slave's labor, who hold no slaves themselves, reap any particular advantage by the slavery of the Africans and their descendants?," Hicks argues:

> They certainly do, especially in relation to the produce of the West-Indies and southern States of America, where the labour is altogether done by slaves. For, was the labour in those parts done by free labourers, it would cost much more than when done by slaves, especially as free hired labourers would not be content to live on such mean scanty fare as is generally dealt out to the poor slaves. Many of whom, if report[s] speak true, are very meanly and scantily fed, so that it is reasonable to judge, that at least the consumers of the produce of the West-Indies, and some of the Southern states, that is raised by the labour of slaves, save to themselves one eighth of the prime cost, or that they now purchase such goods for one eighth less than they could, were the same goods reared by free hands, and are therefore, actually so much benefited by the slavery of their fellow creatures; and, of consequence, so far partakers of the gain of oppression. As it is very evident, that the consumers reap a particular benefit from it, they also furnish the whole fund for carrying on the business of slavery, and which would, of course, stop as soon as they withdrew their support. And, I conceive, agreeable to strict justice, those who are purchasers and consumers of the produce of the West-India slavery, or of the Southern States, are more culpable in the Divine sight, than those who purchase goods of a highway robber, which he hath forcibly taken from his fellow citizen on the highway; by so much as it is more criminal to rob a man of his liberty and property, than only to rob him of his goods. (12–13)

150. Mott quotes part of stanza seven from William Cowper's "Verses, [S]upposed to be [W]ritten by Alexander Selkirk, during [H]is [S]olitary [A]bode in the Island of Juan Fernandez," part of *Poems [b]y William Cowper, [o]f the Inner Temple, Esq.* (London: Printed for J. Johnson, 1782), 305–8. For more information on Cowper, consult the notes on *Life and Adventures of Olaudah Equiano*. Selkirk (1676–1721) was, as James

William Kelly points out in the *Oxford Dictionary of National Biography* (Oxford: Oxford University Press, 2004), vol. 49, the "probable source of inspiration for [Daniel Defoe's character] Robinson Crusoe" (714). Samuel Wood printed and sold at his "Juvenile Book-Store" *The History of Alexander Selkirk, the Real Robinson Crusoe. To Which [A]re Added Sketches of Natural History* (New York: Samuel Wood, 1815). According to the "Advertisement" in *History* (likely written by Wood), "The ingenious fiction[,] called *Robinson Crusoe*, has passed through several editions, and been read with much interest by many, some of whom perhaps have thought it a history of facts. It was founded upon the adventures of Alexander Selkirk, who was left upon a desert island in the Pacific Ocean, in the year 1704, where he remained about four and a half years" (2). *Alexander Selkirk* appears in the list of "Juvenile Books, Published by Samuel Wood & Sons, New York," advertised on the back cover of *Life and Adventures of Olaudah Equiano*.

151. Mott quotes part of Luke 13:24.
152. Mott references parts of John 15:5 and 15:8.
153. Mott quotes most of Luke 9:58.
154. Mott references 2 Samuel 7:6.
155. Mott quotes part of Matthew 6:9, the beginning of the Lord's Prayer.
156. Mott likely refers to British Quaker Mary Thompson Jennings, a York native, who, with her husband, Richard Jennings, established on July 22, 1840, the Friends' School in Cape Town, South Africa. Mott likely read about the Jennings in the article "A Short Notice on Richard Jennings. Presented to the Subscribers to the Cape Town Friends' School" in the April 28, 1849, issue of *Friends' Review. A Religious, Literary and Miscellaneous Journal* (Philadelphia). According to the *Tenth Report of the Friends' School, Cape Town, South Africa, for the Year 1850* (York: James Hunton, 1851), based on the letters of Mary Thompson Jennings, the school comprised about eighty students, "about one half of the whole number are the offspring of coloured parents, thirty of whom are boys" (3). The author of the *Report* also notes that "[e]leven children write in copy-books, and forty-nine on slates. Those who learn Arithmetic are only in the simplest rules[.] Five learn Grammar, and six learn Geography. Six hours in the week are devoted to sewing, but few of the children work with the needle neatly" (3–4). Following the death of her husband in 1848, Mary, along with her oldest daughter, managed the school. Mary Thompson Jennings died in 1861.
157. Editors of the March 1, 1852, issue of *The British Friend: A Monthly Journal, Chiefly Devoted to the Interests of the Society of Friends* (Glasgow) included the November 5 letter/report of Mary Thompson Jennings in which she observed the following on Cape Town: "We see a gradual improvement in the learning and conduct of the children, for some time we numbered from 100 to 110 daily; but the weather being very hot, we found it very exhausting. Our numbers keep up to 90 or 95 regularly, although there has been a great deal of sickness. The effects of the war are felt in Cape Town, provisions being very high; bread twice its usual price." Jennings references the Xhosa Wars (1779–1879), described by a contributor to *A Dictionary of World History*, ed. Anne Kerr and Edmund Wright, 3rd ed. (Oxford: Oxford University Press, 2015), as

> wars between the Xhosa people and Dutch and British colonists along the east coast of Cape Colony, between the Great Fish and Great Kei rivers. From 1811 the policy of clearing the land of Xhosa people to make way for the Europeans began and, following a year of fighting (1818–19), some [four thousand] British colonists were installed along the Great Fish river. As they pushed the frontier east, however, the colonists met with greater resistance, cattle raids resulting in retaliation. The war of 1834 to 1835 yielded [sixty thousand] head of cattle to the colonists and was followed by the longer struggle of 1846 to 1853. The war

of 1877 to 1879, which yielded [fifteen thousand] cattle and [twenty thousand] sheep, was vainly fought by tribesmen returning from the diamond fields in a last bid to regain their land. Afterwards all Xhosa territory was incorporated as European farmland within Cape Colony. (727)

158. The authors of *Memoir* quote Revelation 14:12.

Appendix D

Selected Commentary on the Institution of Slavery in Books Published by Samuel Wood and Sons

"To the Reader," Written by "T[he] P[ublisher]," from *The Penitential Tyrant; or, Slave Trader Reformed: A Pathetic Poem, in Four Cantos*. By Thomas Branagan, Second, "Enlarged" Edition (New York: Samuel Wood, 1807)

The subject of the following pages being of a nature so very important and interesting, we have been induced to swell it beyond what was at first contemplated, and have inserted, towards the close, several pieces that have presented, so beautifully descriptive, that we could not refuse them a place; but should we add all the matter that is good which has been or might be written on this painful theme, instead of a small pocket volume, we should fill huge folios,[1] and not a few;[2] for SLAVERY is in itself so inconsistent, that it seems strange it ever should have had a defender, or its cause should have been espoused by any human being, who had only sense enough to distinguish light from darkness, right from wrong, or happiness from misery. It debases the noble creature man, created but a little below the angels,[3] and reduces him to a level almost with the brutes. Slavery, hateful to God and man, and, in my estimation, the greatest evil under the sun, and inflicted by Americans, the most favoured people, and, may I not say, the most enlightened and highest in profession of liberty and [C]hristianity, must render us the most inexcusable, and draw[n] down, unless expiated by sincere repentance and undoing heavy burdens, the just indignation of Him who does not even let a sparrow fall without [H]is notice: and can we suppose, that [H]is noble creature man shall be trampled on, and the oppressor suffered to pass with impunity? If we can suppose so, our opinion must be very despicable of the Omnipotent Ruler of the Universe. But is it not very conspicuous, that his anger is kindled; for what is the plague frequently let loose in our borders, and many other distressing, alarming, and truly humiliating things, both by sea and land, threatening us? And who, that is not judicially blind, can not discover the finger of an avenging God, in the greatest curse that ever befel[l] this country—ARDENT SPIRITS, the very produce of slavery, which is our greatest scourge.

But a little hope beams on the mind. Since the following sheets were put to press, the very important question has been decided. Enough of virtue has appeared in the council, to declare, that no slave shall be imported after the last day of the present year.[4] But, Oh! the many heart[-]rending scenes, the fruits of avarice, that must occur in the intermediate space, unless by Divine interposition prevented.

You that are parents, husbands, wives, and children, make the case your own.—Twice, within twelve months, there have at a time been about two thousand, in a neighbouring state, of these poor devoted children of affliction, advertised in the public prints, for sale, under the appellation of prime Congo Negroes, prime Windward Negroes, &c.[5]

Here, reader, pause for a moment, and reflect what a mass of misery! Every one of those poor individuals (exclusive of his own distress) in leaving his or her dear and native country, probably left an aged father, a tender mother, a loving husband or wife, an affectionate brother or sister, or dear children to mourn his or her friend and relative; gone not only never to return, but gone into perpetual slavery; and, perhaps, many of them the chief support of dear connexions, who now must suffer for the lack of their attention.

What abundant cause do we, while guilty of such cruelty, administer to the heathen to blaspheme that Holy Name, by which we profess to be saved, if ever we are saved; for natural must be the conclusion; if these are the faithful servants of a crucified Christ; if these are his commands, he must be a cruel tyrant. But, blessed be the great and Holy One, they are not his commands, they are the genuine fruits of sordid avarice, they are direct antipodes.[6] His commands are, "*Whatsoever ye would that men should do to you, do ye even so to them.*"[7]

Pleasing, indeed, must it be to those who are alive to the feelings of another's woe, that the time is fixed for a final termination of the iniquitous commerce: but this is but one step, *slavery must be abolished*, and, no doubt, it will come to an end. I am fully persuaded, that it is the determination of Heaven so to be; and we need not expect to be blessed, or that his correcting hand will spare, unless we are obedient; and how much better cheerfully to resign to [H]is will, than to be scourged into a compliance. The times are big with important events, great commotions are in the earth, nature seems as it were shocked to the centre, and endures the pangs of parturition;[8] a birth will be produced, which, in my opinion, will, through Divine interposition, be the civil and religious rights of man.

Man was made to be happy; it is his duty to be so: and it is incumbent on him, to use his best endeavours, to make his fellow-creatures so, without distinction of name, nation, or colour; and, doubtless, he who most honestly and faithfully uses the faculties and means he may be blessed with, to augment the general mass of happiness, must be most acceptable in the sight of a just and impartial Creator and *vice versa*.

I love my country, I always have loved it; but for this cause, shall I cruelly treat one of another country. God forbid! I am a citizen of the world, and a candidate for heaven; where, I am confident, whoever, by obedient walking, is so happy as to arrive, will never be interrogated in respect to his nation, colour, or profession, for God is no respecter of persons.

I wish that all distinction of parties might be done away. We are all the offspring of the same Universal Parent. How much better would it be, if, instead of teaching our children to regard every other nation or profession, as inferior to ourselves and out of the way, we should take pains to instruct them, that [H]e has other sheep, not of this fold, spread over the whole earth, in every country, and among every people; and that virtue only is to be respected, and vice despised, wherever found; whether arrayed in gold, or clothed in rags; whether in one that wields a sceptre, or begs his bread.[9]

With what a smile of contempt must the judicious foreigner view, on the floor of the capitol, an American slave-holder expatiating on the cause of liberty, virtue, and patriotism, especially when he reflects, that the main tenet, or, as it were, the cornerstone, (may I not rather say the whole fabric) of the religion he professes is simply the divine command already mentioned; and when he looks back to the time "that tried men's souls;"[10] when they could resolve, "We will neither import nor purchase any slave, imported after the first day of December next (1775), after which, we will wholly discontinue the slave-trade; and will neither be concerned in it ourselves, nor will we hire our vessels, or sell our commodities or manufactures, to those who are concerned in it;"[11] and, in their solemn, unequivocal, positive, and pointed declaration of independence,

"We hold these truths to be self evident, that all men are created equal, that they are endowed, by their Creator, with certain unalienable rights; that among these, are life, liberty, and the pursuit of happiness;"[12] when he views this disclaimer in the cause of liberty, &c. when he views our public prints, offering human beings for sale, (and frequently inserted, "for no fault"); when, after a lapse of thirty years, he sees the thirteen stripes stoop so low, in such a base and ignoble traffic, as to waft from their native homes, from every thing near and dear in this life, thousands of (as to us) inoffensive beings; with what disgust must he turn away from such a hypocritical people; and say, well might one of their modern writers exclaim, "I tremble for my country, when I reflect that God is just; that his justice cannot sleep forever;"[13] for, surely, indeed, "we cannot form to ourselves an idea of an object more ridiculous than an American patriot signing declarations of independence with one hand, and with the other brandishing his whip over his affrighted slave."[14]

TYRANNY consists in will and actions, not in power, for a man may be as complete a tyrant over one, as one hundred [million]. Slavery and tyranny are completely inseparable; for, remove one, and the other ceases. There cannot be a slave without a tyrant; for, if the conduct of the master is such, as to do away the appellation of tyrant, of course, that of slave must subside. But he that holds another man in bondage against his will, and that not for his good or comfort, does not do as he would be done by; and, of course, must be a tyrant: and it appears a self-evident truth, that no man who holds a slave ought to be intrusted with a post, either great or small, among a free people.

"Ah! why will kings forget that they are men?
And men that they are brethren? Why delight
In human sacrifice? Why burst the ties
Of nature, that should knit their souls together
In one soft bond of amity and love?"[15]

"A FAMILY [C]ONVERSATION ON THE SLAVERY OF THE NEGROES" FROM *The New-York Reader, No. 2: Being, Selections in Prose and Poetry, for the Use of Schools* (NEW YORK: SAMUEL WOOD, 1813)

Charles. May I be allowed to choose a subject for the present conversation? I want to know how agriculture is performed in the West-Indies; I have understood they have but few if any horses there.

Father. It is true they have not a sufficient number of horses in the West-India islands, to plough and cultivate the land, as farmers do in Europe and America; and, therefore, almost all their laborious operations are performed by Negro-slaves.

Augusta. Are those islands inhabited by Negroes? I thought these people were natives of Africa.

Father. They are, indeed, natives of Africa; but they have been snatched by the hand of violence, from their country, friends, and connections. I am ashamed to confess that many ships belonging to both Americans and Europeans, have been in the habit of going annually to Guinea,[16] to procure slaves from that unhappy country, for the use of not only the West-India islands, but also for this our favoured land; where they were sold as though they were not human beings, entitled to all the privileges inherent to human nature; and afterwards employed in the hardest and most servile occupations; and destined to pass the rest of their days in slavery and wretchedness. But we have to rejoice in believing, that, not only the forcing of these poor children of affliction from their native land, but also slavery itself will be literally annihilated, and they restored to their natural right and dignity; as laws have been passed in this and some other countries, abolishing the trade to Africa for slaves; and some of our states, from a sense of justice, have emancipated all;[17] and we hope and believe others of them will be induced to follow their example.[18] Surely America ought to say as much as England can,

"Slaves cannot breathe in England;
They touch our country, and their shackles fall."[19]

We have already said, "All men are both free and equal."[20]

Sophia. How much my heart feels for them! How agonizing must it be, to be separated from one's near relations! [P]arents perhaps divided from their children forever; husbands from their wives; brothers and sisters obliged to bid each other a final farewell!—But why do the kings of the African states suffer their subjects to be so cruelly treated?

Mother. Many causes have operated to induce the African princes to become assistants in this infamous traffic; and instead of being the defenders of their harmless people, they have frequently betrayed them to their most cruel enemies. The Europeans have corrupted these ignorant rulers, by presents of rum, and other spirituous liquors, of which they are immoderately fond—They have fomented jealousies, and excited wars among them, merely for the sake of obtaining the prisoners of war for slaves. Frequently they use no ceremony, but go on shore in the night, set fire to the neighboring village, and seize upon all the unhappy victims, who run out to escape the flames.

Cecilia. What hardened hearts do the captains of those ships possess! They must have become extremely cruel, before they would undertake such an employment.

Mother. There is reason to believe, that most of them, by the habits of such a life, [become] deaf to the voice of pity: we must, however, compassionate[21] the situation of those, whose parents have early bred them to this profession, before they were of an age to choose a different employment. But to resume the subject of the Negroes. What I have related is only the beginning of their sorrows.

When they are put on board the ships, they are crowded together in the hold, where many of them die, for want of air and room. There have been frequent instances of their throwing themselves into the sea, when they could find an opportunity, and seeking in death a refuge from their calamity.

As soon as they arrive in the West-Indies, they are carried to a public market, where they are sold to the best bidder, like horses at our fairs. Their future lot depends much upon the disposition of the master, into whose hands they happen to fall; for, among the overseers of sugar-plantations, there are some men of feeling and humanity; but too generally the treatment of the poor Negroes is very severe.

Accustomed to an easy, indolent life, in the luxurious and plentiful country of Africa, they find great hardship from the transition to a life of severe labour, with scarcely any mixture of indulgence to soften it.

Deprived of the hope of amending their condition, by any course of conduct they can pursue, they frequently abandon themselves to despair; and die, in what is called the seasoning, which is becoming inured by length of time to their situation. They who have less sensibility and stronger constitutions, survive their complicated misery but a few years: for it is generally acknowledged, that they seldom attain the full period of human life.

Augusta. Humanity shudders at the account!—But I have heard a gentleman, who had lived many years abroad, say, that Negroes were not much superior to the brutes; and that they were so stupid and stubborn, that nothing but stripes and severity could have any influence over them.

Father. That gentleman was most probably interested in misleading those with whom he conversed. People, who reason in that manner, do not consider the disadvantages which the poor Negroes suffer from want of cultivation. Leading an ignorant savage life in their own country, they can have acquired no previous information; and when they fall into the hands of their cruel oppressors, a life of laborious servitude, which scarcely affords them sufficient time for sleep, deprives them of every opportunity of improving their minds.

There is no reason to suppose that they differ from us in any thing but colour; which distinction arises from the intense heat of the climate. There have been instances of a few, whose situation has been favourable to improvement, who have shown strong powers of mind. Those masters, who neglect the religious and moral instruction of their slaves, add a heavy load of guilt to that already incurred, by their share in this unjust and inhuman traffic.

Charles. My indignation rises at the recital; and the beautiful lines of Cowper recur to my mind:

> "Ah! why will kings forget that they are men,
> And men that they are brethren." [22]

Father. Beautiful indeed, my child; and we have a comfortable hope, that the goodness of that Divine Providence, who cares for all his creatures, will not only bring about, but is hastening the day, when their rights will be considered: and there is reason to hope, from the light already cast upon the subject, that the rising generation will prefer justice and mercy, to interest and policy; and will free themselves from the odium we at present suffer, of treating our fellow creatures in a manner unworthy of them, and of ourselves.

Mother. Henry, repeat that beautiful apostrophe to a Negro woman, which thou learned the other day out of Barbauld's [*Hymns*].[23]

Henry. "Negro woman, who sittest pining in captivity, and weepest over thy sick child, though no one sees thee, God sees thee; though no one pities thee, God pities thee. Raise thy voice, forlorn and abandoned one; call upon [H]im from amidst thy bonds, for assuredly [H]e will hear thee." [24]

Cecilia. I think no riches could tempt me to have any share in the slave trade. I could never enjoy peace of mind, whilst I thought I contributed to the woes of my fellow-creatures.

Mother. But, Cecilia, to put thy compassion to the proof; art thou willing to debar[25] thyself of the numerous indulgences thou enjoyest, from the fruit of their labour?

Cecilia. I would forgo any indulgences to alleviate their sufferings.

The [R]est of the [C]hildren [T]ogether. We are all of the same mind.

Mother. I admire the sensibility of your uncorrupted hearts, my dear children. It is the voice of nature and virtue. Listen to it on all occasions, and bring it home to your bosoms, and your daily practice. The same principle of benevolence, which excites your just indignation at the oppression of the Negroes, will lead you to be gentle towards your inferiors, kind and obliging to your equals, and in a particular manner condescending[26] and considerate towards your domestics; requiring no more of them, than you will be willing to perform in their situation; instructing them when you have the opportunity; sympathizing in their afflictions, and promoting their best interests to the utmost of your power.

"**Master and Slave**" FROM *The New-York Reader, No. 3: Being, Selections in Prose and Poetry, from the Best Writers: Designed for the Use of Schools, and Calculated to Assist the Scholar in Acquiring the Art of Reading, and at the Same Time to Fix His Principles, and Inspire Him with a Love of Virtue* (NEW YORK: SAMUEL WOOD AND SONS, 1819)

Master.

NOW, villain! [W]hat have you to say for this second attempt to run away? Is there any punishment that you do not deserve?

Slave.

I well know that nothing I can say will avail. I submit to my fate?

Master.

But are you not a base fellow, a hardened and ungrateful rascal?

Slave.

I am a slave. That is answer enough.

Master.

I am not content with that answer. I thought I discerned in you some tokens of a mind superior to your condition. I treated you accordingly. You have been comfortably fed and lodged, not overworked, and attended with the most humane care when you were sick. And is this the return?

Slave.

Since you condescend to talk with me as man to man, I will reply. What have you done, what can you do for me, that will compensate for the liberty which you have taken away?

Master.

I did not take it away. You was a slave when I fairly purchased you.

Slave.

Did I give my consent to the purchase?

Master.

You had no consent to give. You had already lost the right of disposing of yourself.

Slave.

I had lost the power, but how the right? I was treacherously kidnapped in my own country, when following an honest occupation. I was put in chains, sold to one of your countrymen, carried by force on board his ship, brought hither, and exposed to sale like a beast in the market, where you bought me. What step in all this progress of violence and injustice can give a right? Was it in the villain who stole me, in the slave merchant who tempted him to do so, or in you who encouraged the slave merchant to bring his cargo of human cattle to cultivate your lands?

Master.

It is in the order of Providence that one man should become subservient to another. It ever has been so, and ever will be. I found the custom, and did not make it.

Slave.

You cannot but be sensible, that the robber who puts a pistol to your breast may make just the same plea. Providence gives him a power over your life and property; it gave my enemies a power over my liberty. But it has also given me legs to escape with; and what should prevent me from using them? Nay, what should restrain me from retaliating the wrongs I have suffered, if a favourable occasion should offer?

Master.

Gratitude; I repeat,—gratitude! Have not I endeavoured ever since I possessed you to alleviate your misfortunes by kind treatment, and does that confer no obligation? Consider how much worse your condition might have been under another master.

Slave.

You have done nothing for me more than for your working cattle. Are they not well fed and tended? Do you work them harder than your slaves? Is not the rule of treating both, only your own advantage? You treat both your men and beast slaves better than some of your neighbours, because you are more prudent and wealthy than they.

Master.

You might add, more humane too.

Slave.

Humane! Does it deserve the appellation to keep your fellow-men in forced subjection, deprived of all exercise of their free-will, liable to all the injuries that your own caprice, or the brutality of your overseers, may heap on them, and devoted soul and body, only to your pleasure and emolument?[27] Can gratitude take place between creatures in such a state, and the tyrant who holds them in it? Look at these limbs—are they not those of a man? [T]hink that I have the spirit of a man, too!

Master.

But it was my intention not only to make your life tolerably comfortable at present, but to provide for you in your old age.

Slave.

Alas! is a life like mine, torn from country, friends, and all I held dear, and compelled to toil under the burning sun for a master, worth thinking about for old age? No—the sooner it ends, the sooner I shall obtain that relief for which my soul pants.

Master.

Is it possible, then, to hold you by any ties but those of constraint and severity?

Slave.

It is impossible to make one who has felt the value of freedom, acquiesce in being a slave.

Master.

Suppose I were to restore you to your liberty, would you reckon that a favour?

Slave.

The greatest: for although it would be only undoing a wrong, I know too well how few among mankind are capable of sacrificing interest to justice, not to prize the exertion when it is made.

Master.

I do it, then;—be free.

Slave.

Now I am indeed your servant, though not your slave. And, as the first return I can make for your kindness, I will tell you freely the condition in which you live. You are surrounded with implacable foes, who long for a safe opportunity to revenge upon you and the other planters all the miseries they have endured. The more generous their natures, the most indignant they feel against that cruel injustice which has dragged them hither and doomed them to perpetual servitude. You can rely on no kindness on your part to soften the obduracy[28] of their resentment. You have reduced them to the state of brute beasts; and if they have not the stupidity of beasts of burden, they must have the ferocity of beasts of prey. Superior force alone can give you security. As soon as that fails, you are at the mercy of the merciless. Such is the social bond between master and slave!

Notes

1. In *The Broadview Reader in Book History* (Peterborough, Ontario: Broadview, 2015), Michelle Levy and Tom Mole define a "folio" as "[a] book printed on full-size sheets folded medially once, making two leaves or four pages" (583).
2. After *The Penitential Tyrant* and Branagan's "Notes" on the poem, Wood included the following in the 1807 book: "Messiah: A Sacred Eclogue, in Imitation of Virgil's Pollio," written by Alexander Pope (1688–1744), *Buying Stolen Goods Synonymous with Stealing; or, The Immortality of Using the Produce of Slavery Demonstrated. Addressed to Christians of All Denominations*, "A S[ubject] for C[onversation] and R[eflection] [at] [the] T[ea]-T[able]" (a part of *Life and Adventures of Olaudah Equiano*), *Method of Procuring Slaves* (parts of which appear in *Life and Adventures of Olaudah Equiano*), and *Extract from an Essay in Verse, Entitled, Slavery*, written by Captain Marjoribanks (1758/9–1796) (219–90).
3. Wood draws upon part of Psalm 8:5.
4. Wood refers to legislation enacted by the U.S. Congress to eradicate the slave trade in the United States. As Wood observes, lawmakers brought an end to the transatlantic slave trade in the United States on January 1, 1808.
5. Wood may refer to the following article published in the June 15, 1804, issue of the *Republican Gazette* (Frederick-Town, MD): "In one of our late Charleston newspapers, we observe 367 Congo, 357 Angola, and 148 Winward coast Negroes, lately arrived there, advertised for sale. The inhuman and destructive policy which could legalize such importation must undoubtedly be condemned by every man who has the good of his country at heart, unswayed by the sordid love of gain." He also likely draws from the following article, "Experimental Democracy," published in the September 3, 1804, issue of the *Trenton Federalist*:

    What must be the opinion entertained by Foreigners of a People who talk so much about *liberty* and the *rights of man*, as those of the United States, on seeing in their public prints, such articles as these, directly following each other? Yet such we frequently meet with in the [S]outhern papers, where *Democracy so much abounds*: — "The 4th [of July] was celebrated here with *enthusiasm*!" "There is below an English Guineaman, with 250 *head* of slaves." [*Head* of slaves—like *head of cattle*.] "Just arrived in the ship *Democrat* and to be sold at L—'s wharf to-morrow, by public sale, 150 *prime* Congo Negroes." "*Strayed* into the yard of the subscriber last night, a new Negro, with marks on his cheeks—cannot speak English. The owner may have him again by proving property, &c.

&c." "Runaway from the plantation of the subscriber, on the 12th[,] a Negro Fellow, named Pomp, *branded* with the letters P. B. *on his cheek.*" "Runaway from — plantation, some time since, a Negro man named Tom. Twenty [d]ollars will be given for his apprehension and commitment to any gaol in the state. *Any person may shoot or kill said runaway.*"

The New York publisher and bookseller also included, in *The Mirror of Misery; or, Tyranny Exposed. Extracted from Authentic Documents, and Exemplified by Engravings* (New York: Samuel Wood, 1807), an untitled poem originally published in the *New-Haven Gazette* illustrating the "distress which the inhabitants of Guinea experience at the loss of their children" (45).

6. According to the *Oxford English Dictionary*, this term may be understood as "[t]hose who dwell directly opposite to each other on the globe" and "[t]hose who in any way resemble the dwellers on the opposite side of the globe."
7. Wood quotes Matthew 7:12.
8. According to the *Oxford English Dictionary*, this term may be understood as "[t]he action of bringing forth or of being delivered of young; childbirth."
9. Fifteen years after the publication of Branagan's *The Penitential Tyrant*, Wood and Sons attempted to correct "[m]any wrong ideas" found in the "infant mind" in their *False Stories Corrected* (New York: Samuel Wood and Sons, 1822), 3. One false story concerned children's lack of understanding of individuals of African descent. One part of this book reads: "And shall every Negro be termed an Infidel, Heathen, or Savage? Our own knowledge proves the contrary. We are sensible that there is a considerable number of pious Negroes in this country. . . . [T]here are kind and humane people among them" (15–16). Samuel S. Wood and Company also sold this book in Baltimore.
10. Wood quotes the first sentence from *The American Crisis*, no. 1, first published in December 1776 and written by Thomas Paine (1737–1809).
11. Wood quotes the first sentence from Article 1, Section 9 of the United States Constitution, which the majority of delegates attending the Constitutional Convention approved and signed on September 17, 1787. Richard Beeman, editor of *The Penguin Guide to the United States Constitution: A Fully Annotated Declaration of Independence, U.S. Constitution and Amendments, and Selections from The Federalist Papers* (New York: Penguin, 2010), observes that

> [t]he Convention delegates from South Carolina and Georgia, whose slave economies were still expanding, insisted that no legislation interfering with the African slave trade be permitted until at least twenty years after the adoption of the Constitution. The prohibition of any legislation affecting "the Migration or Importation of such Persons as any of the States now existing shall think proper to admit" was intended to ensure that protection. As in all instances in which the Constitution deals with the institution of slavery, neither the word "slave" nor "slavery" is explicitly mentioned in the text of the document. (36)

12. Wood quotes paragraph 2 from the Declaration of Independence, written principally by Thomas Jefferson (1743–1826). Congressional members approved a revised version of the Declaration on July 4, 1776. Richard Beeman, editor of *The Penguin Guide to the United States Constitution*, maintains that the "opening lines of the second paragraph were, in fact, merely a preface to the real punch line of that paragraph: the assertion of the right to rebel against the government of England. Jefferson reminds his audience that the very purpose of government is to protect the natural rights of mankind" (5).
13. Wood quotes from query 18, "Manners," from *Notes on the State of Virginia. Written by Thomas Jefferson. Illustrated with a Map, Including the States of Virginia, Maryland,*

Delaware and Pennsylvania (London: Printed for John Stockdale, 1787), 272. Before the part Wood quotes, Jefferson observes: "There must doubtless be an unhappy influence on the manners of our people produced by the existence of slavery among us. The whole commerce between master and slave is a perpetual exercise on the most boisterous passions, the most unremitting despotism on the one part, and degrading submissions on the other. Our children see this, and learn to imitate it; for man is an imitative animal" (270). Of course, in query 14, "Laws," Jefferson maintains that the poems of Phillis Wheatley, the first individual of African descent to publish a book written in English, "are below the dignity of criticism" (234). Wood wrote a March 3, 1821, letter to Jefferson in which he quotes the latter's statement from *Notes*. Some of this language also appears in "To the Reader" (appendix D).

14. Wood quotes from *Fragment of an Original Letter on the Slavery of the Negroes. Written in the Year 1776. By Thomas Day, Esq.* (Philadelphia: Francis Bailey, 1784), 7. Day's language in *Fragment* slightly differs from what Wood places in quotes: "If there be an object truly ridiculous in nature, it is an American patriot, signing resolutions of independency with the one hand, and with the other brandishing a whip over his affrighted slaves."

15. Wood quotes part of the poem, *Death: A Poetical Essay* (Cambridge, UK: J. Bentham, 1759), written by Beilby Porteus (1731–1809), who became bishop of London in 1787. Andrew Robinson, the contributor who wrote the entry on Porteus for the *Oxford Dictionary of National Biography* (Oxford: Oxford University Press, 2004), vol. 44, states,

> [he] made full use of his position to further the interest of the campaign to abolish the slave trade; he tried, but failed, to see Sir William Dolben's *Slave Carrying Bill* through the [House of] Lords (1788). He successfully transferred a bequest of Robert Doyle, made in 1691 and intended for missionary work in America, to his own Society for the Conversion and Religious Instruction of the Negroes of the West Indies. (978)

See *Death*, 12, for the portion Wood uses.

16. In *Life and Adventures of Olaudah Equiano* (New York: Samuel Wood and Sons, 1829), Olaudah Equiano provides the following information on Guinea: "The part of Africa known by the name of Guinea, to which the trade for slaves is carried on, extends along the coast above 3400 miles, from Senegal to Angola, and includes a number of kingdoms; the most considerable of which is Benin, as it respects its extent, wealth, and richness of soil" (5).

17. The colony of Vermont, which became a state in 1791, abolished adult slavery in 1777; Massachusetts abolished slavery in 1783. Ira Berlin, author of *The Long Emancipation: The Demise of Slavery in the United States* (Cambridge, MA: Harvard University Press, 2015), writes: "In 1780, when the Pennsylvania legislature enacted abolition, the new law provided only for the liberation of those born after March first of that year, the date designated for freedom's arrival" (68). In other northern states, Berlin continues,

> [e]mancipation eventually prevailed, but not until 1784 in Rhode Island and Connecticut, 1799 in New York, and 1804 in New Jersey. Moreover, everywhere freedom arrived according to the post-nati [born-after] formula of the Pennsylvania law, a stricture that delayed emancipation for decades, sometimes generations, recognized property-in-man, confirmed the idea that freedom had to be purchased, shifted the cost of freedom to black people, and, in some places, provided direct compensation to slaveowners. (69)

18. As of 1813, the year Samuel Wood published *The New-York Reader, No. 2: Being, Selections in Prose and Poetry, for the Use of Schools*, slavery still existed in the state of New York. Patrick Rael, in "The Long Death of Slavery," in *Slavery in New York*, ed. Ira

Berlin and Leslie M. Harris (New York: The New Press, 2005), notes that the Gradual Emancipation Law of 1799

> emancipated all people of African descent born into slavery after July 4, 1799, but liberated no one immediately. Rather, it mandated that women until the age of twenty-five and men until the age of twenty-eight would become the bound "servants" of those who had previously owned them. Excepting instances of individual manumission, 1824 was thus the earliest that blacks covered by the law could become legally free. (132)

19. For this point by Father, the author of "Family Conversation" (likely Wood) draws on part of Book II, "The Time-Piece," from *The Task, a Poem, in Six Books. By William Cowper, of the Inner Temple, Esq.* (London: Printed for J. Johnson, 1785), 47. For more information on Cowper and these lines of poetry (especially his claim that slaves' "shackles fall" when they "touch [England]"), consult the notes on *Life and Adventures of Olaudah Equiano*. Wood and Sons used in *Life and Adventures* numerous lines (including the two quoted by Father) from Cowper's "The Time-Piece." See page 30.

20. For this point by Father, the author of "Family Conversation" (likely Wood) draws upon the second paragraph of the Declaration of Independence:

> We hold these truths to be self-evident, that all men are created equal, that they are endowed by their Creator with certain unalienable Rights, that among these are Life, Liberty and pursuit of Happiness.—That to secure these rights Governments are instituted among Men, deriving their just powers from the consent of the governed.—That whenever any Form of Government becomes destructive of these ends, it is the Right of the People to alter or abolish it, and to institute new Government, laying its foundation on such principles and organizing its powers in such form, as to them shall seem most likely to effect their Safety and Happiness.

For a text written by Wood containing parts from the Declaration, see "To the Reader," written by "T[he] P[ublisher]," from *The Penitential Tyrant; or, Slave Trader Reformed: A Pathetic Poem, in Four Cantos. By Thomas Branagan*, "enlarged" 2nd ed. (New York: Samuel Wood, 1807), in appendix D.

21. According to the *Oxford English Dictionary*, "compassionate," as a verb, may be understood as "[t]o regard or treat with compassion; to pity, commiserate (a person, or his distress, etc.)."

22. For this point by Charles, the author of "Family Conversation" (likely Wood) attributes these poetic lines to William Cowper (1731–1800), a British poet, though they appear in Beilby Porteus's *Death: A Poetical Essay*. For more on Cowper, consult the notes on *Life and Adventures of Olaudah Equiano*. For more on Porteus, consult the notes on "To the Reader" (appendix D).

23. For this point by Mother, the author of "Family Conversation" (likely Wood) references *Hymns in Prose for Children. By the Author of Lessons for Children*, by Anna Letitia Barbauld (1743–1825), first printed in London in 1781 for J. Johnson. In 1816 Wood and Sons printed and sold at their Juvenile Book-Store *Hymns in Prose, For the Use of Children*. U.S. printers published the book in a variety of titles, including *Hymns in Prose for Children*, *Barbauld's Hymns*, *Hymns for Children; in Prose*, and *Hymns for Children; in Prose: Calculated to Impress the Infant Mind with Early Devotion*. In 1813 Wood printed and sold at his Juvenile Book-Store *Pastoral Lessons, and Parental Conversations*, which he intended, according to the title, as a "*[C]ompanion to E.* [sic] *Barbauld's Hymns in Prose*."

24. Henry recites a portion from Hymn VIII in Barbauld's *Hymns*. Consult the 1781 London edition, 60–61.
25. According to the *Oxford English Dictionary*, this verb may be understood as "[t]o set a bar or prohibition against (an action, etc.); to prohibit, prevent, forbid, stop."
26. Samuel Johnson (1709–1784), in his 1755 *Dictionary*, vol. 1, defines the verb "condescend" as "[t]o depart from the privileges of superiority by a voluntary submission; to sink willingly to equal terms with inferiors; to soothe by familiarity."
27. According to the *Oxford English Dictionary*, this term may be understood as "[p]rofit or gain arising from station, office, or employment; dues; reward, remuneration, salary."
28. According to the *Oxford English Dictionary*, the term "obduracy" may be understood as "[s]tubbornness, obstinacy; obstinate hardness of heart, relentlessness; persistence in evil."

www.ingramcontent.com/pod-product-compliance
Lightning Source LLC
Chambersburg PA
CBHW030650230426
43665CB00011B/1027